A READING OF
Sir Gawain and the Green Knight

A READING OF
Sir Gawain and the Green Knight

J. A. BURROW

ROUTLEDGE & KEGAN PAUL
LONDON, HENLEY AND BOSTON

First published 1965
by Routledge & Kegan Paul Ltd.
39 Store Street
London WC1E 7DD,
Broadway House, Newtown Road
Henley-on-Thames
Oxon. RG9 1EN and
9 Park Street
Boston, Mass. 02108, USA

Reprinted 1966
Reprinted and first published as a paperback 1977

Printed in Great Britain
by Redwood Burn Limited
Trowbridge & Esher

ISBN 0 7100 8695 4 (p)

CONTENTS

v

PREFACE

THE CRITICAL METHOD adopted in this book has involved me in a certain amount of miscellaneous, and I hope innocent, comment on individual beauties and subtleties in *Sir Gawain and the Green Knight*; but the reader should perhaps be warned that I also try to develop a somewhat controversial argument about the poem as a whole. My chief point is that *Sir Gawain* is a poem about *truth*, in the medieval sense of the word. From this a number of other points derive, more or less directly. I stress the importance of the hero's two contracts with his adversary; take a relatively serious view of his failure to honour the second of these contracts; and judge the poet's treatment of human character and motive to be generally realistic—according to a medieval Christian mode of realism which I attempt to define in the last chapter.

Mr. C. A. Robson and Mr. A. G. Rigg have kindly given me help, as has my wife, to whom this book is dedicated. I also owe a great deal to the enthusiasm and scepticism of present and former pupils. My debt to other critics is, I am afraid, inadequately acknowledged in the following pages.

All quotations from *Sir Gawain* are taken, by kind permission of the Clarendon Press, Oxford, from the edition of J. R. R. Tolkien and E. V. Gordon. I am grateful to the Princeton University Press for permission to quote from Northrop Frye's *Anatomy of Criticism*.

J. A. B.

Jesus College, Oxford

ABBREVIATIONS

Titles of periodicals are abbreviated as follows:

E.L.H.	*Journal of English Literary History*
J.E.G.P.	*Journal of English and Germanic Philology*
Med. St.	*Mediaeval Studies*
M.L.N.	*Modern Language Notes*
M.L.R.	*Modern Language Review*
M.P.	*Modern Philology*
N. and Q.	*Notes and Queries*
P.Q.	*Philological Quarterly*
P.B.A.	*Proceedings of the British Academy*
P.M.L.A.	*Publications of the Modern Language Association*
R.E.S.	*Review of English Studies* (N.S. = New Series)
Spec.	*Speculum*
S.P.	*Studies in Philology*

I

THE FIRST FITT

Sir Gawain and the Green Knight is a poem for the ear rather than the eye:

> If ȝe wyl lysten þis laye bot on littel quile,
> I schal telle hit astit, as I in toun herde,
>   with tonge. (30–32)

The author does not write his lay, he 'tells' it; and the audience does not read, it 'listens'—as the author himself listened when he heard the story 'in toun'. We are invited to 'listen for just a little while' (about two-and-a-half hours, on my calculation), not to read and ponder at our leisure. Now there is one universal law of literature which is specially binding on poems of this sort: the poet, as one medieval Frenchman put it somewhat plaintively, 'cannot say everything at once—he must say one thing after another'. A reader can stop and turn the pages back or forwards, and in this way he can get a 'view' of several separate parts of a poem more or less at once, almost as if he were looking at a painting; but a listener does not have this freedom—he can only follow the voice of the poet or reciter as it 'says one thing after another' for as long as the poem lasts. The experience of literature as a *linear* art, with a certain necessary extension in time, is therefore stronger in an oral age than in an age of printing and reading.

Even in the Middle Ages there were poets who attempted to escape from this condition of literary communication. Some tried to say many things at once, massing their material rather than lining it up, as it were—the encyclopaedic or synoptic poets; and others tried to say one thing all the time—the thematic or moralizing poets. *Beowulf* is a good example of what I mean, since it has something both of the encyclopaedic and of the thematic about it. But there were also many poets—and the *Gawain*-poet is certainly one of these—who made a virtue of necessity and positively exploited the linear character of the medium in which they worked. The most obvious mark of these writers is that their stories keep the audience in suspense. There is a strong and significant contrast in this matter of suspense between *Beowulf* and *Sir Gawain*. The *Beowulf*-poet had, of course, to 'say one thing after another' like everyone else; but he tells his stories out of their natural order with so much flash-back and flash-forward that he achieves a static effect (noted by Professor Tolkien) which, whatever its other virtues, largely excludes suspense. So, one is told on the eve of Beowulf's fight with the dragon that he was destined ('scolde' is the typical auxiliary) to die in it. Contrast the passage at the end of the third fitt of *Sir Gawain*, where the poet, again on the eve of his hero's decisive encounter, addresses his audience as follows:

> Let hym lyȝe þere stille,
> He hatȝ nere þat he soȝt;
> And ȝe wyl a whyle be stylle
> I schal telle yow how þay wroȝt. (1994-7)

Here, as at the beginning of his work, the author promises to 'tell' if his audience will only sit still and listen; but he does nothing to relieve their anxiety about the outcome. Elsewhere, indeed, he even professes to share this anxiety, as if he were himself ignorant of the hero's future conduct and fate. His advice to Gawain at the end of the first fitt illustrates this:

> Now þenk wel, Sir Gawan,
> For woþe þat þou ne wonde
> Þis auenture for to frayn
> Þat þou hatȝ tan on honde. (487-90)

Critics are sometimes inclined to leave 'suspense' for the simpler kind of reader, as though it could have no bearing on

2

their own interpretations; but this is not a safe assumption. An author who, like the *Gawain*-poet, tells his story in such a way as to keep his audience in suspense about 'what happens next' may do the same sort of thing at those deeper levels which interest the critic or interpreter. He may, that is, keep his audience in suspense about the significance of his people and events, and allow his 'meaning', like his 'plot', to emerge gradually from among a number of more or less deliberately countenanced possibilities. Another comparison with *Beowulf* may help to make this point clear. The passage which introduces Beowulf's first adversary (99 ff.) carefully provides answers for almost every question the audience might think to ask about him. All the important factual details are there—his name, dwelling-place, history and descent; and we also learn exactly where he stands morally—he is a 'hell-fiend', a 'creature of evil', etc. The passage leaves little room for further speculation about the nature and significance of Grendel. By contrast, the *Gawain*-poet gives away very little about the Green Knight on his first appearance—no more than Arthur and his knights could themselves discover. The first fitt leaves the reader in ignorance of his 'right name', his real dwelling-place, his history, his descent—and his significance. It would, in fact, be quite impossible to arrive at a secure 'interpretation' of the Green Knight on the strength of the first fitt alone. The account of his appearance and actions does indeed bristle with suggestions, some of which I shall take up later in this chapter—suggestions of death and fertility, playfulness and hostility, etc.—but the poem does not encourage us to settle for any one of these. We do not even discover whether, at the simplest level, the Green Knight is 'good' or 'bad'.

It follows from what has been said, I think, that an interpretation of *Sir Gawain* must bind itself to the order of events in the poem. The so-called 'spatial' approach—spreading a poem out and viewing it as a synchronous whole, like a picture—is good for *Beowulf*; but in *Sir Gawain* a first fitt is a first fitt and must be studied as such—as a prologue, a beginning. It is no use trying to determine significances whose indeterminacy forms, at a given point, part of the effect—maybe a large part.

The point is not so much that this lets the reader into the secret
and so spoils his pleasure in the suspense (he presumably knows
the story already) as that it misrepresents the nature of the
poem. If *Sir Gawain* were something like a detective story the
case would be different, for there would then be one single and
sufficient truth about, say, the Green Knight, which could be
revealed to a reader of the first fitt (at whatever cost to his
enjoyment), enabling him from the start to distinguish reliable
suggestions from misleading ones. But this is not the case.
To explain that the Green Knight is really Sir Bercilak de
Hautdesert under a magic spell is one thing; to explain that he
is 'really' Death, or a Green Man, or the Old Year, is quite
another. If there is one single and sufficient truth about the
Green Knight of the first fitt, it is that he positively bristles,
bewilderingly, with suggestions and significances.

I

Like most other medieval and renaissance writers, the *Gawain*-
poet has a highly-developed sense of 'decorum'. It is very
common for him, when (as he often does) he wishes to praise
something, to call it 'becoming', 'meet', 'kind', 'seemly', etc.
For a man's dress, speech or conduct to be praiseworthy, it
must be appropriate—appropriate, that is, to such variable
factors as his age and social position, the occasion and his part
in it, and the season of the year.[1] It is desirable, obviously, that
one should be aware of this kind of decorum in older literature,
and particularly that one should keep an eye open for the
unfamiliar points.

The *Gawain*-poet's sense of decorum makes itself felt early
in the first fitt when, after two stanzas of prologue, he embarks
on his description of Arthur's court, keeping the Christmas feast
at Camelot:

[1] This is a fairly full list, and I do not mean to imply that all the
factors mentioned are operative all the time. In case of conflict, for
example, one kind of decorum will overtrump another, as when a
young man at a funeral appropriately dresses and behaves like an
old one.

The First Fitt

Þis kyng lay at Camylot vpon Krystmasse
With mony luflych lorde, ledeʒ of þe best,
Rekenly of þe Rounde Table alle þo rich breþer,
With rych reuel oryʒt and rechles merþes. (37–40)

The stress on 'revel' and 'mirth' in this and the ensuing passage
is so heavy and continuous (tournaments, jousts, carols, feasting,
dancing) that several critics have been led to suppose that the
author may be implying some moral judgment on an immature
or blindly festive company. But before adopting any such
opinion one must reckon with the implications of the 'oryʒt'
in the lines quoted above. From every point of view revel and
mirth are 'right', appropriate, for this company on this occasion.
The people are all young—'al watʒ þis fayre folk in her first
age'—and the year is young too. (The poet's use of the epithet
'ʒep' suggests this linking: the New Year is 'ʒep' in l. 60,
Arthur is 'ʒep in þat Nw Ʒere' in l. 105, and in l. 284 the Green
Knight says 'hit is Ʒol and Nwe Ʒer, and here ar ʒep mony'.)
Again, the occasion is one of the great feasts of the Christian
year, a celebration of Christ at which 'burneʒ blyþe of his
burþe schal sitte / and synge' (922–3). As Arthur observes later,
after the departure of the Green Knight:

Wel bycommes such craft vpon Cristmasse,
Laykyng of enterludeʒ, to laʒe and to syng,
Among þise kynde caroles of knyʒteʒ and ladyeʒ. (471–3)

We should also recognize (and this is a less familiar point of
decorum) that the revelling of Arthur and his knights has
another general sanction in medieval ideas of knighthood; for
the ideal knight was among other things 'jolly' or 'gay'. Medieval
opinion was generally inclined to be suspicious of an un-
bendingly grave, pious or 'sad' demeanour, which it associated
with hypocrisy ('papelardie' in French, 'pope-holiness' in
English):

Seiés jolis devant la gent
Et servés Dieu privéement;
Chantés et volunters jués
Que papelard ne resemblés.[2]

[2] 'Be gay in the company of others and serve God in private. Sing
and play with a will, not like a pious hypocrite.' *Instructio patris regis*

5

Such 'jollity' was particularly admired in knights. One can see this, as Gervase Mathew suggests, in the Chandos Herald's poem on the Black Prince, where the Prince is several times complimented on being a 'jolly' man, as in the following passage:

> De sa volonté noble et france
> Prist la doctrine de largece,
> Car jolieté et noblece
> ffu en son coer parfitement
> Tres le premier comencement
> De sa vie et de sa joenece.[3]

The coupling of 'jolieté' and 'noblece' in this passage is interesting because it throws light on the *Gawain*-poet's somewhat puzzling remarks about King Arthur himself. The New Year's feast was all ready, he says,

> Bot Arthure wolde not ete til al were serued,
> He watȝ so joly of his joyfnes, and sumquat childgered:
> His lif liked hym lyȝt, he louied þe lasse
> Auþer to longe lye or to longe sitte,
> So bisied him his ȝonge blod and his brayn wylde.
> And also an oþer maner meued him eke
> Þat he purȝ nobelay had nomen, he wolde neuer ete
> Vpon such a dere day, er hym deuised were
> Of sum auenturus þyng an vncouþe tale. (85–93)

Whatever the precise implications of this passage, it is surely not, as some critics have maintained, an outright denunciation of the king.[4] The poet devises a double motivation for Arthur's

---

[3] 'From his generous and noble disposition he drew the doctrine of bounty, for gaiety and nobleness were in his heart perfectly from the first beginnings of his childhood up.' *Life of the Black Prince by the Herald of Sir John Chandos*, ed. M. K. Pope and E. C. Lodge (Oxford, 1910), ll. 74–9. See G. Mathew's valuable essay, 'Ideals of Knighthood in Late Fourteenth-Century England', in *Studies in Medieval History Presented to F. M. Powicke* (Oxford, 1948), pp. 354–62.

[4] See especially H. Schnyder, *SGGK: An Essay in Interpretation* (Bern, 1961), pp. 36–9.

---

ad filium Edwardum, in K. de Lettenhove, *Oeuvres de Froissart, Chroniques*, Volume I, Part I (Brussels, 1870), p. 542.

traditional unreadiness to take his place at the table: it is both 'jolieté' ('he watȝ so joly of his joyfnes') and 'noblece' ('he þurȝ nobelay had nomen'). The passage quoted from the Chandos Herald suggests that these are *both* praiseworthy characteristics in a knight: the poet does not, as might at first appear, give with one hand and take away with the other. Arthur is a worthy leader of a company of young and adventurous knights,

> Car jolieté et noblece
> ffu en son coer parfitement
> Tres le premier comencement
> De sa vie et de sa joenece.

But one cannot quite leave the matter there. The *Gawain*-poet is no stern neo-Christian moralist; but neither is he, like the Chandos Herald, a professional publicist. He admires Arthur more than one may at first suspect, but he does not admire him unreservedly. No mere eulogist, it is certain, would have described Arthur as 'sumquat childgered'; for this phrase does undoubtedly imply a criticism. Alexander the Great is said to 'chater with hys chiftanes in hys child gere' in the alliterative *Wars of Alexander*, but he is no more than twelve years old at the time.[5] Arthur may be 'in his first age', but he must be a good deal older than twelve. To be 'joly' is therefore not, for him, the same as to be 'childgered'; and one must therefore recognize in the line a typical ambivalence—typical because it keeps the reader in suspense (forces him to suspend judgment, that is). There is another example of this kind of ambivalence in the line already quoted:

> With rych reuel oryȝt and rechles merþes.

Here, as so often, the disturbance occurs in the second half-line. In their edition of the poem, Tolkien and Gordon gloss 'rechles' 'care-free, joyous', and this genial gloss agrees with one's prevailing sense of the passage in which the word occurs.

[5] See C. A. Luttrell, 'A *Gawain* Group Miscellany', *N. and Q.*, N.S. IX (1962), pp. 447–50. Luttrell quotes several other instances of the expression, all of them derogatory.

However, as the *Oxford English Dictionary*'s article on 'reckless' shows, the Middle English word, like its modern descendant, normally carries sinister implications of heedlessness or rashness; and I think that some such implication plays a part in the *Gawain* use. We should take it as one of the poet's 'suggestions': the knights are carefree and perhaps a little 'heedless', just as their leader is gay and a little ('sumquat') childish.[6]

The poet goes on, after his description of Arthur 'talkkande bifore þe hyȝe table of trifles ful hende', to introduce his hero, Gawain, as one of those who have already taken their seats. This is a significant passage. The first view of any hero helps to establish our sense of the relationship existing between him and the society to which he belongs (*Hamlet* provides an obvious example), and this relationship is usually a matter of some importance. In Arthurian romance it largely determines our view both of the hero and of his society—the Arthurian court. A glance at the two basically different kinds of relationship available to a writer in the Arthurian tradition will show this. In most romances of Arthur the court-hero relationship is a straightforward one. The 'court' consists, in such cases, of those knights who, at a particular time, are not engaged on the current adventure; while the 'hero' is the man who is engaged on it. Some knights, naturally, are braver, more courteous and more pious than others; and it is these who engage on the great adventures. Others (Kay, for example) are less distinguished, and they serve as foils for their superiors. But there is no feeling that the court as a body is in any way inferior to its currently active member. The knights who wish a hero luck at the beginning of his adventure and welcome him

[6] See however M. Borroff, *SGGK: A Stylistic and Metrical Study* (New Haven, 1962), p. 102: '*Rechles* 40 and *dyn* 47 seem to have had mildly derogatory implications which are here neutralized by the context'. Miss Borroff must be referring to the immediate context, for she recognizes similar ironic 'nuances' elsewhere in the first fitt. E. T. Donaldson discusses recklessness in his '*Piers Plowman*': *The C-Text and Its Poet* (New Haven, 1949), pp. 170–5. It may be noted that Langland couples Recklessness with Childishness ('Fauntelte') in *Piers Plowman* B. XI. 33–41.

8

back at the end necessarily cut unremarkable figures; but they are not *fainéants*. Many of them will have their own adventures elsewhere in the cycle: for the moment it is simply not their turn. In some romances, however—notably Grail romances—the case is different. Here one finds a very few knights (Perceval, Galahad, Bors) who are so much superior to their companions that they stand quite apart from them. Where such knights are concerned, the distinction between hero and court takes on a new significance; for they are 'heroes', not merely in a technical, relative sense, but absolutely. They are elect beings, like sheep among goats, and they are graced with a peculiar moral excellence which enables them to engage successfully on high and mysterious adventures where all others fail. In such romances, Arthur and his remaining companions come to figure as representatives of common humanity, sinful sons of Eve, radically inferior to the hero and doomed for their sins to the tragic catastrophe of the *Morte Arthur*. So, whereas in 'ordinary' romances the court is primarily a social group to which the hero belongs, in these it is primarily a spiritual group which he has transcended. A good example of the first type is the *Yvain* of Chrétien de Troyes; but nearly all English Arthurian romances belong here too. Examples of the second type are the French *Queste del Saint Graal* and *Perlesvaus*.

It is fair to say, I think, that all critics of *Sir Gawain* who take a low view of the court regard the poem as belonging to the second of the two types described above. They identify the court with the court of the *Queste-Morte* romances, and treat the hero, more or less explicitly, as a kind of Grail-hero. Charles Moorman, for example, says that the court is morally corrupt and doomed to catastrophe, and that the hero is a superior, 'initiated' being chosen to 'redeem' his fellows (though their moral blindness causes him to fail in this): 'Gawain is the only knight capable of undertaking the quest', he writes; 'Only the returned Gawain, who has himself made the initiatory journey, sees the imminent destruction which he expresses in his condemnation of women, and which he attempts to forestall by the institution of the green baldric'; 'The *Gawain* poet is using the myth of the hero's quest to develop a theme which lies at the

B   9

core of mediaeval literature: that the tragedy of the Round
Table, and of the secular society of which it is a symbol, was
inevitable, and that the seeds of that tragedy were present even
in the "first age" of the youthful and joyous court at Christmas
time.'[7]

I believe that this kind of approach to *Sir Gawain* is fundamentally mistaken, and that nearly all the conclusions to which
it leads are false. For the moment there are two points to be
made. First, I can see no evidence at all that 'the seeds of that
tragedy were present even in the "first age" of the youthful and
joyous court at Christmas time': I cannot detect, as Mr.
Moorman does, the shadow of Mordred in the present scene.
Neither Mordred (not yet born?) nor even Lancelot, the other
tragic agent, are so much as named here—as the Hroþulf of
Beowulf is named, ominously, among the company at Heorot;
and the 'recklessness' of the knights, such as it is, surely
suggests not 'imminent destruction' but an imminent Green
Knight. Again, I cannot agree that Gawain is presented as
'the only knight capable of undertaking the quest', like a Grail-
hero. The Gawain of the first fitt is certainly a 'verray, parfit,
gentil knyght', and he takes upon himself a very dangerous
adventure. But such manifestations of distinction in knights
like Gawain are not at all inconsistent with the conventions of
the ordinary kind of romance, where it is quite common and
natural for the hero to be represented as *primus inter pares*.
Both parts of this formula apply to Gawain. He is, for all the
poem tells us, 'primus'; but he is 'primus *inter pares*', and it is
there that he differs from the 'elect' heroes of the sophisticated
French religious romances. Let me now quote the passage in
which the author first introduces him:

> Thus þer stondes in stale þe stif kyng hisseluen,
> Talkkande bifore þe hyȝe table of trifles ful hende.
> There gode Gawan watȝ grayþed Gwenore bisyde,
> And Agrauayn a la dure mayn on þat oþer syde sittes,
> Boþe þe kynges sistersunes and ful siker kniȝtes;

[7] C. Moorman, 'Myth and Mediaeval Literature: *SGGK*', *Med.
St.*, XVIII (1956), pp. 158–72. My quotations are from pp. 169,
170 and 172.

The First Fitt

Bischop Bawdewyn abof bigineȝ þe table,
And Ywan, Vryn son, ette with hymseluen.
Þise were diȝt on þe des and derworþly serued,
And siþen mony siker segge at þe sidbordeȝ. (107–115)

We see that the hero is first mentioned simply as 'gode Gawan' sitting with his peers, Agravain, Baldwin and Ywain, at the high table and taking part in the celebrations. There is, so to speak, no spotlight on him: indeed, a reader without the benefit of the modern editors' title-page—or a listener—would not realize that Gawain was to be the hero of the poem until the moment, more than 200 lines later, when he first speaks up: 'I beseche now with saȝeȝ sene / Þis melly mot be myne'. The case is very different with such a typical Grail-hero as the Galahad of the thirteenth-century *Queste del Saint Graal* (the source of Malory's Grail book); here a multitude of signs, among them the inscription on the Siege Perilous and the other inscription on the sword in the stone ('Never shall man take me hense but only he by whos syde I ought to honge and he shall be the beste knyght of the worlde'), prepare for the dramatic appearance of the elect hero. The seat and the sword are both waiting for Galahad, 'the beste knyght of the worlde', and only he is worthy of them.

This sense of individual predestination or election is entirely absent in *Sir Gawain*: one does not feel that the beheading adventure, when the Green Knight proposes it, is *for* Gawain alone in any mysterious fashion. Arthur and his knights are challenged as a company, and they respond as a company. They all remain silent at first ('alle þe heredmen in halle, þe hyȝ and þe loȝe', l. 302); then, after a taunting speech from the Green Knight, they all share in the king's anger ('He wex as wroth as wynde, / So did alle þat þer were', ll. 319–20). It is only when the king in person 'as kene bi kynde' has stepped forward to take up the challenge that Gawain proposes himself; and even then, very characteristically, his proposal is debated by the nobles before it is accepted by the king. In all this Gawain acts as a member of the 'hered', a man among his 'cort-feres' (*inter pares*). He offers himself as a good vassal should, with the consent of his fellow vassals, to save his lord

from a dangerous and (as he hints) unseemly act of con-
descension.[8] He is, I would say, essentially the straightforward
'gode Gawan' of many other medieval English romances—
above all a social being, a 'brother of the Round Table'.
Though conspicuously brave and courteous, he is not marked
off from his court-companions by any signs of mysterious
election; and his adventure, though certainly an 'outtrage
awenture of Arthureȝ wondereȝ', is not distinguished, as are
the Grail adventures, by any special portents. It is wonderful,
but not uniquely so. As the author says at the end of his poem:

> Mony auntereȝ here-biforne
> Haf fallen suche er þis. (2527–8)

There is something here of the moderation or 'measure', the
essential conservatism, which distinguishes the English poem
throughout. Though, in the course of events, its hero ceases to
be the simple 'gode Gawan' of the first fitt, he does in the end
return to Camelot. He does not, like Galahad, sail mysteriously
off to the land of Sarras. I shall return to this point in a later
chapter.

II

Having established his court and his hero, the *Gawain*-poet
turns to the third point of the traditional Arthurian triangle—
the challenger or adversary. The sound of drums, pipes and
trumpets which accompanies the first course of the banquet has
hardly died away when 'an oþer noyse ful newe' is heard—the
noise of the Green Knight riding in through the hall door:

[8] Marc Bloch, in his *Feudal Society* (trans. L. A. Manyon, London,
1961), points out that 'it was lawful for the liege vassal to demand
battle on behalf of his lord, and any man could do so, if a member
of his own kin was involved' (p. 125). Gawain is both Arthur's kins-
man (l. 356) and his liege vassal (l. 545, cf. l. 346). Moorman's con-
tention that Arthur, unlike Gawain, was not *able* to behead the Green
Knight (p. 166 of his article cited in note 7) is a typical 'Grail-reading'
error. The idea was first put forward by D. E. Baughan in 'The Role
of Morgan Le Fay in *SGGK*', *E.L.H.*, XVII (1950), pp. 241–51. It is
refuted most convincingly by A. B. Friedman in 'Morgan Le Fay in
SGGK', *Spec.*, XXXV (1960), pp. 260–74.

The First Fitt

Þer hales in at þe halle dor an aghlich mayster. (136)

At this point the poet breaks off for a long and detailed description of the man and his horse (ll. 137–220). The most remarkable feature of this description, it seems to me, is its richness and variety of suggestion. The poet's emphasis on the harmony of the effects (everything 'of a sute', 'of þe same', 'of þat ilke', etc.—green with matching accessories) cannot conceal the basic complexity and ambivalence of the image which he creates. This is already evident in the first group of long lines (ll. 137–46), which are devoted to the Green Knight's physique. There is nothing monstrous about the burly body, slender waist and long, thick limbs. The 'Mirth' of Guillaume de Lorris, an ideal young courtier, has

> shuldris of a large brede,
> And smalish in the girdilstede.[9]

And the equally exemplary figure of Youth in the *Parlement of the Thre Ages* is described in similar terms:

> He was balghe in the breste and brode in the scholdirs,
> His axles and his armes were i-liche longe,
> And in the medill als a mayden menskfully schapen;
> Longe legges and large, and lele for to schewe.[10]

The Green Knight is, in fact, a fine figure of a man, according to the medieval courtly ideal. But it is to be remarked that the poet takes up this conventional contrast between massive body and slender waist and develops it in such a way as to suggest the indeterminate character of the stranger. His body was so massive, he says, that one might consider him 'half etayn'; but then again his waist was so slender and his whole figure so elegant or 'merry' that it might be better to take him simply as a very big man ('mon most'). This expression of doubt is worth noticing, for the whole of the following description hovers in a similar way between the monstrous-supernatural and the merry-human. This is, indeed, the fundamental form

[9] Text of the Middle English translation, ll. 825–6, from *Works of Geoffrey Chaucer*, ed. F. N. Robinson (2nd ed., London, 1957).
[10] Ed. M. Y. Offord, E.E.T.S. 246 (1959), ll. 112–15.

of the Green Knight's 'ambivalence' throughout the first fitt: it is to be detected in his colour, in his behaviour, and in the adventure which he eventually proposes.

When the poet reveals, at the end of the first stanza of his description, that the stranger is 'oueral enker grene', the immediate and obvious effect is to establish him as a supernatural creature of some kind. According to medieval tradition, the colour green was particularly favoured by such creatures. It was the colour of fairies, the colour of the dead, and the colour of the devil.[11] This is the general tradition, no doubt, which lies behind the conclusion later drawn by Arthur's knights themselves from the colour of the knight and his horse: 'Forþi for fantoum and fayryʒe þe folk þere hit demed' (l. 240). And it is the *general* tradition which counts here, for the reader is not invited—at this stage at least—to identify the Green Knight with any particular kind of supernatural creature. Suggestions of the otherworld, the afterworld and the underworld are all appropriate enough in the context; but the context does not particularly favour any one of them. We should perhaps simply recognize the Green Knight as an example, in the romance style, of the 'kind of thing' that is always likely, according to moralists and others, to break in on 'rechles merþes'. The Commendatore and Rumpelstiltskin are other examples in other styles.

Only a supernatural creature, obviously, can have green skin and hair; but green clothes and trappings are another matter. It is here, in the second stanza of the description, that the ambivalence of the colour makes itself felt. Fairies and the like often wear robes of green, but so do other kinds of people; and anyway it should be noted that the Green Knight does not simply wear green—he wears green with gold accessories. We are told this many times. His spurs are of 'bryʒt golde' (l. 159); his silken trappings are embroidered with 'gay gaudi of grene, þe golde ay inmyddes' (167); the green tail, mane and forelock

---

[11] For fairies and the dead, see L. C. Wimberly, *Folklore in the English and Scottish Ballads* (New York, 1928), pp. 175–8 and 240–3. For the devil, see D. W. Robertson, 'Why the Devil Wears Green', *M.L.N.*, LXIX (1954), pp. 470–2.

of his horse are intertwined with gold thread, 'folden in wyth fildore aboute þe fayre grene / Ay a herle of þe here, an oþer of golde' (189–90); the bells on the horse's forelock and tail are of 'brende golde' (195); and the 'grain' of his axe is 'al of grene stele and of golde hewen' (211). The same colour-combination appears in the second of the two similes in which the poet sums up the court's impression of the stranger: he is 'grene as þe gres and grener hit semed, / Þen grene aumayl on golde glowande bryȝter' (235–6); and it appears once again much later in the poem, as a clue, in the description of Bercilak's wife's girdle: 'gered hit watȝ with grene sylke and with golde schaped' (1832).

The significance of this combination of green and gold is not hard to discover. It belongs to the same world as the slender waist and broad shoulders—the merry, luxurious world of courtly youth. In the *Parlement of the Thre Ages*, Youth is said to be 'gerede alle in grene, alle with golde byweuede' (l. 122); and a later passage in the same poem introduces the colours in a similar context:

> Amadase and Edoyne, in erthe are thay bothe,
> That in golde and in grene were gaye in thaire tyme. (614–15)

So too the allegorical Youth of *King Hart* (formerly ascribed to Gavin Douglas) has a green coat adorned with gold; and the young god Jupiter in Robert Henryson's *Testament of Cresseid* has

> His garmound and his gyis full gay of grene,
> With golden listis gilt on everie gair.[12]

Altogether there are sufficient grounds for holding that, while the green of the Green Knight's person carries suggestions of supernatural menace, the green of his clothes and trappings,

[12] *The Poetical Works of Gavin Douglas*, ed. J. Small (Edinburgh, 1874), Vol. I, p. 97, ll. 5–7: 'Bot ȝouthheid had him maid ane courtlie cote / Als grene as gerss, with goldin stremis bricht / Broudin about'; *Testament of Cresseid*, ll. 178–79. It may be noted that the courtly challenger in the prose redaction of the Carados beheading game wears 'fine soie batue en or' and 'satin verd'. See L. D. Benson, 'The Source of the Beheading Episode in *SGGK*', *M.P.*, LIX (1961), p. 3.

combined with the gold, carries sharply contrasting suggestions of gaiety, courtesy and youth. The nature of the Green Knight is such, in fact, that he can be in harmony as well as out of harmony with the court on which he intrudes.

The clearest indication of this is reserved for the very end of the description, where the poet describes the two objects which the Green Knight carries, one in either hand—the 'holyn bobbe' and the battle-axe (ll. 206–20). The implications of the holly, whichever way one looks at it, are seasonable and re-assuring. Holly is obviously associated with the Christmas feast and with the preservation of life through the dead season—it is 'grattest in grene when greueȝ ar bare' (207). The 'bob' of holly carried in the hand is also, as the knight himself later points out, a sign of friendly intentions or 'peace', like an olive-branch:

> Ȝe may be seker bi þis braunch þat I bere here
> Þat I passe as in pes, and no plyȝt seche. (265–6)

As a sign of peace, the branch harmonizes with the Green Knight's unwarlike dress: he has, as he says, left his armour at home—'my wedeȝ ar softer'.[13] It seems to harmonize, too, with the green of his dress and horse-trappings; for there is an interesting piece of evidence to suggest that such equipment was particularly associated with peace-missions and branch-bearing. In Malory's *Morte Arthur* Lancelot (after his breach with Arthur) sets out from Joyous Garde under safe-conduct to return Guinevere to the king, taking with him a hundred knights 'all well clothed in grene velvet, and their horsis trapped in the same to the heelys, and every knyght hylde a braunche of olyff in hys honde in tokenyng of pees'.[14] Substitute

---

[13] The fact that he wears no shoes over his hose ('scholes', l. 160) is a significant detail in this connection. See C. Clark's note, 'The Green Knight Shoeless: A Reconsideration', *R.E.S.*, N.S. VI (1955), pp. 174–7; and M. Rigby, 'The Green Knight Shoeless Again', *R.E.S.*, N.S. VII (1956), pp. 173–4. There can now be no doubt that 'scholes' does mean 'shoeless'.

[14] *The Works of Sir Thomas Malory*, ed. E. Vinaver (Oxford, 1947), p. 1196. The French *Mort Artu* has no green clothes or olive-branches at this point; but both appear, as Vinaver points out (note to 1196.

the seasonable holly-branch for the olive-branch, and you have something very like the Green Knight who claims to 'passe as in pes and no ply3t seche'. It is hardly necessary to stress the peculiar incongruity—a huge battle-axe in the 'other hand' of such a figure. It is as if the Green Knight offers peace with one hand and war with the other.

The figure of the Green Knight, then, has about it a wide range of 'suggestions' calculated to evoke, in a medieval reader at least, conflicting expectations about his future actions and eventual significance—'al þe wonder of þe worlde what he worch schulde'. When the figure is set in motion again, we can see that the poet contrives with considerable virtuosity to keep up this suspense. Let us look first at his behaviour immediately after entering the hall:

> Þis haþel helde3 hym in and þe halle entres,
> Driuande to þe he3e dece, dut he no woþe,
> Haylsed he neuer one, bot he3e he ouer loked.
> Þe fyrst word þat he warp, 'Wher is', he sayd,
> 'Þe gouernour of þis gyng?' (221–5)

This passage raises the question of the Green Knight's 'rude-ness', which has been made much of by some critics. There can be no doubt that he *is* rude, both here and in what follows: he rides up to the high dais without a word of greeting ('haylsed he neuer one'), and he later addresses Arthur and Gawain as 'thou' (ll. 258–9, 272–3, 379–80, etc.). None the less, it seems to me very misleading to speak, as does Gollancz, of his 'uncouthness'

9–12), in the English Stanzaic *Morte Arthur* (N. W. Midlands, *c.* 1400): 'The other knyghtis euerychone / In samyte grene of heythen lande . . . / Ichone a braunche of olyffe in hande' (2364–9). Later in the same poem, Lancelot sends a damsel to plead for truce with Arthur: 'Hyr par*a*ylle all of one hewe / Off a grene weluette, / In hyr hand a braunche newe / Forwhy that no man sholde her lette; / Therby men messangerys knewe / In ostes whan that men them mette' (2614–9). In this case, however, Malory does not preserve the green clothes and branch. It may be noted here that H. L. Savage has found evidence for the use of the holly-branch, in place of the more usual olive-branch, as a sign of peaceful intentions in Lancashire. See his *The 'Gawain'-Poet* (Chapel Hill, 1956), pp. 15–16.

(see the note to l. 1071 in his edition); or to say, as Speirs does, that 'his demeanour and his behaviour in this castle of courtesy are outrageously discourteous; he behaves, as if radically a "villeyn", with contemptuous humorous rudeness'.[15] The proper inference from the Green Knight's behaviour is not that he is 'uncouth' or 'radically a "villeyn"', but that he is a *hostile challenger*. There is a pretty clear, though unfamiliar, point of decorum here. The role of challenger involves, in Arthurian romance at least, certain conventions of behaviour, the object of which is to distinguish challengers from other kinds of stranger (suppliants, gift-bearers, etc.) who may walk or ride into Arthur's hall in the course of a story.[16] These conventions vary somewhat according to circumstances, for some challengers are more hostile in intention, and therefore more arrogant in bearing, than others; but we need be concerned here only with the more hostile type. Three examples from French romance will illustrate the way such strangers were expected to behave. The earliest is from the *Chevalier de la Charrete* of Chrétien de Troyes, where Méléagant of Gorre comes to Arthur's court to deliver a hostile challenge:

> Li chevaliers a tel conroi
> S'an vint jusque devant le roi
> La ou antre ses barons sist,
> *Nel salua pas*, einz li dist:
> 'Rois Artus, j'ai en ma prison
> De *ta* terre et de *ta* meison
> Chevaliers, dames et puceles. . .'.[17]

[15] John Speirs, *Medieval English Poetry: The Non-Chaucerian Tradition* (London, 1957), p. 226. This chapter is a revised version of Speirs' original essay in *Scrutiny*.

[16] Riding into the hall is not in itself distinctive of challengers, as one might expect. Challengers quite commonly do 'ride up to the high dais', but so do suppliants and gift-bearers. See references in B. J. Whiting, 'Gawain: his Reputation, his Courtesy and his Appearance in Chaucer's *Squire's Tale*', *Med. St.*, IX (1947), p. 232, note 360.

[17] 'So attired the knight went right before the king where he sat among his barons. He did not greet him, but said: "King Arthur, I have in my power knights, ladies and maidens of your land and of your household".' Ed. M. Roques (Paris, 1958), ll. 47–53. My italics in these examples.

Precisely the same pattern of behaviour may be observed in two episodes of the so-called 'Vulgate' cycle—a group of thirteenth-century prose romances which the *Gawain*-poet almost certainly knew. In one, a knight arrives while Arthur is at supper to challenge him on behalf of Galehaut, King of the Strange Isles: 'Li chevaliers fu armés fors sa teste et ses mains, et vint tres devant le rois, s'espée chainte. *Ne salue pas le roi*, ains li dist tres devant sa table: "Rois, a *toi* m'envoie le plus preudom qui orendroit soit de son ëage"'.[18] Compare this with the speech, much later in the same cycle, of the 'valet' who brings Mordred's defiant message: 'Rois Artus, *je ne te salu mie*, car ge sui hom a un *tuen* ennemi mortel: c'est Mordrés, li rois del roiaume de Logres. Il *te* mande par moi que *tu* ies folement entrez en sa terre'.[19]

To omit a greeting and to address a nobleman as 'thou' were certainly, under ordinary circumstances, 'outrageous discourtesies'; but such discourtesies were conventional, even decorous, in a hostile challenger. The Green Knight, in fact, observes the decorum of his particular role just as much as does the friendly and courteous emissary of Chaucer's *Squire's Tale*, with his 'heigh reverence and obeisaunce / As wel in speche as in his contenaunce'; and Chaucer's approving comment might apply equally to him:

> Accordant to his wordes was his cheere,
> As techeth art of speche hem that it leere.

[18] 'The knight was armed except for his head and hands, and he went before the king with his sword at his side. He did not greet the king, but said to him before his table: "King, the most valiant man of his time sends me to you".' *The Vulgate Version of the Arthurian Romances*, ed. H. O. Sommer (Washington, 1909-16), Vol. III, p. 201, ll. 35-8. The Scottish author of *Lancelot of the Laik*, when he translated this passage (ll. 542 ff.), had the knight salute Arthur and address him as 'you'. Not all British writers shared the *Gawain*-poet's knowledge of the conventions of French courtly romance.

[19] 'King Arthur, I do not salute you, for I follow one of your mortal enemies—Mordred, king of the realm of Logres. He sends you word by me that you have rashly entered into his lands.' *La Mort le Roi Artu*, ed. J. Frappier (Geneva, 1954), p. 229.

The First Fitt

He is no more radically a 'villeyn' than Chrétien's Méléagant, or the valet or the knight of the Vulgate romances—the last, according to the author, 'uns chevaliers d'ëage qui moult sambloit preudom'. The episode of Perceval's first appearance at court, as described in the fourteenth-century English *Sir Perceval of Galles*, provides a point of contrast here. Perceval is not a 'villeyn', of course; but he is uncouth and discourteous, having been brought up by his mother in ignorance of courtly manners. Riding on a mare and wearing (apparently) a goatskin, he gallops into the hall without a greeting, and addresses the king with an unceremonious 'thou'. The king's reaction is made quite clear:

> The childe hadde wonnede in þe wodde:
> He knewe noþer evyll ne gude;
> The kynge hymselfe understode
> He was a wilde man.[20]

Perceval comes to ask to be made a knight, and his behaviour (not to speak of his horse, dress, etc.) is therefore absurdly inappropriate. It marks him in the king's eyes as a 'wild man', which is what he is. This is a plain case of the 'contrast between "nature" and "sophistication"' which Mr. Speirs also finds in *Sir Gawain*. But the Green Knight is a different matter. His behaviour is, unlike Perceval's, appropriate to his intentions—indeed it is, if I am right, a very conventional sign of them; so it cannot help to establish a thematic antithesis of the kind that Mr. Speirs proposes, between wild nature and courtly civilization. I suspect that all the other apparent similarities between the Green Knight and a 'wild man' are equally illusory.

The Green Knight's behaviour on first entering the hall, then, seems to resolve the conflict between the axe and the holly-bough in favour of the axe; and the court certainly respond to him (in what follows) as a hostile and dangerous stranger:

[20] In *Middle English Metrical Romances*, ed. W. H. French and C. B. Hale (New York, 1930), ll. 593–6.

Þerfore to answare watȝ arȝe mony aþel freke,
And al stouned at his steuen and stonstil seten
In a swoghe sylence þurȝ þe sale riche. (241-3)

But his answer to Arthur's invitation (in the next stanza) complicates matters once more. He has not come to join the feast, he says; but neither has he come 'in feȝtyng wyse'—

> Bot if þou be so bold as alle burneȝ tellen,
> Þou wyl grant me godly þe gomen þat I ask. (272-3)

And again:

> Forþy I craue in þis court a Crystemas gomen,
> For hit is Ȝol and Nwe Ȝer, and here ar ȝep mony. (283-4)

The hostile challenger submits, surprisingly, to the decorum of the Christmas season. His holly-bough symbolizes peace— 'pax' in both the Christian and the schoolboy sense (compare his 'barlay' in l. 296, a word which still survives among schoolchildren as a truce-term). All he wants of Arthur is a 'Christmas game'.

In one way, obviously, this is a deceitful description of what the Green Knight goes on to propose; but it is also an appropriate one. The element of game or play is a distinguishing feature of many romantic, as against most heroic, adventures; and the *Gawain*-poet is certainly right when he recognizes this in what is aptly referred to nowadays as the 'Beheading Game'. Unlike Beowulf's monster-fights, for one thing, the adventure is a gratuitous or unnecessary one, in that it is undertaken not under the pressure of practical need but—as Old English poets expressed it—'for wlence'. The Green Knight does not threaten to ravage Arthur's lands or to occupy his hall. He simply dares some member of the court to 'strike a strok for an oþer' and so vindicate the reputed 'joliete' and 'noblece' of the Round Table:

> Þe wyȝtest and þe worþyest of þe worldes kynde,
> Preue for to play wyth in oþer pure laykeȝ. (261-2)

Again, unlike Beowulf's fights, and like a game, Gawain's adventure is governed by specially agreed *rules*. This is appropriate for a season of 'pax', and particularly so since the rules suggest (however deceptively) that the contest is scarcely more than a customary bit of Christmas dramatics—hardly even a 'game' in the competitive sense. There is no doubt that dramatic 'interludes' had a place in fourteenth-century Christmas festivities: and the evidence suggests that these pieces sometimes involve the kind of ritual episode which bulks so large in the Mummers' Plays collected in modern times—a mock beheading followed by a revival of the beheaded actor. Such a supposition lends point to Arthur's later comment on the beheading episode, 'Wel bycommes such craft vpon Cristmasse, / Laykyng of enterludeȝ, to laȝe and to syng'; and it strengthens our own sense of the congruity, the 'becomingness', of that episode in its festal context. The Green Knight's 'game', like his holly-bough, is seasonable.[21]

One has only to read the passage in which the Green Knight first announces the rules of his Christmas game, however, to see that this is not the whole story. This passage, ll. 285–98, is notable for its grave, formal and rather legalistic language: 'I schal gif hym of my gyft' . . . 'I quit-clayme hit for euer' . . . 'þou wyl diȝt me þe dom' . . . 'gif hym respite' . . . 'a twelmonyth and a day'.[22] This is more like the language of a legal contract than of a Christmas game. The Green Knight is inviting some one of Arthur's knights to bind himself 'bi statut', as Gawain later puts it, to fulfil the conditions which he proposes. Clearly this is 'earnest' rather than 'game'—a vein of legal earnest which can be traced later in the scene. Thus,

[21] The distinction suggested here between a 'romantic' and a 'heroic' adventure comes out clearly in the first part of *Beowulf*. The swimming-match with Breca is in my sense 'romantic'. It is a gratuitous trial of strength, undertaken as Unferþ says 'for wlence'—out of bravado (508); and Beowulf in his reply emphasizes that he and Breca were only youngsters at the time (535–8). The contrast with the 'heroic' Grendel adventure seems deliberate.

[22] 'Quit-clayme' is an Anglo-French law term (commonly used in legal formulae together with 'release', another of the Green Knight's technical terms (2342): see R. Blenner-Hassett, 'Autobiographical Aspects of Chaucer's Franklin', *Spec.*, XXVIII (1953), pp. 796–9). The 'twelmonyth and a day', though common enough in literature, is an interval in law: 'a period constituting a term for certain purposes, in order to ensure the completion of a full year', *O.E.D.*, 'year' 7b.

after Gawain has received the axe from Arthur and steps forward to deliver the blow, the Green Knight insists that he 'refourme'—that is 'restate'—the 'forwardes', or terms of agreement, first announced to Arthur. This Gawain does (ll. 382–5); and the Green Knight congratulates him on having 'rehersed' the whole 'couenaunt' without omissions ('clanly'). He then adds a new clause: that Gawain shall seek him out to receive the return blow. Gawain agrees, on condition that he reveals his 'cort' and his 'name'; and the Green Knight promises to do this after he has had his 'tape'. He fulfils this promise in his parting speech (ll. 448–56), and at the same time repeats the terms of the agreement once more before leaving. These elaborate exchanges suggest that Gawain is entering into a solemn quasi-legal agreement; and this impression is confirmed by the frequent occurrence of the pregnant words 'trawþe', 'trwe' and 'truly' (see ll. 380, 392, 394, 401, 403, 406). These are not mere tags. When Gawain is asked by the Green Knight to swear to his extra clause 'bi þi trawþe' (394), he duly does so, solemnly repeating the substance of the clause and adding, as part of the form of agreement:

> And þat I swere þe for soþe, and by my seker trawþe.

Here, as in the exchange-of-winnings agreement later in the poem, the 'rules of the game' are stated and agreed to like clauses in a contract. The Green Knight's Christmas game is a seasonable contribution to the festivities; but it engages the hero in a test of the most fundamental of all knightly virtues— 'trawþe'. This is the most important of all the paradoxes associated with the figure of the Green Knight in the first fitt.

III

In the course of the action of *Sir Gawain* the hero makes two contracts with his adversary, the beheading agreement and the exchange agreement, and the outcome of his adventure is made to depend on his fidelity to these contracts—what the poet calls his 'trawþe'. His trial is essentially one of 'truth' in this medieval sense; and we are expected to accept this truth-trial as a

sufficient basis for the life-and-death moral judgment passed on
him by the Green Knight in the last part of the poem. It is not
surprising that most modern readers should, consciously or
otherwise, find this assumption difficult to accept. Gawain's
phrase 'by my seker trawþe' will not go into modern English.
'By my troth' is a mere Wardour-Street archaism, and the
word 'truth' itself is not normally used nowadays to denote a
moral quality. To express the sense of Gawain's 'trawþe' we
have to resort to some such other words as 'good faith', 'trust-
worthiness' or 'fidelity to contract'; and none of these renders
the force of the Middle English term at all adequately. The
main reason for this, I suppose, is that the ideal itself has lost
much of its force in societies which—outside one or two
eccentric institutions like the Stock Exchange—put all but the
most trivial contracts in writing and enforce them with effective
legal sanctions. Anyway, it is clear that the fourteenth century
attached far more importance to 'good faith' than we do.
'Truth' is one of the key words of later medieval English
literature. We shall see in the next chapter that it expresses a
powerful, though now largely unacknowledged, complex of
ideas, in which the notion of good faith assumes a dignity quite
strange to modern thinking. Gawain's 'truth', as symbolized by
the pentangle, is not a trivial matter. There is no need to cast
about, as some critics have done, for a graver and more worthy
moral theme. (It usually turns out to be chastity.)

These difficulties are further aggravated by the peculiar
nature of the agreements which engage Gawain's 'trawþe'. The
fantastic character of both the beheading game and the exchange of winnings, together with the circumstances under
which the hero agrees to them, make it hard for us to take his
obligations at all seriously. But it is clear that these considerations do not, in the poet's eyes, impair the gravity of the tests to
which Gawain is submitted. Rather the reverse. The complicated game-earnest ambivalence of the Green Knight in the
first fitt makes it *possible* for the hero to treat his obligations
lightly, but it does not make it *right* for him to do so. The
Christmas game which is not a game involves Gawain in a real
obligation, however tempting it may be for hero or reader to

suppose otherwise. The *Gawain*-poet, whether one likes it or not, was certainly casuist enough to enjoy contemplating the subtleties of such a test. A comparison with Chaucer may be helpful here. The *Franklin's Tale*, like *Sir Gawain*, turns on a question of 'truth', and it too has a strong vein of casuistry in it.[23] Dorigen, dancing with friends after dinner, receives the unwelcome advances of the squire Aurelius. 'In pley', as Chaucer puts it, she proposes an agreement: she will accept his love if he will remove the rocks from the coast of Brittany. Aurelius takes this fantastic proposal in earnest, enlists the help of a magician, and holds Dorigen to her word. So the heroine finds herself involved in a kind of test-case of 'truth' not unlike Gawain's: she has to honour an agreement made on her part 'in pley', and fulfilled on the part of Aurelius 'agayns the proces of nature'. Either consideration might now be thought sufficient to invalidate Aurelius' claim upon her: she did not really mean it, and anyway she was not to know that Aurelius would resort to magic. Yet Chaucer recognizes these arguments only insofar as their availability makes Dorigen's truth the more notable and praiseworthy. He simply assumes that it is right and noble of her not to entertain such thoughts: 'Trouthe is the hyeste thyng that man may kepe'. This shows how far a fourteenth-century writer was ready to go in exalting the claims of the pledged word.

In one way, however, the *Gawain*-poet's case is, in the first fitt at least, less extreme than Chaucer's. Despite the festive surroundings, Gawain does not exactly pledge his word 'in pley'; nor can he claim to be entirely surprised when a green knight survives decapitation 'agayns the proces of nature'. The interest of his case is, one might say, rather more straightforward and heroic in character. He has given his word, and the 'renoun of þe Rounde Table' depends upon his keeping it,

[23] Both these aspects of the *Franklin's Tale* are well brought out in P. F. Baum, *Chaucer: A Critical Appreciation* (Durham, N.C., 1958), pp. 122–33. Mr. Baum's discussion of Dorigen's obligation to Aurelius illustrates the modern reader's difficulties in accepting the ideal of 'trawþe'.

even in the face of what seems certain death. For once the Green Knight has survived the blow, it seems clear that the hero has bound himself 'by his seker trawþe' to seek out his own death; and the tensions in the last part of the scene derive entirely from this simple fact. There is nothing ambivalent, for once, in the Green Knight's parting speech. Gawain is, as he later says, 'summoned'—like Everyman—to keep an appointment with Death:

> To þe Grene Chapel þou chose, I charge þe, to fotte
> Such a dunt as þou hatz dalt—disserued þou habbez—
> To be ȝederly ȝolden on Nw Ȝeres morn.
> Þe Knyȝt of þe Grene Chapel men knowen me mony;
> Forþi me for to fynde if þou fraystez, faylez þou neuer.
> Þerfore com, oþer recreaunt be calde þe behoueus.[24] (451–6)

There are a number of passages in the first fitt where the idea of Death may suggest itself, momentarily, as one of the many and various significances playing round the figure of the Green Knight. It is not difficult, for example, to hear the voice of the Preacher in the speech which he makes after proposing his game and receiving no reply:

> 'What, is þis Arþurez hous,' quoþ þe haþel þenne,
> 'Þat al þe rous rennes of þurȝ ryalmes so mony?
> Where is now your sourquydrye and your conquestes,
> Your gryndellayk and your greme, and your grete wordes?'
>
> (309–12)

In these words one sees the court, for a moment, exactly as one might see it in a Morality Play, a Tragedy of Princes, or an 'ubi sunt' lyric ('Where is now your sourquydrye . . .?'). But it is only in the Green Knight's parting speech that the idea of Death can be said positively to demand recognition—the kind of recognition suggested by the phrase 'The Summoning of

[24] The capitals in 'þe Knyȝt of þe Grene Chapel' are my own. Editors have not taken the phrase as a proper name; but Bercilak has previously promised to announce 'my hous and my home and myn owen nome', and this is what he does in l. 454. 'The Green Knight' is a more convenient name, but it does not seem to be used as such in the text. (The phrase occurs twice, ll. 390 and 417; also, with inversion, l. 704.)

Gawain'. I do not mean to suggest that the bewildering creature turns out after all to 'be' Death—what he turns out to 'be' (or claim to be) is 'The Knight of the Green Chapel'. I mean rather that the speech has for me a peculiar resonance which I cannot explain except by reference to the traditional figure of Death in the moral allegories. Consider these lines, for example:

> Þe Knyȝt of þe Grene Chapel men knowen me mony;
> Forþi me for to fynde if þou fraysteȝ, fayleȝ þou neuer.

The vagueness of the directions needs no explanation, for it is common enough in romance; but what about the mysterious certainty of the promise, 'you cannot fail to find me if you look'? True, the Green Knight explains the promise; but his explanation—'men knowen me mony'—is itself mysterious. It cannot be reconciled with what he says at the end of the poem, where he clearly implies that Morgan turned him into a green knight for the one occasion only; and it is positively supported elsewhere only by the speech of the guide in the fourth fitt, itself a peculiar passage which, as we shall see later, comes closer than anything else in the poem to an actual identification of the Green Knight with Death. In fact, of course, such an identification is never made—it would be out of keeping with the conventions of this kind of romance—but there is a partial association; and it is this association, I think, which explains the slight liberty the poet took with his story in the guide's speech and the Green Knight's speech of summons; for it led him to ascribe to Gawain's adversary something of the universality and inevitability of Death itself—'Forþi me for to fynde if þou fraysteȝ, fayleȝ þou neuer'. What I take to be the same sinister note is struck by the Old Man in Chaucer's *Pardoner's Tale* when he directs the 'rioters':

> 'Now, sires,' quod he, 'if that yow be so leef
> To fynde Deeth, turne up this croked wey,
> For in that grove I lafte hym, by my fey,
> Under a tree, and there he wole abyde;
> Noght for youre boost he wole him no thyng hyde.
> Se ye that ook? Right there ye shal hym fynde'.

and by the Death who summons Everyman:

> And now out of thy syght I wyll me hy.
> Se thou make the redy shortely,
> For thou mayst saye this is the daye
> That no man lyuynge may scape awaye.[25]

IV

The two Canterbury Tales mentioned in the last section—the *Franklin's Tale* and the *Pardoner's Tale*—together suggest something of the range of the poet's conception in *Sir Gawain*. Like the Pardoner's 'exemplum', his poem is a 'moral tale'. It is also, like the Franklin's romance, a 'laye' such as 'thise olde gentil Britouns' might have read 'for hir plesaunce'. We have already seen these aspects of the poem in the first fitt: on the one hand, feasts, games and wonders, on the other, intimations of moral trial and mortality. The balancing of contraries is most delicately done; and it is difficult, if not impossible, to do it justice in a general summary. Let me instead suggest very briefly how the balance stands in the last part of the fitt, after the departure of the Green Knight.

The Green Knight 'hales out' without leavetaking, just as earlier he had 'haled in' without greeting,[26] and even the poet himself needs a short line (a 'bob') to gather his wits before describing the reactions of Arthur and Gawain:

> To quat kyth he becom knwe non þere,
> Neuer more þen þay wyste fram queþen he watȝ wonnen.
> > What þenne?
> Þe kyng and Gawen þare
> At þat grene þay laȝe and grenne,
> Ȝet breued watȝ hit ful bare
> A meruayl among þo menne. (460–6)

The poet's treatment of the court's reactions to the Green Knight is, throughout the first fitt, scrupulously balanced. He

[25] *Canterbury Tales*, VI, 760–5; *The Summoning of Everyman*, ed. A. C. Cawley (Manchester, 1961), ll. 180–3.
[26] The 'valet' who carries Mordred's defiant message in the *Mort Artu* also leaves 'sanz congié prendre', ed. cit. p. 230.

neither merely eulogizes and idealizes Arthur and his men nor scores cheap moralizing points at their expense, as we see, typically, in his comment on the 'swoghe sylence' which greeted the first appearance of the Green Knight, where he allows for both noble and ignoble feelings:

> I deme hit not al for doute,
> Bot sum for cortaysye. (246-7)

There is a similar balancing in the quatrain (or 'wheel') quoted above, for here we find both the heroic laughter of Arthur and Gawain and its offset, the suggestion of 'doute' in 'ʒet breued watʒ hit ful bare . . .' (the 'ʒet' is typical).[27] So too in the next stanza:

> Þaʒ Arþer þe hende kyng at hert hade wonder,
> He let no semblaunt be sene, bot sayde ful hyʒe
> To þe comlych quene wyth cortays speche. . . . (467-9)

The wit and elegance, the *self-possession*, of Arthur's 'courteous speeches' to Guinevere and then to Gawain (note particularly the play on the phrase 'heng vp þyn ax' in the latter) demonstrate that the Green Knight has not, as he claimed, 'ouerwalt' the revelry of the Round Table, its 'joliete' and 'noblece'. Yet Arthur does not attempt to deny that he has 'sen a selly', and the poet makes us aware of his 'wonder' as well as his courtesy. We are not allowed to take his self-possession for granted, as though it cost him no effort to achieve. The poet's view is beautifully inclusive and human. Arthur and his knights (including Gawain, be it noted) are neither degradingly unnerved nor superhumanly nerveless in the face of Morgan's testing marvel.

Once the 'interlude' of the Green Knight has been put in its place 'among þise kynde caroles of knyʒteʒ and ladyeʒ' and the

[27] One may contrast an episode in the French *Perlesvaus* where the laughter and the fear are divided between a hero and a foil. A 'valet', exploring a deserted castle, finds a room full of severed heads and feet, and returns 'toz esfreez' and nearly fainting. Lancelot goes to look for himself, and returns 'tot riant'. *Perlesvaus*, ed. W. A. Nitze and T. A. Jenkins (Chicago, 1932-7), ll. 6413-25.

axe has been hung up as a token 'abof þe dece on doser', Arthur
and Gawain are free to return to the feast:

> Þenne þay boȝed to a borde þise burnes togeder,
> Þe kyng and þe gode knyȝt, and kene men hem serued
> Of alle dayntyeȝ double, as derrest myȝt falle;
> Wyth alle maner of mete and mynstralcie boþe,
> Wyth wele walt þay þat day, til worþed an ende
> in londe. (481–6)

It is almost as if the 'rechles merþes' of the beginning of the
scene were restored; but the effect is qualified here by the
fine modulation of tone in the last long line and the 'bob':
'Wyth wele walt þay þat day, til worþed an ende / in londe'. This
has a melancholy effect of withdrawal, as a lengthening shot
may have in a film; and it prepares us for the author's stepping
forward, in the 'wheel', with his earnest and ominous words
of advice:

> Now þenk wel, Sir Gawan,
> For woþe þat þou ne wonde
> Þis auenture for to frayn
> Þat þou hatȝ tan on honde.

II

THE SECOND FITT

I

THE FIRST FITT, after engrossing the reader in the fictional world of Camelot, ended with a movement of withdrawal, the author stepping in between reader and fiction to address his hero; and two stanzas of the second fitt pass before we are restored to the court at Camelot.[1] There is, first of all, a passage of summary and comment (ll. 491-9) in which the author turns from hero to audience, directing their attention back to what has gone before, then forward to what will follow. The passage, though short, has several noteworthy features. The first lines

> This hanselle hatʒ Arthur of auenturus on fyrst
> In ʒonge ʒer, for he ʒerned ʒelpyng to here (491-2)

recall the dominant gaiety of the first fitt—the young year and its gifts, the young Arthur and his yearning for adventures. At the same time the traditional heroic irony in the reference to Gawain's adventure as a 'hanselle' or New Year's Gift (compare ll. 66-70) recalls the irony of the Green Knight's game which is not a game.[2] Arthur's knights got more than they bargained for:

[1] On the division of the poem into fitts, see L. L. Hill, 'Madden's Divisions of *Sir Gawain* and the "Large Initial Capitals" of *Cotton Nero A.X.*', *Spec.*, XXI (1946), pp. 67-71. I adopt the conventional four-fold division here. Note, however, that the second fitt, unlike the first, is subdivided at two points: in addition to the four-line capital at l. 491, there are three-line capitals at ll. 619 and 763. The 'second fitt' is indeed something of a piecemeal, Balkan affair by comparison with the first.

[2] Malory's Sagramoure refers to a knock-down blow as a 'hansell'

31

Thaȝ hym wordeȝ were wane when þay to sete wenten,
Now ar þay stoken of sturne werk, stafful her hond. (493–4)

The Green Knight's challenge (the 'wordeȝ' of 'ȝelpyng') re-
leased Arthur from his vow, but involved Gawain in 'sturne
werk'. To receive a 'hanselle' 'on fyrst'—at the beginning of a
day or year—was traditionally an omen of good luck and
prosperity;[3] but not in Gawain's case:

> Gawan watȝ glad to begynne þose gomneȝ in halle,
> Bot þaȝ þe ende be heuy, haf ȝe no wonder. (495–6)

This, the last of three terse couplets, makes the game-earnest
antithesis explicit in the chiastic balance of 'glad' and 'heuy',
'begynne' and 'ende'; and it leads on to the more expansive
generalizing comment with which the passage ends:

> For þaȝ men ben mery in mynde quen þay han mayn drynk,
> A ȝere ȝernes ful ȝerne, and ȝeldeȝ neuer lyke,
> Þe forme to þe fynisment foldeȝ ful selden. (497–9)

These lines must carry something of a shock even for readers
who have recognized already that the *Gawain*-poet stands, in
some ways, outside the tradition of high courtly French romance. We should, when reading the first fitt, have acknowledged Gawain as a more 'human' hero than Galahad; but we
can hardly have been prepared for the 'mayn drynk'. And it is
surprising to find the hero coupled in such a broad and frankly
realistic generalization with men who cannot very often afford
such drink—as if Gawain were not a Knight of the Round Table,

---

[3] See J. Brand, *Observations on Popular Antiquities*, rev. H. Ellis
(London, 1813), I, 8–18 and II, 572. Robert Mannyng refers to the
superstition sceptically, rather as the *Gawain*-poet does: 'For many
hauyn glad hancel at þe morw / And to hem or euyn comþ mochyl
sorw' (*Handlyng Synne*, ed. F. J. Furnivall, Part I, E.E.T.S. O.S.
119 (1901), ll. 373–4).

(*Works*, ed. Vinaver, p. 398—compare the reference to 'gifts' on
p. 17). See also Gavin Douglas' translation of the *Aeneid*, Small, Vol.
III, p. 257, l. 4. On such ironic metaphors in the 'epic style', see G. V.
Smithers (ed.), *Kyng Alisaunder*, Vol. II, E.E.T.S. 237 (1957),
pp. 32-34.

sure of at least five great feasts a year.[4] These things seem to spring from an impulse in the poet to see Gawain not only as a knight among his peers but also as a man among men, a representative of 'humanum genus' without distinction of social class—as an Everyman, in fact, whose experiences, though in many ways fantastic and out of the common, are in the end central to common experience in a way that Galahad's are not. This is for me an important feature of the poem, and I shall return to it later.

With 'Þe forme to þe fynisment foldeȝ ful selden' the poet ends his passage of summary and comment, and in the next line the poem gets vigorously under way again: 'Forþi þis ȝol ouerȝede, and þe ȝere after'. Notice, though, that the famous seasons passage which follows is attached to the preceding generalization by 'Forþi', and that the attachment which that word implies is a genuine one. The year which ensues for Gawain after the Christmas feast is to him what all years are to the common 'men' of l. 497: it 'ȝernes ful ȝerne, and ȝeldeȝ neuer lyke'. The passing seasons—Lent, Spring (called 'softe somer' in the text), Summer and Autumn ('heruest')—do not involve him in the everyday life of ploughing, sowing and reaping; but neither do they 'yield the like' of Christmas, with its games in hall. There is the great feast of All Saints' Day (l. 536); but this, for all its 'much reuel and ryche of þe Rounde Table', is overshadowed for the court by the approach of Gawain's 'anious uyage': 'Al for luf of þat lede in longynge þay were' (540). Despite his privileges, Gawain shares the common experience: 'Þe forme to þe fynisment foldeȝ ful selden'.

The attachment of such a moral to a description of the changing seasons is, of course, by no means peculiar to *Sir Gawain*: the cycle of the year is naturally associated with thoughts of mutability and death at any period. It is worth noticing, none the less, how the *Gawain*-poet handles this general theme within the particular time-scheme of his story. Normally, in a moralized

---

[4] 'Drynking redde wyne' is the characteristic occupation of December in such popular pieces as 'Occupations of the Months', no. 67 in *Secular Lyrics of the XIVth and XVth Centuries*, ed. R. H. Robbins (Oxford, 1952).

seasons passage, the 'forme' of the year is spring, and it is the spring which corresponds to the period of youthful 'game' in man's life, as in this passage of Lydgate's:

> Thus four tymes makith vs a merour cleer
> Off mannys lyff and a ful pleyn ymage.
> Ver and Iuuentus togedir haue sogeer,
> Estas folwith, longyng to saddere age;
> To vs Autumpne bryngeth his massage
> Off Senectus, Wynter last of alle,
> How Dethys orlogge doth on vs calle.[5]

The *Gawain*-poet draws on the tradition represented in these lines. His Michaelmas moon, especially, with its 'wynter wage' ('earnest of winter') making Gawain think of his impending winter voyage to death, has something of the ominousness of Lydgate's allegorical Autumn, who 'bryngeth his massage / Off Senectus'. On the other hand, despite the richness and beauty of his spring passage, the 'ʒonge ʒer' of the *Gawain*-poet is not the spring season (at the beginning of the zodiacal year) but the season of New Year (at the beginning of the calendar year). It is the New Year, not Ver, and Juventus which 'togedir haue sogeer' in the first fitt and the opening lines of the second.

Few readers, however, will feel any inconsistency in this. The poet is improvising, but his improvisation comes off. As one reads one can accept both the joys of the Christmas feast and the 'solace of þe softe somer' as equally types of the 'forme', or glad beginning. Each, one recognizes, has its own proper 'fynisment': there is Lent, which follows after Christmas and 'fraysteʒ flesch wyth þe fysche and fode more symple'; and there is autumn, which catches up on the 'wynne wort' of summer and 'warneʒ hym for þe wynter to wax ful rype'. It is specially important, here, to recognize the double value of the mid-winter season, which emerges for the first time in this passage and is sustained throughout the rest of the poem. It is a season of both

---

[5] Lydgate and Burgh's *Secrees of Old Philisoffres*, ed. R. Steele, E.E.T.S. E.S. 66 (1894), ll. 1457–63. The theme is strongly represented in moral lyrics, as in 'A Winter Song', no. 9 in *Religious Lyrics of the XIVth Century*, ed. Carleton Brown (Oxford, 1952).

birth and death, glad beginnings and heavy ends. Indoors there is, as in the first fitt, feasting and drinking in celebration of the birth of Christ and of the New Year. Outdoors (the 'þeroute' of l. 518, probably) there is cold, hardship and death:

> Þenne al rypeȝ and roteȝ þat ros vpon fyrst,
> And þus ȝirneȝ þe ȝere in ȝisterdayeȝ mony,
> And wynter wyndeȝ aȝayn, as þe worlde askeȝ,
> no fage. (528–31)

The outdoor winter played no part in the first fitt; but from this point on it is to have an important place, alternating and contrasting with the indoor world of mid-winter festivities, just as it does in a famous and beautiful passage in Chaucer's *Franklin's Tale*:

> Phebus wax old, and hewed lyk laton,
> That in his hoote declynacion
> Shoon as the burned gold with stremes brighte;
> But now in Capricorn adoun he lighte,
> Where as he shoon ful pale, I dar wel seyn.
> The bittre frostes, with the sleet and reyn,
> Destroyed hath the grene in every yerd.
> Janus sit by the fyr, with double berd,
> And drynketh of his bugle horn the wyn;
> Biforn hym stant brawen of the tusked swyn,
> And 'Nowel' crieth every lusty man.[6]

Since the greater part of the action of *Sir Gawain* takes place in the winter, there is no room in it, outside the seasons passage, for spring, summer or autumn. But the double, Janus-like character of the mid-winter season—on the one hand wine, boars' heads and lusty men crying 'Nowel', on the other the old, pale sun, frost, sleet and rain—provides the poet with a set of strong contrasts which can serve him, in place of more conventional contrasts between spring living and winter living, as physical correlatives for his moral theme. His two winters, indoor and outdoor, 'makith vs a merour cleer / Off mannys lyff' as effectively as do Lydgate's four 'times' or seasons. They are not allegorical types of Juventus or Senectus, any more than the

---

[6] Ed. Robinson, *C.T.*, V, 1245–55.

The Second Fitt

Green Knight is an allegorical type of Death; but they do—and increasingly as the poem progresses—carry a load of moral implication. Perhaps I might repeat here that the seasons passage is itself introduced as demonstrative of a moral truth.

That passage ends with a wheel which answers the closing wheel of the first fitt: 'Now þenk wel, Sir Gawan . . .', 'Þen þenkkeʒ Gawan ful sone . . .'. This echo serves to mark the end of the passage of moral comment and 'withdrawal' on the part of the narrator; and at the beginning of the next stanza he returns to Camelot and to feasting:

> ʒet quyl Al-hal-day with Arþer he lenges;
> And he made a fare on þat fest for þe frekeʒ sake,
> With much reuel and ryche of þe Rounde Table. (536–8)

The description of the All Saints' Day feast never really gets under way, however, and it is cut off, somewhat abruptly, after only one stanza. The poet does not—to use his own expression (l. 1009)—'point' the revels here, partly, no doubt, because we have already had a good deal of revelling in the first fitt, but also because these revels are not relevant to his purpose anyway. For one feels here—as one did not even at the end of the first fitt—that Gawain, though still for the moment among the 'compayny of court', is no longer quite of it. The very fact that the feast is made in his honour ('for þe frekeʒ sake') suggests that he is now set apart by virtue of his impending 'errand'. The feeling that he is alone with his 'destinés derf and dere' is already strong—so strong that it may colour one's response even to something as conventional as the list of knights who offer him advice:

> Aywan, and Errik, and oþer ful mony,
> Sir Doddinaual de Sauage, þe duk of Clarence,
> Launcelot, and Lyonel, and Lucan þe gode . . . etc. (551 ff.)

The naming of so many knights at this particular point in the poem—for the first and last time in most cases—serves as a reminder that the court, though elsewhere it is always (barring ll. 109–13) presented as a corporate, anonymous whole, is in fact a company of knights with names, and adventures, of their own: individuals, like Gawain.

The Second Fitt

The emergence of Gawain as an individual knight-hero is completed in the following four stanzas. Here, in the description of the arming of Gawain and his departure from Camelot, the court has no part to play except to wish the hero well in one brief passage: Gawain, for the first time in the poem, has the stage to himself. The scene is an important one, for it marks the beginning of a new phase in the presentation of the hero and to a large degree establishes the character of the presentation in this phase. I would distinguish three such major phases in the poem as a whole, the first of which extends up to the point which we have now reached. The Gawain of the first phase is the 'gode Gawan' of the first fitt—essentially, as I have suggested, a straightforward figure, presented in the tradition of the English romances as an eminently brave and courteous 'brother of the Round Table'. We must now consider the Gawain of the second phase who emerges out of his chrysalis in the course of the arming scene.

The action of this scene can be summarized very briefly. On the morning after the feast of All Saints Gawain rises early, puts on his armour, hears Mass, takes leave of his companions, is escorted to the mounting stage, and there dons his helmet, receives his shield and lance, and rides off. This summary may leave one wondering why a scene devoted to such routine incidents should occupy four whole stanzas, running to more than a hundred lines; but there are, in fact, at least two good reasons for this. The first consideration is one that applies pretty generally to the arming scenes of traditional poetry. There is a convenient statement of it in A. B. Lord's discussion of Greek and Yugoslav oral epics, where he considers the function of the Arming of the Hero as a conventional 'theme': 'The varying degrees of elaboration of the theme of arming used by Homer are similar to those of the Yugoslav singers, extending from the single line to longer passages. As with the South Slavic poets, the very presence of the theme has a meaning beyond that of description for description's own sake. If the ritual in the Yugoslav poems and in the *Digenis Akritas* seems to be one of initiation, that in the *Iliad* is probably one of dedication to the task of saving the hero's people, even of sacrifice. Each of these men is about to set out upon a mission of deep significance, and the "ornamental" theme is a signal and mark, both "ritualistic" and artistic, of the role of the hero.'[7] What is said here of the *Iliad* may be applied to *Sir Gawain* (and to *Beowulf*). The sense of Gawain as a 'dedicated' hero set apart from his fellows, already present in the stanza preceding the arming passage, certainly gains strength in the course of his ceremonious preparations for departure.

But there is another, more important, consideration. The arming scene is concerned not only with the hero's preparations for departure, but also, equally, with the hero himself: it provides, in effect, that description of Gawain which was missing in the first fitt. It is not a formal, static description, like that of the Green Knight; but it is, for all that, clearly conceived as one of those 'descriptiones personarum' beloved of medieval rhetoricians. 'Notandum quod cujuslibet personae duplex potest esse descriptio: una superficialis, alia intrinseca; superficialis, quando membrorum elegantia describitur vel homo exterior; intrinseca, quando interioris hominis proprietates, scilicet ratio, fides, patientia, honestas, injuria, superbia, luxuria et cetera epitheta interioris hominis, scilicet animae, ad laudem vel ad vituperium exprimuntur.'[8] The description of the hero in *Sir Gawain* can, I think, usefully be characterized in terms borrowed from this passage of Matthew of Vendôme. It is a double description of the kind distinguished by Matthew as eulogistic ('ad laudem'), praising both the 'homo exterior' and the 'interioris hominis proprietates'. The 'descriptio superficialis' is somewhat peculiar, in that it is devoted to armour and weapons to the exclusion of 'membrorum elegantia' (we never get any clear idea of what Gawain looks like); but this is natural

[7] A. B. Lord, *The Singer of Tales* (Cambridge, Mass., 1960), p. 91.

[8] 'Note that the description of any person can be of two kinds, one external, the other inward. The external kind is when we describe the beauty of the bodily parts, or the outer man; the inward kind is when we portray, whether for praise or blame, the properties of the inner man, such as reason, faith, patience, honesty, injustice, pride, lustfulness, and other attributes of the inner man, that is, the soul.' Matthew of Vendôme, *Ars Versificatoria*, I, 74, in E. Faral, *Les Arts Poétiques du XII' et du XIII' Siècle* (Paris, 1924), p. 135.

in an arming scene. It is for the same reason that the 'descriptio intrinseca' is itself formally subordinated to the description of the equipment. Both peculiarities follow from the one act of artistic economy—the combining of the rhetoricians' set 'descriptio' with the traditional arming scene of the oral poets. The 'descriptio intrinseca' is what matters here, for this plays a most important part in establishing the Gawain of the 'second phase'. The pentangle passage, especially, with its formal exposition of the 'interioris hominis proprietates', demands some attention; and there are also other passages in the scene which, though less explicitly, contribute to one's newly-enriched sense of the moral values which Gawain is to represent in the course of his impending adventure. Modern readers may find the poet's method somewhat devious; but people in the late Middle Ages were well accustomed to seeing connections between items of a knight's equipment and moral properties. Allegorical elaborations of the Pauline 'armour of God' were common in contemporary religious writings; while the many late medieval books on chivalry regularly incorporated some account of the moral significance of shields, spears and the like: 'That whiche the preest reuestyth hym whan he syngeth the masse hath somme sygnefyaunce whiche concordeth to his offyce; and the offyce of preesthode and of chyualry haue grete concordaunce. Therfor thordre of chyualry requyreth that al that whiche is nedeful to a knyght as touchynge the vse of his offyce haue somme sygnefyaunce by the whiche is sygnefyed the noblesse of chyualrye and of his ordre.'[9] Such writings would have prepared the original audience of *Sir Gawain* to accept the poet's exposition of the 'significance' of the pentangle, as well as to see other, unexpounded, significances elsewhere. Let me briefly give two examples of the latter, before going on to the pentangle itself.

The first, a small but cunning example of moral symbolism, concerns *gold*. Gold appears frequently in the first part of the

[9] *The Book of the Ordre of Chyvalry*, ed. A. T. P. Byles, E.E.T.S. O.S. 168 (1926), p. 76. For an elaborate example in religious writing, see Lydgate's translation of Deguileville, *The Pilgrimage of the Life of Man*, ed. F. J. Furnivall, Part I, E.E.T.S. E.S. 77 (1899), ll. 7225 ff.

The Second Fitt

arming scene as an item in the 'superficial' description of
Gawain's body-armour and Gryngolet's horse-trappings.
Gawain's armour is 'gyld gere' (569), with 'knoteʒ of golde'
(577), 'gold soreʒ' (587), and laces that 'lemed of golde' (591).
Gryngolet's saddle has 'mony golde frenges' (598), his bridle is
'with bryʒt golde bounden' (600), and everywhere there are
'ryche golde nayleʒ' (603). All these details are quite conventional in a eulogistic description of knightly equipment.
Notice, however, that the 'ryche golde nayleʒ' are all 'rayled on
red'. This colour-combination has a heraldic significance; for,
as one learns at the beginning of the next stanza, Gawain's
heraldic device is a pentangle 'depaynt of pure golde hweʒ' on a
field of 'schyr gouleʒ' (i.e. red). And these heraldic 'pure golde
hweʒ' in their turn have a further, moral, significance, as one
discovers in the course of the same stanza:

> Gawan watʒ for gode knawen, and as golde pured,
> Voyded of vche vylany. . . . (633-4)

So one is led on from the 'gyld gere', through the 'pure golde
hweʒ' of the heraldic device, to the 'golde pured' which, in a
comparison of biblical origin, signifies the righteous man
'voyded of vche vylany'.[10] The gold belongs, as a mark of
excellence, both to the exterior and to the interior man.

Significances of a more secular kind are to be found in the
poet's description of the 'vrysoun', or embroidered covering,
on Gawain's helmet. This is adorned with gems and embroidered
with

> bryddeʒ on semeʒ,
> As papiayeʒ paynted pernyng bitwene,
> Tortors and trulofeʒ entayled so þyk
> As mony burde þeraboute had ben seuen wynter
> in toune. (610-4)

These things, the parrots, the turtle-doves and the love-knots,
are alike in their significance: they all belong to the medieval

[10] See *Zechariah* 13.9, *Malachi* 3.2-3. The figure is commonplace
enough, but developments later in the poem (where it is recalled,
l. 2393) suggest that its biblical connections may be relevant.

iconography of love. Cupid's robe in the *Romance of the Rose* is 'ypaynted al with amorettes' (that is, love-knots), and Cupid himself is 'all with briddes wryen, / With popynjay, with nyghtyngale'. The 'papeiai' is coupled with the 'trewe tortle' as an image of the mistress in the love lyric *Annot and John*. The turtle-dove, in turn, is coupled with the 'treweluf' in the *Quatrefoil of Love*.[11] But there is no need to multiply examples to show that parrots, turtle-doves and love-knots were, singly and in combination, recognized emblems of 'true love'. The point to stress is that they occur together on an 'vrysoun' embroidered for Gawain by the young ladies of Camelot. This should put us on our guard against taking too narrowly ascetic a view of the ideal which he represents.

Let me turn now to the pentangle, for it is the pentangle which, by its shape, most completely symbolizes Gawain's ideal—just as, by its colour, it symbolizes his perfect realization of it. Here one must follow the poet's argument rather closely. After describing the 'vrysoun' and the diamond-studded circlet on the helmet,[12] he goes straight on to the shield (without, incidentally, remembering to mention that Gawain mounts his horse, which he would do at this point, as in ll. 2060–1):

> Then þay schewed hym þe schelde, þat was of schyr goule3
> Wyth þe pentangel depaynt of pure golde hwe3.

[11] *Romance of the Rose*, M.E. version, ll. 892, 912–3; *Annot and John*, no. 3 in *The Harley Lyrics*, ed. G. L. Brook (Manchester, 1948), ll. 21–22; *Quatrefoil of Love*, ed. I. Gollancz in *An English Miscellany Presented to Dr. Furnivall* (Oxford, 1901), pp. 112 ff.

[12] This 'device' of diamonds (see *Middle English Dictionary* under 'devis', 4a) is useful as well as decorative: 'The lapidarie seith þt muche vertue yaue god to þe diamaunde & many graces. Hit yeuyth to a man þat berith hym strencthe & vertue, and kepith hym fro greuouse metynge & temptacions & fro venym. Also *hit kepeth þe boones & þe membres whoole*', *English Mediaeval Lapidaries*, ed. J. Evans and M. S. Serjeantson, E.E.T.S. O.S. 190 (1933), p. 30. The lapidaries, incidentally, suggest that 'bry3t' and 'broun' in l. 618 are not synonyms, as editors have believed: 'þe diamaundes þat commen oute of ynde ben cleped þe males, & arne broun of colour & of violet; & tho þat commen oute of arabie be cleped þe femmales and ben whitter', ed. cit. p. 30. 'Broun' here corresponds to Marbod's 'ferruginei coloris' (*De Gemmis; Patrologia Latina*, Vol. 171, col. 1739).

He braydeʒ hit by þe bauderyk, aboute þe hals kestes,
Þat bisemed þe segge semlyly fayre.[13] (619–22)

It is the word 'bisemed' that provides the cue for the digression
that follows; for the poet 'tarries' to explain why it is that the
pentangle beseems, or 'apendeʒ to', his hero—why, that is, it is
not only a conventional heraldic device but also an emblem
proper to its bearer's character. It is an argumentative digression, running from the 'quy' of l. 623 to the 'þerfore' of
l. 662. The poet first explains that the pentangle is 'a syngne þat
Salamon set sumquyle / In bytoknyng of trawþe, bi tytle þat hit
habbeʒ'. This is the major premiss of his argument, and it is
established by a characteristically medieval recourse to both
Nature and Authority. The pentangle, on the authority of
Solomon and also by its very nature ('bi tytle þat hit habbeʒ'),
is a sign of *trawþe*.[14]

The idea of 'trawþe', as I have already suggested, plays a
vitally important part in *Sir Gawain*; and it is without a doubt
the key idea in the present passage. So it is worth pausing here
to discover what this complex word meant to fourteenth-century
writers and readers. To do this, one must take some account of
its semantic history.[15] The source of the Old English noun
'triewþ' (or 'treowþ') was the adjective 'triewe' (or 'treowe'), and
this adjective (itself derived from an earlier noun meaning
'good faith, fidelity') meant 'faithful, loyal, constant, trusty'.
Correspondingly, the meaning of the Old English noun was
(in the definition of the *O.E.D.*): 'The character of being,
or disposition to be, true to a person, principle, cause, etc.;
faithfulness, fidelity, loyalty, constancy, steadfast allegiance'.
This sense (*O.E.D.* 1), together with a closely related objective
sense, 'a solemn engagement or promise, a covenant' (*O.E.D.* 2),
is the only one recorded for the word during the Old English
and earlier Middle English periods. It is not until the early

[13] The extra large capital T at the beginning of these lines (see
above, n. 1) should be noted.

[14] See Appendix One.

[15] See, apart from the very substantial *O.E.D.* article, W. Hérau-
court, *Die Wertwelt Chaucers* (Heidelberg, 1939), pp. 131 ff. The new
Middle English Dictionary has not reached T at the time of writing.

fourteenth century—according to the evidence of the *O.E.D.*—
that new senses begin to develop. During that century, however,
they develop profusely.

Three of these new senses concern us here.[16] The first,
religious 'faith, trust, confidence' (under *O.E.D.* 3), is originally,
no doubt, simply a specialization of *O.E.D.* 1, religious faith
being regarded as a kind of loyalty or fidelity to God. 'Trawþe'
in this sense is one of the three theological virtues, along with
Hope and Charity. In the early fourteenth-century *Cursor
Mundi*, where this sense is first recorded, the word is regularly
associated with Abraham, the traditional type of Faith. The
second new sense (also, as it happens, first recorded in *Cursor
Mundi*) is less unfamiliar; it is 'disposition to speak or act truly
or without deceit; truthfulness, veracity, sincerity' (*O.E.D.* 4).
This in turn—no doubt with the support of its parent sense,
O.E.D. 1, which was still flourishing—gave rise to a third, and
much more generalized, new sense. This third sense is defined
by the *O.E.D.* (classing it, somewhat questionably, simply as a
'wider sense' of truthfulness, etc., under 4) as: 'honesty, up-
rightness, righteousness, virtue, integrity'.

The evidence of the Dictionary, therefore, suggests that
'truth'—insofar as it was a moral term, denoting the 'properties
of the inner man'—had four main distinguishable meanings at
the time when *Sir Gawain* was composed. To praise a man for
his 'truth' might mean (*a*) that he was loyal to people, principles
or promises, (*b*) that he had faith in God, (*c*) that he was without
deceit, or (*d*) that he was upright and virtuous. These various
meanings are, of course, closely related one to another; but they

---

[16] The present discussion is entirely restricted to senses falling
under *O.E.D.* I, 'The quality of being true (and allied senses)'.
Branch II senses ('Conformity with fact', 'accuracy', etc.) are
not recorded before the late sixteenth century. Branch III senses
('Something that is true'—'true statement', 'true religious doctrine',
'spiritual reality', etc.) are first recorded in the fourteenth century. I
have excluded them because I do not think them relevant. One can see
from Holy Church's exposition of Truth in *Piers Plowman*, Passus I,
that these objective Branch III senses could become entangled with
the subjective moral senses of Branch I; but this does not seem to happen
in *Sir Gawain*.

leave room for a certain amount of semantic manoeuvring, and the *Gawain*-poet exploits this to the full in his exposition of the pentangle.

The pentangle, he says first, has a natural right, or 'tytle', to be considered a sign of 'trawþe' because

> . . . hit is a figure þat haldeʒ fyue poynteʒ,
> And vche lyne vmbelappeʒ and loukeʒ in oþer,
> And ayquere hit is endeleʒ. . . . (627–9)

The exact sense of 'trawþe' in this context is difficult to identify. The sense 'fidelity (to contract)' may suggest itself first, on the strength of the conversation between Gawain and the Green Knight in the first fitt, where the word occurs in that sense (*O.E.D.* 1). We may, that is, take the pentangle as symbolic of exactly that quality which is engaged, in Gawain, by the beheading agreement. True, it will not be immediately clear to a modern reader why the geometrical properties described should give pentangles a 'tytle' to symbolize truth in this sense. But the poet's explanation, on this reading, is no more far-fetched than many other medieval attempts to demonstrate a 'natural' appropriateness in signs (in the field of 'etymology', for example). The interlocking lines are 'loyal' to each other, like the 'lel letteres loken' of the prologue; so they may perhaps appropriately symbolize a man's loyalty to people, principles, or promises.

Nevertheless, I think it is better to take 'trawþe' here in the more inclusive sense—'integrity', or perhaps 'righteousness' (under *O.E.D.* 4). The advantage of this is that it makes much better sense in the general argument of the passage. The poet, after having established his major premis (the pentangle is a sign of truth) and anticipated his conclusion (it 'acordeʒ to þis knyʒt and to his cler armeʒ'), goes on to establish what is logically his minor premis: that Gawain is 'true'. His lengthy exposition of this point strongly suggests that he understands his middle term ('truth') in a wide sense—here and, presumably, in his major premis too. We need to take account of the full semantic range of the word, in fact, if we are not to dismiss half

44

the ensuing passage as irrelevant to the argument about the pentangle.

It begins with the statement that Gawain was 'ay faythful in fyue and sere fyue syþeȝ'. Here 'faythful' is, I take it, an alliterative stand-in for 'true': Gawain's perfection, the poet claims, is a perfection of fivefold 'truth'. Before going on to expound this obscure statement, however, he gives us a kind of summary of his whole argument:

> Forþy þe pentangel nwe
> He ber in schelde and cote,
> As tulk of tale most trwe
> And gentylest knyȝt of lote. (636–9)

This is both premature and partial, as if the poet did not quite know what to do with his spare wheel. The fact that Gawain is 'true of speech' is certainly relevant ('truthfulness' being, as we have seen, one sense of 'trawþe'); but the argument from it seems a little feeble, and the last line is a mere fill-up.

The exposition of Gawain's fivefold truth follows in the next stanza: he was faultless in his five senses; he never failed in his five fingers; he trusted in the five wounds of Christ; he drew his strength from the five joys of Mary; and he practised five virtues—franchise, fellowship, cleanness, courtesy, and pity. It is a strange list, but one thing at least emerges clearly from it: that 'trawþe', for the *Gawain*-poet, involves not only fidelity and truthfulness but also (as in *Cursor Mundi*) Faith. Gawain's 'afyaunce' in the five wounds and his dependence upon the five joys are both, plainly, representative of 'trawþe' in this sense (*O.E.D.* 3). The significance of the remaining three pentads, however, is less obvious. The first of them—that Gawain was 'funden fautleȝ in his fyue wytteȝ'—has been taken to mean that his sensory perceptions were vivid and acute;[17] but this reading, though a possible one, is not consistent with the overall argument (vivid sense-perception having nothing to do with truth, on any definition), and I would therefore prefer an interpretation recently put forward by R. W. Ackerman. According

[17] G. Mathew, art. cit. (Chap. I, note 3), p. 361.

to Mr. Ackerman, the key to the line is to be found in medieval penitential writings, which certainly contain frequent references to the sins of the five senses ('misspending the five wits'). Gawain, on this reading, was 'found without sin in the five senses.'[18] This agrees, I think, much better with the poet's argument, since the line so taken does contribute to the demonstration of Gawain's truth (in the 'wider sense'); and it gains some further support from the 'argument' of the poem as a whole, which, as I shall suggest later, makes considerable use of penitential ideas. However, Mr. Ackerman is less convincing when he extends his interpretation to include the second pentad ('fayled neuer þe freke in his fyue fyngres'). 'The second five-fold significance of the pentangle', he writes, 'is an entirely natural development of the first. Wishing to extend his series of pentads, the poet singled out the sense of touch for special mention.' But why should the poet single out the sense of touch? Simply to 'extend his series of pentads'? There seems no other reason. However, other interpretations of the line (e.g. that it refers to Gawain's physical strength) are equally unsatisfactory; and I am inclined to think that the demands of the poet's elaborate numerical scheme were simply too much for him at this point.[19]

There remains the group of virtues which make up the 'fyft fyue'. These have a special importance for our understanding of Gawain's truth, most of all because they remind us—like the emblems on his helmet—that the ideal of 'pured' perfection which he represents is not to be identified too exclusively with 'righteousness'—religious faith and sinlessness. When the poet says that his hero is 'voyded of vche vylany', he means both that he is righteous and that he is courteous. Here, and in other

[18] R. W. Ackerman, 'Gawain's Shield: Penitential Doctrine in *GGK*', *Anglia*, LXXVI (1958), pp. 254–65. The passage quoted from John of Gaunt's will (p. 264) is specially interesting for its association of the five wits with the five wounds.

[19] R. H. Green, in his recent article, 'Gawain's Shield and the Quest for Perfection', *E.L.H.*, XXIX (1962), pp. 121–39, suggests that the five fingers are an allegory of the five virtues, justice, prudence, temperance, fortitude and obedience. But he quotes only one relevant authority for this 'conventional figure'.

contemporary writings, secular and religious graces are involved
in each other:

> Clerkys þat canne þe scyens seuene
> Seys þat curtasy came fro heuen
> When Gabryell owre lady grette,
> And Elyzabeth with here mette.
> All vertus be closyde in curtasy
> And alle vyces in vilony.[20]

This conception of courtesy, which the *Gawain*-poet would
certainly have understood (witness his handling of 'cortaysye'
in *Pearl*), implies, among other things, that spiritual perfection
involves the perfection of the social man—as in the grace
of Gabriel's approach to Mary. So one need not be surprised
to discover that the virtues of Gawain's fifth five are, for
the most part, distinctively secular or social in character.
'Fraunchyse' (generosity, magnanimity), 'felaȝschyp' (com-
panionableness) and 'cortaysye' itself are all virtues already
apparent in the social Gawain of the first fitt—in his generous
readiness to praise Arthur (compare the use of 'fraunchis' in
l. 1264), in the laughter which he shares with the king, in his
behaviour towards the queen, etc. The ideal of 'truth' does not
require a knight to transcend these things: it involves the
perfection of a man before society as well as before God. In
many cases, anyway, the two sets of obligations coincide. It
would be both churlish and sinful for a knight to ignore a
legitimate request for help. Pity, that is, is both an aspect of
charity (the supreme Christian virtue which 'passeȝ alle
poynteȝ') and a mark of knightly 'gentillesse'.[21] The remaining

---

[20] *The Young Children's Book*, ll. 5–10. In *Early English Meals and
Manners*, ed. F. J. Furnivall, E.E.T.S. O.S. 32 (1868), pp. 17–25.

[21] In fourteenth-century English the cognate forms 'piety' and 'pity'
were not differentiated in meaning; so the *Gawain*-poet's 'pité' can
correspond to either modern word. Gollancz takes it to mean 'piety'
here (note to 651–4); but 'pity' makes rather better sense in the context. On the connection between pity and charity, see *The Book of
Vices and Virtues*, ed. W. N. Francis, E.E.T.S. O.S. 217 (1942),
p. 143; also R. K. Root's note in his edition of *Troilus and Criseyde*,
p. 427. Note that Langland's Samaritan 'þat was so ful of pité' (B.
XVII. 84) is the knightly representative of Charity.

member of the pentad, 'clannes', is to be understood, I think, in a similar fashion. It should not, at least, be identified with the celibacy of the Grail-hero, the virtue which above all distinguishes the Galahad of the *Queste* as a special kind of person. Cleanness, in *Sir Gawain* as in *Cleanness* itself, involves abstention from fornication, adultery, unclean thoughts and the like; but it is not, for a layman, inconsistent with marriage (see the passage in praise of marriage and its 'play of paramours' in *Cleanness*, ll. 697–705) or with 'trweluf' outside marriage. Lydgate's account of Arthur's court is a safe guide, I believe, to the *Gawain*-poet's intention:

> . . . al they mente in honest wyse,
> Vnleful lust was set asyde.
> Women thanne koude abyde,
> And loveden hem as wel ageyn
> Of feythful herte hool and pleyn,
> Vnder the yok of honeste,
> In clennesse and chastite . . .
> Wher so as her sort was set
> The knot never was vnknet.
> Their choys was nat for lustynesse,
> But for trouth and worthynesse,
> Nor for no transitorie chaunce
> Nor, shortly, for no fals plesaunce.[22]

The introduction of 'cleanness' among Gawain's virtues does not mean that the hero has, by special grace, risen above a supposedly 'normal' ideal of adulterous courtly love. It is not in any way provocative or tendentious. The poet understood 'cleanness', I am sure, as the generally accepted condition of knightly love—a condition which ruled out the 'vnleful lust' of adultery as a matter of course, but not true-love or even 'love-talking' with one's hostess. To suppose otherwise is to ignore the symbolism of the 'vrysoun'—and also to miss much of the subtlety in the ensuing castle scenes.

[22] *Reson and Sensuallyte*, ed. E. Sieper, E.E.T.S. E.S. 84 (1901), ll. 3188–94 and 3201–6. On this ideal of 'chastity, constancy in love, and prowess in chivalry', see D. A. Pearsall (ed.), '*The Floure and the Leafe*' and '*The Assembly of Ladies*' (London, 1962), pp. 38–41.

The Second Fitt

That these crucial scenes were already present in the author's
mind is apparent in the concluding passage of his exposition of
the pentangle. On a first reading, these lines (656–61) are apt to
seem obscure and over-emphatic. One may appreciate their
virtuosity, as an elaborate metaphorical counterpart to the
earlier description of the pentangle itself, without quite understanding what they mean—and this despite the fact that the
poet seems to be insisting that one should understand; as if, for
once, he is *anxious* to put an idea over. The passage might
almost come from *Piers Plowman*:

> Now alle þese fyue syþeȝ, for soþe, were fetled on þis knyȝt,
> And vchone halched in oþer, þat non ende hade,
> And fyched vpon fyue poynteȝ, þat fayld neuer,
> Ne samned neuer in no syde, ne sundred nouþer,
> Withouten ende at any noke aiquere, I fynde,
> Whereeuer þe gomen bygan, or glod to an ende. (656–61)

Plainly the poet has an 'idea': we are to understand that the
qualities which go to make up Gawain's 'trawþe' (fidelity, truthfulness, faith, cleanness, etc.), though, like the constituent lines
of a pentangle, they are distinguishable one from another ('ne
samned neuer in no syde'), nevertheless in some way form a
continuous whole as well—'vchone halched in oþer, þat non
ende hade', 'withouten ende at any noke'.

The idea that the virtues are inter-connected ('connexae',
'concatenatae', etc.) is quite common in patristic and medieval
writers. Aquinas has a *quaestio* on the subject ('De connexione
virtutum', *Summa Theologiae* I–II, Q. LXV) in which he quotes,
among others, Ambrose ('connexae sibi sunt, concatenataeque
virtutes, ut qui unam habet, plures habere videatur'), Augustine
('virtutes quae sunt in animo humano, nullo modo separantur
ab invicem') and Gregory ('una virtus sine aliis aut omnino
nulla est, aut imperfecta'). The *Gawain*-poet may have had
passages such as these in mind (compare 'vchone halched in
oþer' with 'connexae sibi', and 'ne sundred nouþer' with 'nullo
modo separantur ab invicem'). But the precise interpretation of
the patristic passages is itself a complex matter, as Aquinas'
discussion shows; and it is difficult to determine exactly what
the *Gawain*-poet meant from the pentangle passage alone, even

49

with their help. However, if we assume that the poet is saying something relevant to the poem as a whole—and the insistent tone suggests that this is so—we may distinguish a possible interpretation. Gregory says that 'one virtue without others is either entirely null, or imperfect', and Aquinas explains how this works with the cardinal virtues: firmness (fortitude), he says, is not praised as a virtue ('non habet laudem virtutis') if it is without moderation (temperance), rectitude (justice) and discretion (prudence)—and so with the others. The *Gawain*-poet may—and I would stress *may*—be saying something similar: that each of the virtues making up the five fives of Gawain's moral pentangle is 'entirely null, or imperfect' without the others. The virtues, therefore, stand and fall together, and there can be no question, for the hero, of sacrificing one in order to preserve another—as he is tempted to do in the scenes with the lady in the third fitt. Courtesy, one might say, is not praised as a virtue if it is without cleanness and loyalty; nor loyalty without courtesy and cleanness—and so with the others. Just as a broken pentangle loses its magical power,[23] so 'truth' loses its moral power if it is 'sundered' in any of its parts; for it is an ideal of *integrity* or oneness.

The dominant note of the pentangle passage, and of the arming scene generally, is one of optimistic idealism. The Gawain of the second phase is, indeed, the very mirror of Christian chivalry, a flawless reflector of the ideals of Camelot. The 'accord' between the man and the ideal is so perfect that both can be symbolized in the one geometrical figure, the 'pure pentaungel'. This is very much a 'descriptio ad laudem', revealing a vein of extreme moral idealism which one would not have suspected in the poet of the first fitt and the seasons passage. One might wonder, indeed, on what terms such idealism can coexist at all with the sober and realistic awareness which finds expression in passages such as

> . . . þaʒ men ben mery in mynde quen þay han mayn drynk,
> A ʒere ʒernes ful ʒerne, and ʒeldeʒ neuer lyke,
> Þe forme to þe fynisment foldeʒ ful selden.

[23] Mephistopheles, in Goethe's *Faust*, is able to enter Faust's room because the pentangle on the threshold has an unjoined corner.

The Second Fitt

The awareness of the instability of human experience, its in-congruities and complexities, found here and in the many ironies and ambiguities of the first fitt—how is it to be reconciled with the geometric absolutism of the pentangle passage? It seems hardly possible for the hero to justify the claims made for him there—hardly possible, that is, in the world which the poet has created for him.

II

Gawain's journey in search of the Green Knight begins at Camelot on All Souls' Day (November 2, the day after All Saints') and ends, temporarily, at Bercilak's castle on Christmas Eve. The journey lasts nearly eight weeks, and the poet divides it into four stages. Gawain rides first through the kingdom of Logres (Arthurian England), then east across North Wales; then, having forded the Dee, he crosses the Wirral, and from there enters the 'contraye3 straunge' where he eventually comes upon the castle. The blend of realistic and romantic geography in this itinerary may seem somewhat arbitrary; but it is coherent enough if we look at it from the point of view of the author and his original audience—if, that is, we will imagine ourselves to be in Cheshire or thereabouts. We should see Gawain coming towards us through Arthurian England, entering our country by way of the familiar coast-road from North Wales, fording the Dee and crossing the notorious Wirral, before riding off again into the countries of romance.

By making his hero pass from friendly into hostile territory at the Dee, the poet neatly reconciles romance and local realities. Behind him Gawain has the well-trodden coast-road and the friendly kingdom of Logres; in front he has the 'wyldrenesse of Wyrale' and, beyond that, the 'contraye3 straunge' with their romantic counterparts to the Wirral outlaws—dragons, wild men, ogres, etc.[24] The poet further strengthens the effect by

[24] On the notoriety of the Wirral in the fourteenth century, see H. L. Savage, 'A Note on *SGGK* 700–2', *M.L.N.*, XLVI (1931), pp. 455–7. H. J. Hewitt's *Mediaeval Cheshire* (Manchester, 1929) gives an excellent account of this and other features of what I take to be the *Gawain*-poet's 'country'.

having Gawain cross the Dee where he does—'ouer at þe Holy Hede' (700). The head in question, that of St. Winifred, was cut off by a ravisher and caused a healing well to spring up where it fell. From this well a stream ran down to the Dee. The phrase 'ouer at þe Holy Hede' probably means that Gawain crossed the Dee from a point on its southern side near where that stream flowed into the estuary. A local audience would be reminded both of St. Winifred's Well, the big pilgrim centre at the head of the stream, and of the Cistercian abbey of Basingwerk near its mouth. The Flintshire shore would therefore figure in their minds as a place of piety and hospitality, in contrast to the Wirral on the other side of the estuary, where there 'wonde bot lyte / Þat auþer God oþer gome wyth goud hert louied'. So it is, for Gawain, the last outpost of his civilization (before he comes to the castle, that is), a place where saints are honoured as they are at Camelot. Yet it also brings with it a 'wage', or foretaste, of what is to come—and one which would hardly be lost on the original audience. St. Winifred was, notoriously, beheaded. True, her head—like the Green Knight's —was restored to her shoulders; but Gawain, as he himself later points out, cannot rely on either magic or miracle:

> . . . þaȝ my hede falle on þe stoneȝ,
> I con not hit restore. (2282-3)[25]

The dangers of Gawain's journey begin at the Dee, but its hardships are emphasized from the moment he leaves Camelot:

> Now rideȝ þis renk þurȝ þe ryalme of Logres,
> Sir Gauan, on Godeȝ halue, þaȝ hym no gomen þoȝt.
> Oft leudleȝ alone he lengeȝ on nyȝteȝ
> Þer he fonde noȝt hym byfore þe fare þat he lyked. (691-4)

The phrase 'þaȝ hym no gomen þoȝt' is specially interesting, because it refers us back (via the 'Crystmasse gomneȝ' mentioned in l. 683) to the first fitt, suggesting a deliberate contrast between the winter feast and the winter journey. Gawain is no longer buoyed up with good food and strong drink—'he fonde noȝt hym byfore þe fare þat he lyked'; and he is 'fer floten fro his frendeȝ' (714), for, as he promised the Green Knight, he

[25] For further discussion of 'þe Holy Hede', see Appendix Two.

travels 'al hym one', without even a squire ('leudleȝ'—compare
the use of 'leude' in l. 851). The *Gawain*-poet, as I have suggested, was far from regarding the feasting and company of
Camelot as evils; but he is sufficiently medieval to regard their
absence as a possible source of spiritual benefit. Gawain rides
through Logres 'on Godeȝ halue', he has 'no gome bot God bi
gate wyth to karp', and his journey ends on Christmas Eve with
a prayer to Mary and Christ:

> And perfore sykyng he sayde, 'I beseche þe, lorde,
> And Mary, þat is myldest moder so dere,
> Of sum herber þer heȝly I myȝt here masse,
> Ande þy matyneȝ to-morne, mekely I ask,
> And þerto prestly I pray my pater and aue
> and crede.'
> He rode in his prayere,
> And cryed for his mysdede,
> He sayned hym in syþes sere,
> And sayde 'Cros Kryst me spede!' (753–62)

Supplicatory prayers such as this are by tradition penitential in
character, and the fact that Gawain 'cried for his misdeed' here
would hardly be worth noticing were it not that penance, more
particularly penance coupled with winter hardship, assumes
such importance in the fourth fitt, where, as we shall see, the
outdoor winter is strongly associated not only with the idea of
Death (as in the seasons passage) but also with ideas of sin,
penance and judgment. These ideas are, of course, not stressed
in the present passage: at this point in the poem the hero,
though he thinks he is to die, does not know that he is to be
'judged', and he has, so far as the poem is concerned, no sins to
repent. However (and it is worth noticing this even though we
may have assumed it), the poet clearly does not expect us to
have taken the claims of the pentangle passage too literally, in
defiance of common sense and Christian orthodoxy. The 'faultless' Gawain *has* faults, and it is to be taken for granted that he
would cry for them on such an occasion. For winter, and
especially the wintry journey, is a traditional occasion for
penance in medieval literature. 'Winter-care', part physical and
part spiritual, is by no means peculiar to the Old English

53

elegies;[26] nor is it as foreign to the traditions of romance as one might, perhaps, imagine. The best-known of all penitential scenes in Arthurian literature, the Good Friday episode of the Perceval story, opens, in Wolfram's *Parzival*, with the hero riding through a great wood, in bitter cold, with the snow lying on the ground; and these hardships are plainly regarded by Wolfram as a fitting prelude to Parzival's meeting with the hermit who hears his confession.

Parzival's winter journey takes place on Good Friday, near the end of the penitential season of Lent; and this fact reminds one that medieval poets commonly tried (where it was possible to do so) to set their episodes at the right season, not only of the natural, but also of the ecclesiastical year. The *Gawain*-poet, unlike Wolfram, was working with a strict time-scheme, and he was not free to choose that Gawain should take his wintry ride in 'crabbed lentoun'; but his scheme does permit him to find appropriate associations in other parts of the ecclesiastical calendar. For one thing, as H. L. Savage has pointed out, 'Gawain departs on his quest on All Souls' Day, on whose morn the three masses are offered for the souls of the faithful departed and *Dies Irae* is sung. We are to consider him a dead man, one as good as gone'.[27] We are told that Gawain 'herkneȝ his masse / Offred and honoured at þe heȝe auter' before he sets out (592–3), and it does seem fair to suppose that a medieval listener, having identified this as the Requiem Mass of All Souls, would see in it an ominous appropriateness. True, Gawain's setting out on this particular day, immediately after the traditional All Saints' feast at Camelot, is, like his crossing the Dee at the Holy Head, entirely natural; and he is well-known in the romances for his eagerness to hear Mass at any time.[28] But these considerations do not invalidate Savage's point. Indeed, one may safely go further and notice that part of Gawain's

[26] See E. G. Stanley, 'Old English Poetic Diction and the Interpretation of *The Wanderer, The Seafarer* and *The Penitent's Prayer*', *Anglia*, LXXIII (1955), pp. 413–66.

[27] *The 'Gawain'-Poet*, p. 27.

[28] *Perlesvaus*, ed. cit., ll. 4435–7: 'Misire Gavains ne se partist ja d'ostel ou il geüst qu'il n'oïst messe ançois qu'il em partist, si le peüst avoir'.

The Second Fitt

journey, including his forest ride on Christmas Eve, takes place in the season of Advent (which begins on the Sunday nearest November 30), and that Advent is, like Lent, a season of penitential preparation: 'During this time the faithful are admonished to prepare themselves worthily to celebrate the anniversary of the Lord's coming into the world as the incarnate God of Love, thus to make their souls fitting abodes for the Redeemer coming in Holy Communion and through grace, and thereby to make themselves ready for His final coming as Judge, at death and at the end of the world' (*Catholic Encyclopedia*). Notice that, here as in the medieval authorities, Advent is regarded as a period of preparation, not only for the celebration of Christ's first coming at Christmas, but also for 'His final coming as Judge, at death and at the end of the world'. So in John Mirk's sermon (*c.* 1400) for Advent Sunday: 'Þys day holy chyrch makyth mencyon of two comyngys of Crist, Godys sonne, ynto þys world: forto by mankind out of þe deueles bondage, and to bryng hym and weldoers to þe blys þat euer schall last; and his oþer comyng þat schall be at þe day of dome forto deme all wikytdoers ynto þe pyt of hell for euermor'.[29] So when Gawain 'cries for his misdeed', one may think ahead not only to the coming Christmas feast, but also to the New Year encounter which lies beyond it: for, as I shall try to show later, that New Year's Day is a kind of death-and-doom day for the hero.

However, such eschatological and penitential matters are no more than faintly adumbrated in the present section of the poem. Gawain, unlike Parzival, rides 'meryly' through the wood on Christmas Eve, and his prayer for harbour is answered not with a hermitage but with a castle:

> Nade he sayned hymself, segge, bot þrye,
> Er he watȝ war in þe wod of a won in a mote,
> Abof a launde, on a lawe, loken vnder boȝeȝ
> Of mony borelych bole aboute bi þe diches:
> A castel þe comlokest þat euer knyȝt aȝte. (763–7)

The scribe of the Nero Manuscript gave the word 'Nade' at the beginning of this passage an extra-large capital, and he seems to

---

[29] *Festial*, ed. T. Erbe, E.E.T.S. E.S. 96 (1905), p. 1.

have followed the author's intentions in doing so.[30] For the appearance of the castle marks the end—or rather suspension—of Gawain's winter hardships and the beginning of another phase of Christmas feasting, in a household almost as congenial as Camelot. The castle is 'þe comlokest þat euer knyȝt aȝte'; the porter who appears on its wall is 'pure plesaunt'; the castle-folk come 'frely' out to receive the hero; knights and squires bring him 'wyth blys' into the hall; the lord greets him 'wyth menske'; and so on. The whole of the rest of the second fitt, in fact, is devoted to a glowing account of the courtesies and comforts which Gawain enjoys in his 'bone hostel', first on Christmas Eve, and then on three days of the Christmas feast.

III

A striking feature of this latter part of the second fitt is the generosity which the author displays towards his characters. His plan required that Gawain should be 'disarmed', metaphorically as well as literally, before being submitted to his crucial tests; and this disarming of the hero required that the castle should seem to him to be another Camelot—a house of mirth, full of friendly and congenial people, and presided over by a high-spirited lord with a beautiful and amiable wife. In the event this not only seems to be but *is* so. Not that the poet allows us to lose sight of the dangers of Gawain's situation—there are, as we shall see, enough ominous suggestions to keep us aware of that. Yet Bercilak, his wife and (with one obvious exception) his household gain, and keep, our goodwill as well as Gawain's. Their gaiety and piety, their joy at Gawain's arrival and their friendliness and respectful courtesy towards him, impress the reader as spontaneous and genuine; and this impression is somehow not qualified by our suspicions at the time, any more than it is cancelled, towards the end of the poem, by the Green Knight's explanations. We know that Gawain is de-

---

[30] The *Beowulf* manuscript similarly indicates a break at a turning-point in the hero's fortunes, in the middle of his fight with Grendel's mother (l. 1557). See Klaeber's interesting discussion in the introduction to his edition, pp. c-ci.

ceived; but we do not respond to his hosts merely as deceivers. The poet brings this off with a good deal of genuine dexterity and a little cheating.

The kind of response required of the reader in these scenes may be illustrated from the poet's account of the dinner served to Gawain in his private chamber shortly after his arrival (ll. 884–927). The most impressive aspect of this scene is the powerful sense of well-being that is conveyed. After the hardships of his journey, Gawain finds himself, warm and comfortably dressed, sitting down to eat an elaborate dinner off a table laid with a clean cloth and silver spoons. The author enters into the spirit of the thing so thoroughly that it is surely impossible, even in retrospect, to feel anything of deliberate testing or 'temptation' in the scene. Gawain's hosts cannot be seen as Satanic ministers of the 'table richly spread'; and we do not lose faith in their goodwill even when the poet introduces, as he certainly does, a disturbing note into the merrymaking:

> Þe freke calde hit a fest ful frely and ofte
> Ful hendely, quen alle þe haþeles rehayted hym at oneȝ
> as hende:
> 'Þis penaunce now ȝe take,
> And eft hit schal amende.'
> Þat mon much merþe con make,
> For wyn in his hed þat wende. (894–900)

Here, as so often in the poem, the wheel has a peculiar reverberating effect, calling up in the back of the mind memories of what has gone before. Gawain's meal on the fast-day before Christmas is, technically, a 'penaunce'; yet it hardly 'fraysteȝ flesch wyth þe fysche and fode more symple'. Indeed, Gawain's condition at the end of it is such as to remind us (despite the attendants' assurances) of the poet's ominous observation at the beginning of the fitt: 'þaȝ men ben mery in mynde quen þay han mayn drynk . . . þe forme to þe fynisment foldeȝ ful selden'. All the same, it is hard to see Gawain's tipsiness moralistically, as a dangerous weakness in the face of artful temptation. One might contrast an episode in Malory (following the French *Queste*) where Perceval is tempted by a devil in female form: 'And anone there was leyde a table, and so muche meete was sette thereon that he had mervayle, for there was all maner of meetes that he cowde thynke on. Also he dranke there the strengyst wyne that ever he dranke, hym thought, and therewith he was chaffett a lityll more than he oughte to be . . .'.[31] Here, as in a preacher's 'exemplum', the hero is being subjected to diabolical temptation, and his every concession is to be explicitly deplored: 'therewith he was chaffett a lityll more than he oughte to be'. Such a comment would be quite out of place in *Sir Gawain*, where the relation between the hero and his 'tempters' is more subtle and, one might add, truer to most people's experience of actual moral trial.

The first part of the following stanza describes how Gawain, in response to discreet promptings, reveals his identity:

> Þenne watȝ spyed and spured vpon spare wyse
> Bi preué poynteȝ of þat prynce, put to hymseluen,
> Þat he beknew cortaysly of þe court þat he were,
> Þat aþel Arthure þe hende haldeȝ hym one,
> Þat is þe ryche ryal kyng of þe Rounde Table,
> And hit watȝ Wawen hymself þat in þat won sytteȝ. (901-6)

One may detect a sinister touch of cunning in the attendants' behaviour here; but it should be remembered that it was not a matter of course for a knight to reveal his name. This is indicated by the very fact that Gawain is particularly noted in the romances for his readiness to do so.[32] The attendants could not take it for granted that the unknown knight would be 'cortaysly' ready to disclose his identity: it is because they themselves are courteous, simply, that they refrain from putting a direct question. But what is one to make of the behaviour of the lord in the lines which follow?

> When þe lorde hade lerned þat he þe leude hade,
> Loude laȝed he þerat, so lef hit hym þoȝt. (908-9)

[31] Ed. Vinaver, p. 918.

[32] *Perlesvaus*, ed. cit., ll. 1490–3: 'Sire chevalier, font il, arestez, si nos dites vostre non sanz mentir. Seigneur, fet il, molt volentiers. Mes nons ne fu onques celez par moi, se on le me demanda. On m'apele Gavain.' See the editors' note on this passage, and B. J. Whiting, art. cit., p. 196, note 25.

The Second Fitt

It may seem natural to read these lines too in a sinister sense: Bercilak (who, whatever may be true of the attendants, is certainly in the plot) rejoices at having caught his victim. But he should, of course, already have recognized Gawain while embracing him (with his helmet off) in the hall. Are we to think, then, that he is putting on a genial act to deceive Gawain? The poet does not really make this point either; for he leaves one with the distinct impression that Bercilak receives the news at second hand ('when þe lorde *hade* lerned'), and if this is so,.who is he trying to deceive?[33] So, in the absence of any clearly articulated sinister meaning, one finds oneself thinking simply of a genial host rejoicing at the prospect of a distinguished and interesting guest. Whether this is a faked clue or simply a slip does not matter here: the point is significant because it illustrates the author's general tendency (conscious or unconscious) to block, and sometimes even falsify, our view of Bercilak's feelings and thoughts during the castle scenes. This works almost entirely in Bercilak's favour, and it goes a long way to explain why one carries away such a favourable view of him at the end of the poem.

This is an appropriate place to note that Bercilak, though he 'discovers' Gawain's name early on, and is explicitly said (l. 937) to employ it when addressing him later, himself remains nameless throughout the castle scenes. As usual, the author protects him from our criticism. We do not *see* him failing to reciprocate his guest's courtesy; indeed, the point is never raised—Bercilak, like his wife and all the other members of his household, simply remains anonymous. But this, though it is not meant to affect our opinion of Bercilak's character, does—or should—affect our opinion of Gawain's situation. Proper names, in romance as in other medieval writing, are instruments of knowledge and power. A knight who reveals his identity to others gives them, as in the modern metaphor, a 'handle'—something to get hold of. They may know his

---

[33] There is no mention of Bercilak's presence in the chamber, and ll. 933–8 suggest that, when he meets Gawain in the chapel, he does so for the first time since greeting him in the hall. Line 937 in particular would otherwise be pointless.

strengths and weaknesses by report; or his name may itself, more or less obviously, reveal them ('Agravayn a la Dure Mayn', etc.). Such considerations—together, certainly, with survivals of more primitive ideas of word-magic and name-souls[34]—explain why it should be a mark of courtesy or 'franchise' for a knight to be ready, like Gawain, to tell his name to all comers. They explain too the curious piece of advice given to Perceval by his mother at the beginning of his career, in the *Perceval* of Chrétien de Troyes:

> Biax fix, encor vos veil dire el,
> Que en chemin ne en hostel
> N'aiez longuement compaignon
> Que vos ne demandez son non;
> Et ce sachiez a la parsome,
> Par le sornon connoist on l'ome.[35]

So in *Sir Gawain* one must feel that Gawain's ignorance of his host's name involves ignorance of 'the man', and further that this ignorance is a potential source of advantage to the host and danger to the hero.

Now let us turn, with these ideas in mind, to the last and most interesting part of the dinner scene, where the poet describes how the news of Gawain's identity, already known to the attendants and the host, is received by the rest of the castle household (ll. 910–27). Episodes such as this, dealing with the reactions of a crowd of observers or common people to some notable event, are quite frequent in medieval narrative. There are several animated examples in the *Canterbury Tales*, where we find crowds speculating about the tournament in the *Knight's Tale*, the mysterious gifts in the *Squire's Tale*, and the

[34] See E. Clodd, *Magic in Names* (London, 1920) and E. Cassirer, *Language and Myth*, trans. S. K. Langer (New York, 1946), Chap. IV.

[35] *Roman de Perceval*, ed. W. Roach (Geneva, 1956), ll. 557–62: 'My son, I want to tell you another thing: never have a companion on the road or in a lodging for any length of time without asking his name. For you must understand that one knows a man by his name.' Compare the response of Malory's Balyn and Balan when Merlin refuses to reveal his name: 'Hit ys an evyll sygne ... that thou arte a trew man, that thou wolt nat telle thy name', ed. Vinaver, p. 73.

affairs of Walter in the *Clerk's Tale*; and similar 'tableaux de
foule' are to be found, as a French critic has pointed out, in
such earlier works as Chrétien's *Chevalier de la Charrete*.[36]
Medieval writers did not take mass opinion of this kind very
seriously, and their tone in such passages ranges from amused
superiority (as in the *Squire's Tale*) to downright indignation
(as in the *Clerk's Tale*). The *Gawain*-poet himself clearly, I
think, meant us to feel ourselves superior to those 'segges' who,
earlier in the second fitt, criticized Arthur for allowing Gawain
to get involved with the Green Knight (ll. 674–83). We were to
feel that they recognized knightly excellence, but not the obligations which it entails. In Chaucer's words:

> . . . lewed peple demeth comunly
> Of thynges that been maad moore subtilly
> Than they kan in hir lewednesse comprehende;
> They demen gladly to the badder ende.

The present episode, however, is rather more subtle than this.
It is not immediately obvious here that we are concerned with
'lewed peple' at all:

> . . . alle þe men in þat mote maden much joye
> To apere in his presense prestly þat tyme,
> Þat alle prys and prowes and pured þewes
> Apendes to hys persoun, and praysed is euer,
> Byfore alle men vpon molde his mensk is þe most. (910–14)

This may leave the impression that the author is generously
allowing the men of Bercilak's household as perfect a knowledge
of knightly ideals as he has himself—as if the subordinate part
of the sentence, which sounds so much like a recapitulation of
the pentangle passage, could be either indirect (the men's view)
or direct (the author's view) indifferently. But this is not quite
the case. The men are not mere churls, or conspirators—they do
have an appreciation of chivalry, and their joy at seeing one of
its notable representatives is meant to ring true. But, as the
following passage more clearly suggests, their ideal of 'prys
and prowes and pured þewes', though perfectly acceptable so
far as it goes, is not coextensive with the author's ideal of 'truth':

36 *Le Chevalier de la Charrete*, ed. Roques, Introduction, pp. xxix–
xxx.

The Second Fitt

Vch segge ful softly sayde to his fere:
'Now schal we semlych se sleȝteȝ of þeweȝ
And þe teccheles termes of talkyng noble,
Wich spede is in speche vnspurd may we lerne,
Syn we haf fonged þat fyne fader of nurture.
God hatȝ geuen vus his grace godly for soþe,
Þat such a gest as Gawan graunteȝ vus to haue,
When burneȝ blyþe of his burþe schal sitte
                            and synge.
        In menyng of manereȝ mere
        Þis burne now schal vus bryng,
        I hope þat may hym here
        Schal lerne of luf-talkyng.' (915–27)

What, according to this passage, do the 'segges' expect from
Gawain? A display of the social graces of chivalry. It is as if, in
terms of the arming scene, Gawain were all 'vrysoun' and courtesy. The key phrases are 'sleȝteȝ of þeweȝ', 'talkyng noble',
'spede in speche', 'fader of nurture', 'manereȝ mere', and 'luf-
talkyng'; and there is nothing whatever to qualify the impression which they create.

It may be objected that the men could not reasonably have
been shown rubbing their hands in expectation of displays of
loyalty or faith in the five wounds of Christ. This is true. The
men are certainly not meant to seem godless or stupid, and my
point against them could not be pressed—and would not be
worth pressing—were it not supported by other parts of the
poem, especially the temptation scenes. Here, indeed, is the
place to notice how the author is preparing us for those scenes,
building up for his hero the difficult situation which the lady
is later to exploit. His conception of this situation is one of the
most subtle and persuasive things in the poem. Gawain, the
representative of all that is best in the great court of Camelot,
finds himself spending Christmas in a provincial household.
This household is very far from uncouth. Indeed it is in many
ways exemplary, not least in its gracious recognition of its own
remoteness from the centre of things. Its members (Bercilak
and his lady included) show an extreme respect for Gawain,
coupled with an almost childish glee at having captured

The Second Fitt

('fonged') such a distinguished guest (see ll. 906, 920–1, 1035–6, etc.). Yet they do not grasp—or do not admit to grasping—the full nature of his distinction: Gawain, to his own great embarrassment, is in some ways 'maad moore subtilly / Than they kan in hir lewednesse comprehende'. Not that the kind of conduct which they constantly press upon him, by their expectations and (in the case of the lady) demands, is in itself alien to him. His situation would be much easier if it *were*—if, that is, he were committed to an ascetic ideal in which courtesy and love-talking had no place. It is rather that the members of the household reflect back at him his own values a little distorted, as it were a slightly lopsided pentangle. This is a fascinating variation on the theme of the acknowledged identity and the disadvantages which attend it; and the poet makes the most of it in what follows, both as a source of social comedy (particularly acceptable if one remembers that the poet and the original audience would identify themselves with the north-western 'provincials') and as a source (though, in the event, only a potential one) of tragedy.

The murmured 'deemings' of the household conclude the dinner scene, and Gawain, having finished his meal, goes off to a chapel to hear Vespers, 'þe hersum euensong of þe hyʒe tyde' (932). It is after this service that he first meets the lady, whom the poet introduces, together with the 'auncian' who accompanies her, in a set 'descriptio' (943–69). The passage is one of the few parts of the poem (Gawain's attack on women in the last fitt is another) which may strike a modern reader as crudely 'medieval'; for it takes the form of a quite brutally frank contrast between the physical attractions of the two women ('More lykkerwys on to lyk / Watʒ þat scho hade on lode', etc.). The coupling of two such contrasted descriptions, one 'ad laudem' and the other 'ad vituperium', was in fact a conventional trick in medieval poetry.[37] But that hardly excuses the crudity of the present passage—which can only be understood,

[37] Faral, op. cit., pp. 76–77. Matthew of Vendôme couples descriptions of a beautiful and an ugly woman (Helen and Beroe) in *Ars Versificatoria*, I, 56–58 (Faral, pp. 129–32). See D. A. Pearsall, 'Rhetorical "Descriptio" in *GGK*', *M.L.R.*, L (1955), p. 131.

and perhaps tolerated, if we take account of the poet's general intentions. There are two points to be made here, the first a matter of audience psychology. At the end of his poem the author is to use Morgan le Fay as a dumping-ground for all the suspicions and resentments which we have stored up on Gawain's behalf in the course of his adventure—'stored up' because, as I have already suggested, we are discouraged from releasing them upon Bercilak or his dependants. The author, therefore, has every reason for setting up Morgan as an unsympathetic figure from the first. Indeed, since we should already be feeling somewhat uneasy on Gawain's behalf after the previous scene, the author's uninhibited attack on the old lady in the chapel (contrasting with Gawain's respectful courtesy towards her) may afford some relief in its own right.

At the time, however, we are likely to understand the attack in a less tender-minded way, as an attack on the lady not for being an adversary, but simply for being old. Even at this level, though, the passage is not quite as gratuitous as it may seem. One way to see this is to compare the portrait of Morgan with Guillaume de Lorris' almost equally unsympathetic portrait of Old Age in the *Romance of the Rose* (Middle English translation, ll. 355–8):

> Ful salowe was waxen her colour;
> Her heed, for hor, was whyt as flour.
> Iwys, great qualm ne were it non,
> Ne synne, although her lyf were gon . . . etc.

The two writers agree in their treatment of old age here because they are both, for once, acting as advocates for the same cause. Guillaume speaks on behalf of his garden of Mirth, the *Gawain*-poet on behalf of his younger lady:

> . . . vnlyke on to loke þo ladyes were,
> For if þe ȝonge watȝ ȝep, ȝolȝe watȝ þat oþer. (950–1)

The old lady gives offence simply by being old and 'ȝolȝe' in a household where, as in Arthur's hall, the whole company is otherwise presented as 'ȝonge' or at least 'ȝep'; and it is just so with the image of Old Age painted on the wall of Mirth's garden. But the point is, surely, that by the time one gets to the present passage one knows quite well that the *Gawain*-poet is not, like Guillaume, unreservedly committed to Mirth's cause. We should, that is, know him well enough to appreciate the contextual or dramatic value of his contrasted portraits.

The scene which these portraits introduce marks the beginning of the real Christmas festivities at the castle. Gawain, having eaten, performed his religious duty, and met the ladies, is conducted by them to another private chamber where

> . . . chefly þay asken
> Spyceȝ, þat vnsparely men speded hom to bryng,
> And þe wynnelych wyne þerwith vche tyme.
> Þe lorde luflych aloft lepeȝ ful ofte,
> Mynned merthe to be made vpon mony syþeȝ,
> Hent heȝly of his hode, and on a spere henged,
> And wayued hom to wynne þe worchip þerof,
> Þat most myrþe myȝt meue þat Crystenmas whyle. (978–85)

It is from this point on until the end of the second fitt that the poet makes his most sustained effort to confront hero and reader with 'another Camelot'. Indeed, the A-B-A structure of the first half of the poem is completed in these five stanzas with what is almost a first fitt done over again in little. The parallels are made very striking. We see from the passage just quoted that Bercilak, though a man 'of hyghe elde' (in the prime of life), shares Arthur's boyish gaiety and unwillingness 'auþer to longe lye or to longe sitte', and whips up the Christmas festivities with 'gomneȝ in halle'.[38] The Christmas feast itself, which follows 'on þe morne' and is described rather briefly in one stanza ('for to telle þerof hit me tene were'), clearly recalls the New Year's feast at Camelot. 'Dainties' are again brought in with trumpets, drums and pipes, and Gawain is again on the dais, sitting next to the 'gay' lady of the house. The comparison of Bercilak's wife with Arthur's has in fact already occurred to Gawain himself (she strikes him—despite ll. 83-4—as 'wener þen Wenore'), and he treats her quite as courteously as he did

---

[38] The phrase 'gomneȝ in halle' is formulaic. It is not aptly used here, since Bercilak is entertaining Gawain in a chamber. Contrast l. 495.

Guinevere in the first fitt. It is to be noted that the poet rules out any suspicions we might feel about this:

> Such comfort of her compaynye ca3ten togeder
> Þur3 her dere dalyaunce of her derne worde3,
> Wyth clene cortays carp closed fro fylþe,
> Þat hor play wat3 passande vche prynce gomen. (1011–14)

The phrase 'clene cortays carp' seems designed to recall the line 'His clannes and his cortaysye croked were neuer'. Indeed Gawain's behaviour here, as throughout this phase of the poem, is to be taken as a vindication of the claims made for him in the pentangle passage.

However, the most important parallel between the first fitt and the last part of the second remains to be mentioned. In both, the Christmas festivities lead up to a point at which the hero makes a *contract* with his adversary. And it is this point that the author now hurries to reach. After truncating his account of the feasting on Christmas Day, he goes straight on, with no more than a bare mention of the intervening festivities, to the evening of the third day of Christmas (St. John's Day), when Bercilak, having said goodbye to his other guests, leads Gawain to his chamber and, after an exchange of civilities, asks him to stay longer:

> Þe lorde fast can hym payne
> To holde lenger þe kny3t;
> To hym answare3 Gawayn,
> Bi non way þat he my3t. (1042–5)

Perhaps this offer of further hospitality is meant to reawaken our suspicions of the nameless host, with the suggestion that he is trying to entertain Gawain so well that he will forget or abandon his quest. One might note that Bercilak seems to be taking advantage of Gawain's promise a moment before to 'worch youre hest, / As I am halden þerto, in hy3e and in lo3e,/ bi ri3t'; and that he sets in motion what, on this theory, is Plan 2 immediately after a very similar promise from Gawain later in the scene. However this may be, one is certainly meant to admire the determination with which Gawain refuses the host's offer:

Forþi, iwysse, bi ȝowre wylle, wende me bihoues,
Naf I now to busy bot bare þre dayeȝ,
And me als fayn to falle feye as fayly of myyn ernde. (1065-7)

The remainder of the episode is most subtly and beautifully contrived. Once Gawain has explained his 'errand' Bercilak immediately reveals the whereabouts of the Green Chapel ('not two myle henne'), and invites Gawain again to stay longer, until New Year's Day itself. This time Gawain accepts the invitation:

Þenne watȝ Gawan ful glad, and gomenly he laȝed:
'Now I þonk yow þryuandely þurȝ alle oþer þynge,
Now acheued is my chaunce, I schal at your wylle
Dowelle, and elleȝ do quat ȝe demen.' (1079-82)

'Now that my object is as good as attained, I will stay on as you desire, and do whatever else you may like to ask of me.' It is at this point, when the hero, and the audience with him, feels that he is at last sure of 'achieving' the task originally set him, that he unwittingly gives Bercilak the opportunity of setting him another. This opportunity is more substantial than it may seem to us now. Gawain's two promises are not mere courtesies—he is 'halden' to obey his host 'bi riȝt'; and his obligation to fulfil the second is all the stronger because he has been forced to break the first as soon as it was made, by refusing the host's invitation to stay longer.[39] This explains Bercilak's excitement on this occasion (though, as usual, even when there is an obvious sinister sense, the poet leaves a favourable one open too). He seizes hold of Gawain, sits him down, calls the ladies in, and talks, the poet says, like mad—'as wyȝ þat wolde of his wyte'. Finally he cries out:

'Ȝe han demed to do þe dede þat I bidde;
Wyl ȝe halde þis hes here at þys oneȝ?'
'Ȝe, sir, for soþe,' sayd þe segge trwe,
'Whyl I byde in yowre borȝe, be bayn to ȝowre hest.'

(1089-92)

[39] The phrase 'in hyȝe and in loȝe', used by Gawain in his first promise (l. 1040), is a legalism (corresponding to the Latin formula 'in alto et basso'). It is used twice in the *Canterbury Tales* in similar contexts—I, 817 (see notes of Skeat and Robinson) and II, 993.

The Second Fitt

At this point we may suspect that Gawain has involved himself in one of those traditional Rash Promises, from which, as a 'segge trwe', he will be unable to withdraw. But it is not so. The host merely proposes, first, that he should stay in bed late on the following mornings and enjoy his wife's company while he is out hunting, and, second, that he should join him in an exchange-of-winnings agreement. Gawain 'grants' both.

The exchange-of-winnings agreement is even more difficult for the modern reader to swallow than the beheading agreement. Gawain was 'merry' in more senses than one in the first fitt; yet one did feel that he agreed to the beheading game with at least one eye open, insofar as the Green Knight more or less announced himself as a hostile challenger from the first. By depriving the reader of this consolation on the present occasion the author pushes his case up to the brink of absurdity, as Chaucer does in the *Franklin's Tale* and, in different ways, in the tales of the Clerk and the Man of Law. This kind of brink-manship, indeed, is common in fourteenth-century literature, even characteristic of it. Over and over again authors of this period present us with 'test-cases' in which some superlatively good (humble, true, obedient, etc.) hero or heroine is subjected to some superlative test of virtue. The *Gawain*-poet is pursuing the logic of such a case at this point. He does not, in fact, pursue it right through to the end of his poem (an important point, to which I must return later); but even if he had done so, we ought still to feel that he played fair here—on medieval rules, at least. The exchange agreement is assented to by Gawain merely in order to pass the holidays more agreeably ('þat yow lyst for to layke, lef hit me þynkes'); but the legalism of the medieval mind was such that a contemporary audience would have accepted even this as a genuine contract—though, as the case required, only just so. There is a closely analogous contract in the *Canterbury Tales*, when the pilgrims on their first evening together swear an oath (accompanied, as in *Sir Gawain*, by the drinking of a confirmatory 'beverage') that they will accept Harry Bailey as their 'governor' for the period of their pilgrimage (I, 810–21). On several later occasions Bailey has cause to appeal to this holiday agreement, and the right-thinking pilgrims are shown to respect his position. The exchange between him and the Man of Law is, as one might expect, particularly illuminating:

> 'Ye been submytted, thurgh youre free assent,
> To stonden in this cas at my juggement.
> Acquiteth yow now of youre biheeste;
> Thanne have ye do youre devoir atte leeste.'
> 'Hooste,' quod he, '*depardieux*, ich assente;
> To breke forward is nat myn entente.
> Biheste is dette, and I wole holde fayn
> Al my biheste, I kan no bettre sayn.
> For swich lawe as a man yeveth another wight,
> He sholde hymselven usen it, by right;
> Thus wole oure text.'

It would be a mistake to imagine that Bailey and the Man of Law are merely being pompous (though they are that) in their use of legalistic argument and language here.[40]

The poet ends his second fitt, like his first, with one of his most powerful wheels:

> To bed er ȝet þay ȝede,
> Recorded couenaunteȝ ofte;
> Þe olde lorde of þat leude
> Cowþe wel halde layk alofte. (1122-5)

The 'recording' of the covenants here is like the 'reforming' or 'rehearsing' (ll. 378 and 392) of the beheading agreement towards the end of the first fitt: on both occasions Bercilak is making sure that Gawain understands the exact terms of their contract. I think one may fairly assume that the author meant us to notice this ominous parallel—particularly as the assumption allows a strong explanation for the odd use of 'olde' in the following line. This has caused difficulty because Bercilak is said to be 'in the prime of life', and behaves so throughout. But the word makes good sense if we take it as a colloquial 'expression of familiarity', used 'in addressing or speaking of persons

---

[40] *C.T.*, II, 35-45. See Robinson's notes, on the 'technical language' of the passage. The Man of Law's attitude to his obligation may be compared with that of the Franklin, V, 696-708.

with whom one has an acquaintance of some standing, or whom one treats as such' (*O.E.D.*, 'old' 8a). Such an expression of familiarity would come very aptly here, immediately after a reminder of our previous acquaintance with the nameless host. An alternative is to take the word in *O.E.D.* sense 5: 'practised, experienced, skilled; also, in slang use, clever, knowing'. Some such meaning would go well with the next line, and the reader may find it preferable. In my own opinion, there is no reason why we should not accept both possibilities at once.[41] This seems the best way to account for the powerful and rather obscure effect which the word creates in its context here. It conveys a sense of (almost affectionate) familiarity both with Bercilak himself, and with the skill which he habitually shows in reconciling his duty as host with his duty as tester, pursuing the hero with tricky covenants while at the same time 'halding layk alofte'.[42]

[41] The colloquial shades of meaning in 'old' are rather elusive. The word is not recorded by the *O.E.D.* as an 'expression of familiarity' before Shakespeare. But the use presumably developed from sense 7c ('known or familiar from of old'); and 7c is recorded as early as Alfred. Like Chaucer, the *Gawain*-poet seems often to use 'old' in advanced colloquial senses. All three remaining occurrences of the word in *SGGK* present this possibility: 'þe olde auncian wyf', l. 1001 (a tautology? or *O.E.D.* 1c?); 'nobot an olde caue, / Or a creuisse of an olde cragge', ll. 2182–3 (*O.E.D.* 3? or 1c?).

[42] The phrase 'halde layk alofte', coming right at the end of the fitt, is in a position which strongly favours 'reverberations'. 'Hold aloft' is no more than a variant (for rhyme) of 'hold up', in the sense 'support, sustain'; but it recalls Bercilak's earlier efforts to 'move mirth', with a hood held up on the end of a spear, and with his head held up in his hand.

III

THE THIRD FITT

I

AS I POINTED OUT EARLIER, the second fitt is something of a piecemeal, Balkan affair—just a string of scenes, lacking any unity of place, time or action. The third fitt, on the other hand, is unmistakably planned as a whole, a *unity*; and one may be sure that the author would have approved the fitt-division here, even if he was not himself responsible for it. The action takes place in and around Bercilak's castle; it occupies three consecutive days (the last three days of the old year); and it consists, basically, of a single sequence of events three times repeated. On each occasion the poet first describes how Bercilak rises and goes hunting; then how his wife visits Gawain's room; then how Bercilak hunts his prey down and returns home; and finally how he and the hero meet, exchange 'winnings' and spend the evening together. The only section which falls outside this repeated fourfold scheme is the brief opening description of the departure of the other Christmas guests (ll. 1126–32).

It is obvious that the author expects us to observe and enjoy the symmetry of his plan—and at the same time keep an eye open for significant variations in the repeated pattern. Notice, for example, how on all three occasions he uses a similar (though not identical) phrasing to carry him from the hunting-field to the bed-chamber. On the first day:

> Þus layke3 þis lorde by lynde-wode3 eue3,
> And Gawayn þe god mon in gay bed lyge3. . . . (1178–9)

The Third Fitt

On the second:

> Þis day wyth þis ilk dede þay dryuen on þis wyse,
> Whyle oure luflych lede lys in his bedde,
> Gawayn grayþely at home, in gereȝ ful ryche
>   of hewe. (1468–71)

On the third:

> And ȝe he lad hem bi lagmon, þe lorde and his meyny,
> On þis maner bi þe mountes quyle myd-ouer-vnder,
> Whyle þe hende knyȝt at home holsumly slepeȝ
> Withinne þe comly cortynes, on þe colde morne. (1729–32)

In each case the transition from the first to the second phase of the day's events is managed in mid-sentence, according to a common pattern: thus (with this same deed, in this manner) the lord hunts, while (and) Gawain lies at home in his gay (rich, comely) bed. The same kind of repetition-with-variation is to be observed when, later each day, the poet crosscuts back from the castle to the hunt. On the first day:

> And ay þe lorde of þe londe is lent on his gamneȝ,
> To hunt in holteȝ and heþe at hyndeȝ barayne. (1319–20)

On the second:

> Bot þe lorde ouer þe londeȝ launced ful ofte,
> Sweȝ his vncely swyn. . . . (1561–2)

On the third:

> Ȝet is þe lorde on þe launde ledande his gomnes.
> He hatȝ forfaren þis fox. . . . (1894–5)

It is notable that each of these passages begins with a half-line of the type (*and ay*, etc.) *þe lorde of* (*ouer, on*) *þe londe* (*londeȝ, launde*). This is an interesting example of purposive formulaic writing.[1]

This, then, is one peculiarity of the third fitt: it demands a specially close attention to its pattern of action—the repetition of details and the variations (sometimes, as we shall see, very

[1] See R. A. Waldron, 'Oral-Formulaic Technique and Middle English Alliterative Poetry', *Spec.*, XXXII (1957), pp. 792–804.

significant) which they undergo. In other ways, too, this fitt makes special demands on the reader. Consider its time-scheme. *Sir Gawain* is in general a very time-conscious romance: the prologue and epilogue place the story in historical time, and the body of the text keeps us constantly informed of the season of year and hour of day. But this is nowhere more evident than in the present fitt, where the events of the three days of hunting and temptation are plotted with particular precision. The action of the first day (December 29) begins with the host rising before dawn (he is on horseback 'by þat any dayly3t lemed vpon erþe', l. 1137), and hunting through the day until sunset ('to þe derk ny3t', 1177). Then, in the second phase, we turn back to Gawain, lying in bed until dawn ('quyl þe dayly3t lemed on þe wowes', 1180) when the lady steals in on him. They talk until after 'mydmorn' (1280). Gawain then rises, hears Mass, dines, and 'made myry al day, til þe mone rysed' (1313). This brings us to the point of the day at which we left Bercilak, to whom we now therefore return. Bercilak, we are told, had slain a great number of deer by evening ('bi þat þe sunne heldet', 1321). The hunters, having 'undone' the deer, return to the castle, and are all in by nightfall ('bi þat þe dayly3t wat3 done', 1365). Bercilak and Gawain meet in the great hall and make merry until bedtime. For the two following days the time-scheme is only a little less circumstantial. On the second day, for example, Bercilak is again said to rise before dawn ('bi þat þe coke hade crowen and cakled bot þryse', 1412; 'er any day sprenged', 1415) and hunt until evening ('til þe sunne schafted', 1467); while on the third day he gets ready 'ful erly' (1689), sets out at sunrise (1695), and chases the fox until 'myd-ouer-vnder' (1730).[2]

---

[2] The meaning of 'myd-ouer-vnder' is obscure (lit. 'the middle of the period succeeding "undern" '). 'Undern' originally meant about 9 *a.m.* (monastic tierce); but it could also mean *midday* in the fourteenth century; and there is evidence in late M.E. and in modern dialects for its meaning *afternoon* or *evening*. It probably had different meanings in different places in the fourteenth century; and the same would seem to be true of 'myd-ouer-vnder'. In its two recorded occurrences outside *SGGK* it translates Lat. 'meridies' (noon) and 'circa horam undecimam' (about 5 in the afternoon) respectively—for

The Third Fitt

By such means the *Gawain*-poet achieves an effect very rare in romance: the illusion of separate events taking place concurrently hour by hour throughout a given day. This is something more than the 'interlacing' technique which allowed French prose romancers to keep several stories going at the same time. That technique, though it involves much 'cross-cutting', and sometimes a precisely calculated time-scheme too, does not, I think, create the illusion of which I am speaking. Of course, there must be some degree of synchronization if two errant knights are to converge in a forest glade; but the romances rarely make any sustained attempt, beyond such occasional requirements, to run two adventures neck-and-neck.[3] The truth is, I suspect, that the *Gawain*-poet is here playing a trick not out of romance but—unlikely though it may seem—out of fabliau. Parallels for his carefully synchronized time-scheme are, at least, more readily found in fabliau than in romance. The action of Chaucer's *Shipman's Tale*—the most typical of all his fabliau-tales—opens with a merchant and his wife entertaining their friend, John the Monk. On the third day, we are told, the merchant goes up and locks himself in his counting-house:

> . . . he nolde that no man sholde hym lette
> Of his acountes, for the meene tyme;
> And thus he sit til it was passed pryme.
> Daun John was rysen in the morwe also,
> And in the gardyn walketh to and fro. . . .[4]

The monk meets the lady, and they entertain each other in the garden until John suggests that they should go to dinner, 'for by my chilyndre it is pryme of day'. The lady, having been to the

---

[3] On 'interlacing', see especially Chapter II of F. Lot's *Étude sur le Lancelot en prose* (Paris, 1918). See also, on time-schemes, Chapter III of the same. Lot gives (p. 56) one striking example of synchronization from the *Lancelot* (ed. Sommer, Vol. V, pp. 292–4 and 303–6).

[4] Ed. Robinson, *C.T.*, VII, 86–90.

---

references, see C. Brett, *M.L.R.*, VIII (1913), pp. 163–4. So it seems best to allow the context to dictate the meaning in *SGGK*; and the analogy of ll. 1177 and (probably) 1467 strongly favours 'late afternoon'.

kitchen to order dinner, calls her husband down from the counting-house, and they all three hear Mass and dine together. This is the very technique used by the *Gawain*-poet in his third fitt. The time-scheme is less elaborate but, as far as it goes, even more exact. Between leaving the monk at prime and knocking up her husband, the woman goes to the kitchen. It is, therefore, precisely 'passed pryme' when the merchant is disturbed—as we were told it would be, a hundred lines earlier. The two actions—husband in counting-house, wife in garden—are concurrent, and Chaucer, like the *Gawain*-poet, does everything in his power (though it would be much easier for a painter) to make us realize the fact.[5]

This comparison brings us on to another of the distinctive features of the third fitt. If the author uses a trick out of fabliau here, it is because his poem is at this point moving through, or at least close to, fabliau country. When Gawain first hears the 'littel dyn at his dor' and sees the lady stealing in, neither he nor the reader is to know that her husband is in the secret. So her presence at once provokes the characteristic fabliau question: where is the husband, and when will he come back? An answer to this question, here as in the *Shipman's Tale*, has already been carefully prepared. The sunlight which 'lemed on þe wowes' of Gawain's chamber before the lady's entry is the same which 'lemed vpon erþe' in the surrounding country where Bercilak is out hunting; and a knight can be trusted to stay on the hunting-field, just as a merchant can be trusted to stay in his counting-house. Indeed the author has already said that he does stay there, 'to þe derk nyȝt'. We can therefore trust the lady when she assures Gawain that they will not be disturbed:

> My lorde and his ledeȝ ar on lenþe faren,
> Oþer burneȝ in her bedde, and my burdeȝ als,
> Þe dor drawen and dit with a derf haspe. (1231-3)

So the reader is permitted to discount one major fabliau possibility, the sudden return of the husband, while following the bedroom scenes. But this does not mean that these scenes are

[5] Another example of this kind of 'fabliau time-scheme' may be found in Boccaccio's *Decameron*, the fifth story of the seventh day.

lifted free of all fabliau connections. On the contrary—to discount a possibility is to admit its existence. A wife who calculates on her husband's absence and a strong door-catch will hardly establish herself as not the fabliau type, however much she may reassure hero or reader that she is not the type to be caught.

The notion that the third fitt may to some extent be distinguished by the presence of 'fabliau elements' gains support when we turn our attention from the concurrent hunting and tempting, which occupy the first three phases of each day's action, to the exchange of winnings, which follows in the fourth. I would not lay much stress on the fact that the only known parallel to this exchange motif (which is not found in any of the beheading or temptation analogues) is provided by one of the so-called 'Latin fabliaux' of the twelfth century, the *Miles Gloriosus*,[6] because I do not think that the exchange of winnings is *in itself* particularly distinctive. Its character depends on the circumstances of the exchange and the nature of the commodities exchanged; and in these respects the *Miles Gloriosus* differs significantly from *Sir Gawain*. In the *Miles* the hero, having agreed with a rich citizen that they should divide all their worldly possessions, gets involved (without identifying her) with the citizen's wife, and on several occasions pays over to the husband half the sum which he has received for his services to the wife. The point is that the citizen should be paid in his own coin, and know it. This is one kind of fabliau joke to be made out of the exchange idea; but the point in *Sir Gawain* is different, and even more distinctively 'fabliau' in character. Gawain 'wins', at first, nothing but kisses from his partner's wife—there being no coin or commodity involved until he receives the rich girdle on the third day. Yet, unlike the hero of the Latin poem, he decides to treat the wife's favours as themselves a kind of commodity or 'winning'; so each evening he 'pays' them over to the husband in return for the proceeds of the day's hunt. One may see this decision as evidence of Gawain's high romantic scrupulosity, his perfect 'truth'; yet the fact remains that it is based on an idea much more characteristic of

[6] Ed. R. Baschet, in G. Cohen's *La 'Comédie' latine en France au XIIe siècle*, Vol. I (Paris, 1931), pp. 179–210.

The Third Fitt

fabliau than romance—the 'mercantile' idea of sexual favours as a commodity to be exchanged against other commodities or cash.[7] Chaucer's *Shipman's Tale* again provides an excellent illustration, for its basic plot consists entirely in a series of transactions in which sexual favours and money are treated as commensurable and therefore exchangeable—an attitude which, as one critic has pointed out, finds perfect expression in the wife's punning remark to her husband: 'I am youre wyf; score it upon my taille, / And I shal paye as soone as ever I may'.[8] We shall find a similar use of commercial jargon when we come to look more closely at the exchange scenes in *Sir Gawain*.

So far I have been concerned, in a general way, with some of the distinctive features of the third fitt—its symmetrical structure, its use of repetition-with-variation, its carefully synchronized time-scheme, and its incorporation of 'fabliau elements'. Let me now follow the action through in greater detail.

II

There is nothing to arrest the attention in the first two stanzas of the fitt. The Christmas guests, who have already taken their leave (ll. 1024–8), depart; and the host, who has already promised as much to Gawain (ll. 1101–2), rises early for the hunt. The description of the deer-hunt which follows is vivid, but in no way out of the ordinary.[9] One notices simply that Bercilak is a

[7] The idea that kisses can be 'stolen' or 'restored' is more widely current. See, for example, Charles D'Orléans' 'Confession of Love', no. 185 in *Secular Lyrics of the XIVth and XVth Centuries*, ed. Robbins; and Gower's *Confessio Amantis*, V, 6493 ff.

[8] See A. H. Silverman, 'Sex and Money in Chaucer's *Shipman's Tale*', *P.Q.*, XXXII (1953), pp. 329–36.

[9] Deer-hunts are common in romances (see Tolkien and Gordon's note to l. 1139); and it is quite natural that Bercilak should spend his time hunting once all his guests, except Gawain, have gone home, and he is left alone with his household, or meinie. Compare Arthur at Cardoil in the First Continuation of Chrétien's *Perceval*: 'A privée mesnie estoit, / Si vos di bien que il aloit / Sovant ou bois por archoier / Et an riviere esbenoier / Les plusor jors de la semeine', Long Version, ed. W. Roach and R. H. Ivy (Philadelphia, 1950), ll. 6879–83.

77

skilled and eager huntsman, that he stays out till nightfall, and
that, consequently, his winnings in the wood are likely to be
substantial—difficult, perhaps, for Gawain to match when it
comes to the exchange. There is in these stanzas no question of
surprise (or, I might add, of symbolism). They create the impression that everything is going according to plan—an impression that is strengthened when, after the crosscut at the
beginning of the following stanza, we find Gawain still peace-
fully asleep in his bed, just as Bercilak would have wished:

> ʒe schal lenge in your lofte, and lyʒe in your ese
> To-morn quyle þe messequyle, and to mete wende
> When ʒe wyl, wyth my wyf, þat wyth yow schal sitte
> And comfort yow with compayny, til I to cort torne. (1096-9)

Gawain is to lie in bed until Mass, be joined by the lady for
dinner (though in retrospect the lines may appear a little vague
on this), and spend the rest of the day in her company. These
expectations, however, are dramatically disturbed by the little
noise at the door which announces the first of the 'temptation
scenes'.

This scene opens, as other critics have noticed, with a sustained and brilliantly effective piece of dumb-show. The door
opens—Gawain peeps out through the bedcurtain—the lady
approaches the bed—Gawain lies down quickly and pretends
to sleep—the lady sits on the side of the bed—Gawain keeps up
his pretence of sleep—decides that he must wake up—stretches
and turns towards the lady—starts and crosses himself—the
lady speaks. All this is pure comedy, the comedy of embarrassment ('shame' in Middle English, as in l. 1189); and it sets the
tone for the first part of the conversation which ensues. The
lady, with Gawain pinned down and at a disadvantage in his own
bed, laughingly claims him as her prisoner; and he, accepting
the role, gives himself up and begs for mercy ('I ʒelde me
ʒederly, and ʒeʒe after grace'). These exchanges represent very
well, I think, what the author understood by 'dalyaunce'—the
kind of courtly conversation between a man and woman which
could mean anything or nothing. The lady's opening words—
'Now ar ʒe tan astyt; bot true vus may schape, / I schal bynde

yow in your bedde, þat be ȝe trayst'—are practically the same
as those used by Troilus at the most passionate moment in
Chaucer's *Troilus and Criseyde*:

> O swete, as evere mot I gon,
> Now be ye kaught, now is ther but we tweyne.
> Now yeldeth yow, for other bote is non.[10]

But the courtly-love conceit of the prisoner, which means
everything to Troilus, means almost nothing to Gawain, who
accepts it as one of the lady's 'bourdeȝ' (l. 1212) and 'bourded
aȝayn with mony a blyþe laȝter' (1217). The sexual innuendo is
there, of course; but Gawain is perfectly at ease with this kind
of dalliance (compare ll. 1010–15), and when he asks the lady
to allow him to get up and dress, he does so with an unruffled
courtesy which recalls his first speech in the poem—the elaborate, measured request to Arthur and Guinevere for permission
to leave the high table at Camelot (compare ll. 1218–21 with
343–7).

It is while refusing this request that the lady introduces for
the first time—in this fitt—an idea which is to dominate both
this and the succeeding temptation scenes:

> Ȝe schal not rise of your bedde, I rych yow better,
> I schal happe yow here þat oþer half als,
> And syþen karp wyth my knyȝt þat I kaȝt haue;
> For I wene wel, iwysse, Sir Wowen ȝe are,
> Þat alle þe worlde worchipeȝ quere-so ȝe ride;
> Your honour, your hendelayk is hendely praysed
> With lordeȝ, wyth ladyes, with alle þat lyf bere. (1223–9)

The position which the lady takes up here is exactly that

---

[10] Ed. Robinson, Book III, ll. 1206–8. Compare 'now be ye kaught'
with 'now ar ȝe tan astyt' (*SGGK*, 1210); 'now is ther but we tweyne'
with 'and we bot oure one' (1230); and 'now yeldeth yow, for other
bote is non' with 'I ȝelde me ȝederly . . . for me byhoueȝ nede' (1215–
16). Generally in *Troilus*, as in *SGGK*, it is the woman who dominates
(emprisons, commands) the man. The present passage is exceptional.
On the part played by such courtly conversation in the 'game of
love', see J. Stevens, *Music and Poetry in the Early Tudor Court* (London, 1961), pp. 159–64.

The Third Fitt

adopted by the unnamed 'segges' in the dinner-scene of the second fitt:

> Wich spede is in speche vnspurd may we lerne,
> Syn we haf fonged þat fyne fader of nurture.
> God hatȝ geuen vus his grace godly for soþe,
> Þat such a gest as Gawan graunteȝ vus to haue. (918–21)

The lady's 'Sir Wowen ȝe are' is neither a truism nor merely a compliment. It introduces the first of her attempts to manoeuvre Gawain into acting in accordance with *her conception* of what his identity involves. Unlike the 'segges', however, she does not want to make her expectations too explicit at first, and her catalogue of Gawain-qualities is truncated and rather vague ('honour' and 'hendelayk'). She does appear to share something of her household's consuming interest in 'luf-talkyng' ('syþen *karp* wyth my knyȝt', compare l. 1236); but her talk of the 'derf haspe' on the door leads one to suspect that this is no more than a manner of speaking. And this suspicion is confirmed, seemingly in the baldest possible fashion, by her closing words:

> Ȝe ar welcum to my cors,
> Yowre awen won to wale,
> Me behoueȝ of fyne force
> Your seruaunt be, and schale. (1237–40)

This is the point at which to observe that the role of 'temptress', like the corresponding masculine role of challenger, has an established place in the repertoire of courtly romance. A modern reader well instructed in the 'theory of courtly love' may feel that the lady, by boldly taking the initiative upon herself, runs the risk of disqualification—if, as seems otherwise evident, she is appealing to Gawain as the 'fyne fader of nurture'. But the notion that such an initiative necessarily marks a lady as 'uncourtly'—though it seems to follow as a natural conclusion from accepted accounts of the 'courtly code'—is not supported by the evidence of the medieval romances. It is indeed an important part of our very definition of the courtly *lyric* that the mistress should be portrayed as remote and 'dangerous'; but in *romances* one can find many courtly ladies who, without in any way forfeiting their status, behave quite differently. In *Perlesvaus*, for example, we find the Queen of the Tents (who woos Perceval), the wife of Marin the Jealous (who woos Gawain), the two Damsels of the Tent (who woo Gawain and Arthur), the Queen of the Castle of the Beards and the Damsel of the Castle of the Griffon (both of whom woo Lancelot.)[11] The accommodation of romance to the strict rules of the orthodox love-lyric—though, from the time of Chrétien onwards, it went a long way—was never complete, and could perhaps never have been so. Romance-writers always reserved the right to match their greater variety of roles and situations with a correspondingly greater variety of permissible behaviour. Their knights can deliver a rough challenge without ceasing to be chivalrous, and their ladies can press a suit without ceasing to be ladylike.

One might grant all this and still feel, with Gollancz, that 'the lady's bluntness in coming to the point testifies to her inexperience' in the role of temptress. But even this is doubtful. The line chiefly responsible for the impression of bluntness and inexperience, '3e ar welcum to my cors', is less blunt (though not less suggestive) than it sounds. In Middle English 'my (your, his) corse (body)' could mean no more than 'me (you, him)'. This idiom, which is based on a corresponding use of 'cors' in French, is sufficiently illustrated by what God says to Abraham in *Cleanness*:

How my3t I hyde myn hert fro Habraham þe trwe,
Þat I ne dyscovered to his corse my counsayl so dere?[12]

There is, then, a saving ambiguity about the lady's offer. She can claim to have said no more than she says in the following lines: 'I am at your service' (compare her husband's words in ll. 835-7). One can find the corresponding French idiom used quite innocently in just this way, as part of a polite expression of gratitude or obligation; as when a perfectly respectable rescued maiden says to Gawain:

[11] *Perlesvaus*, ed. cit., pp. 74, 95, 133, 153, 288, 315.
[12] *Cleanness*, ll. 682-3. On the idiom, see T. F. Mustanoja, *A Middle English Syntax*, Part I (Helsinki, 1960), pp. 148-9.

The Third Fitt

> Sire, dist-elle, guerredon
> Vous doi; tout vous met à bandon
> Mon cors et trestot mon avoir.[13]

On the other hand—and here there is very clear evidence of ambiguity, in French at least—almost the same words can be used by another lady with a plainly erotic intention:

> Sire, fait elle, an abandon
> Vos met mon cors et vos presant
> M'amor a toz jors loiaumant.[14]

Of course the lady's offer of service is itself highly 'ambiguous'. When such an offer is made by a man, it may mean almost nothing; but this cannot be so, I think, when it is made by a woman—unless she has a very strong and obvious reason for gratitude.[15] So, though Gawain could readily accept the offered role of prisoner or vassal, he cannot accept that of suzerain. He demurs:

> 'In god fayth,' quoþ Gawayn, 'gayn hit me þynkkeȝ,
> Þaȝ I be not now he þat ȝe of speken;
> To reche to such reuerence as ȝe reherce here
> I am wyȝe vnworþy, I wot wel myseluen.' (1241–4)

---

[13] '"Sir," she said, "I owe you a reward. I put myself and all my goods entirely at your disposal".' *Perceval le Gallois*, ed. C. Potvin (Mons, 1866–71), ll. 37893–5. Notice that 'cors' is here coupled with 'avoir'. The idiomatic use of 'mon cors' for 'me' may have originated in this contrasting phrase.

[14] ' "Sir," she said, "I put myself at your disposal and offer you loyally my love for ever".' First Continuation of Chrétien's *Perceval*, Long Version, ed. cit., ll. 6322–4. Ten lines later the maiden is deflowered. Compare the Queen of the Tents' suggestive use of 'vostre cors' to Perceval in *Perlesvaus*, ed. cit., l. 3282: 'li cuers me semont que je face joie de vostre cors'.

[15] Though Lancelot refuses the love of the Damsel of the Castle of the Griffon, he offers himself in her 'servise' (*Perlesvaus*, l. 7541). But the Damsels of the Tent are plainly tempting Gawain when they offer him *their* service: 's'apoient desus la coche, et li presentent molt leur service. E Messire Gavains ne leur respont autre chose que granz merciz, car il ne pense fors a dormir e a reposer' (*Perlesvaus*, ll. 1811–13; cp. 1907–8).

The Third Fitt

Gawain's 'I be not now he þat ȝe of speken' is a subtle and revealing stroke. The lady appeals to him, as I have said, to act on her conception (or what for the occasion she adopts as her conception) of what he is. His reply says both '*I* am not that' and 'I am not *that*'. It demonstrates both his courtesy and (covertly) his awareness that courtesy is not everything. The same kind of double significance runs right through the ensuing dialogue. In form this is no more than an extended exchange of compliments. The lady praises Gawain, his 'prys', 'prowes', 'daynté wordeȝ', 'bewté', 'debonerté' and 'blyþe semblaunt'; and he replies (very much as he had replied to her husband, ll. 1037–8) by attributing everything to her own courtesy and 'fraunchis'. But the poet makes us aware—though only vaguely as yet—of the moral issues stirring beneath the surface of the dialogue:

> Scho made hym so gret chere,
> Þat watȝ so fayr of face,
> Þe knyȝt with speches skere
> Answered to vche a cace. (1259–62)

'The knight' (a cool, appraising expression, as often in the wheels) faces a challenge in the lady's compliments.

The dialogue at this point is extremely artificial (notice specially the play on the word 'pris', repeated in ll. 1247, 1249 and 1277), and it is something of a relief when Gawain brings it to an end. Excess of self-depreciation is a social evil—as well as, according to Aristotle and Aquinas, a moral one—and Gawain has, in the end, to accept something of the 'pris' which the lady attributes to him:

> 'Iwysse, worþy,' quoþ þe wyȝe, 'ȝe haf waled wel better,
> Bot I am proude of þe prys þat ȝe put on me,
> And, soberly your seruaunt, my souerayn I holde yow,
> And yowre knyȝt I becom, and Kryst yow forȝelde.' (1276–9)

This is an ingenious bit of 'dalliance'. There is modesty in the praise of Bercilak and in the acceptance of the lady's suzerainty; but there is also a calculated expression of pride, sufficient to concede a kind of victory to the lady in the battle of compliments—Gawain left gracefully holding the baby.

Þus þay meled of muchquat til mydmorn paste,
And ay þe lady let lyk as hym loued mych;
Þe freke ferde with defence, and feted ful fayre. (1280–2)

Nobody reading this scene can doubt the poet's interest in, and indeed love of, the 'teccheles termes of talkyng noble'. He is not in any way critical of courtesy here. It is true that he has no truck with adulterous 'courtly love'. But such love, though an important element in some continental courtly writing, seems to play little or no part in fourteenth-century English ideals of courtesy.[16] The poet, so far from thinking his hero's concern for 'cleanness' remarkable or controversial, simply takes it for granted—he would know not to make love to a married woman, particularly the wife of his host—and contents himself with pointing out that Gawain would not be very interested in women anyway, considering his circumstances:

Þaȝ ho were burde bryȝtest, þe burne in mynde hade
Þe lasse luf in his lode, for lur þat he soȝt
     boute hone,
Þe dunte þat schulde hym deue,
And nedeȝ hit most be done.[17] (1283–7)

The comment is somewhat ambiguous. It might be compared, perhaps, with the comment on the Gawain of *Perlesvaus*, who, because he is on the Grail quest, resists the wife of Marin the Jealous: 'il avoit si son cuer lié e estraint q'il ne li lessoit penser chose qui a vilenie tornast, por le haut pelerinage qu'il avoit enpris'.[18] But the phrasing suggests a less noble reading: Gawain's fear of impending death is so great that it overpowers his other instincts. One may recall that he has only just, the evening before, learnt of the whereabouts of the Green Chapel.

[16] See especially G. Mathew, 'Marriage and *Amour Courtois* in Late Fourteenth-Century England', in *Essays Presented to Charles Williams* (Oxford, 1947), pp. 128–35.

[17] Gollancz's emendations. Tolkien and Gordon manage to avoid emendation; but their punctuation is tortuous, and I doubt whether we should be told at this point what the lady is thinking.

[18] 'His heart was so tied and bound up that it did not allow him to think of anything base, because of the high pilgrimage which he had undertaken.' *Perlesvaus*, ed. cit., ll. 1259–61.

The Third Fitt

He received the news heroically ('Þenne watȝ Gawan ful glad,
and gomenly he laȝed'); but it is not beyond the range of the
poem's realism to credit him with a shock of fear—'nedeȝ hit
most be done'. Taken so, the present passage anticipates the
crucial moment in the third temptation when the lady shifts the
ground of her attack and, appealing at last—and successfully—
to an overpowering instinct, offers not love but life.
The lady does not make this appeal in the first temptation,
however; and the present scene ends with a kiss and a victory
for the hero. The lady, just as she is about to go, turns on Gawain
and reproaches him:

> Now he Þat spedeȝ vche spech Þis disport ȝelde yow!
> Bot Þat ȝe be Gawan, hit gotȝ in mynde. (1292–3)

It is one of those 'ramposnes' or mocking reproaches which are
to be found in French romance: 'You cannot be Gawain. A
knight as courteous as Gawain would already have asked me for
a kiss.'[19] The argument is, of course, highly typical of the lady's
strategy—appealing to her guest's acknowledged identity—but
she is not yet, as the poet later puts it, 'pressing him near the
thread'. Gawain feels a momentary anxiety (the 'freschly' of
l. 1294 is very expressive); but she 'blesses' (reassures) him,
and makes a request which she knows he can grant. Notice that
there is no question, either here or anywhere else in the poem,
of Gawain's being wrong to accept the lady's kisses. They are
not in themselves adulterous, and—always providing Gawain
pays them over at the exchange—they do not, apparently, involve any breach of faith with his host. So Gawain accepts the
present one:

> Iwysse, worÞe as yow lykeȝ;
> I schal kysse at your comaundement, as a knyȝt falleȝ,
> And fire, lest he displese yow, so plede hit no more. (1302–4

The syntax is somewhat loose (as so often in the poem when
people are being polite), but the general meaning is clear.

---

[19] Compare *Perlesvaus*, ll. 1814–16: 'se ce fust cil Gavains qui niés
est le roi Artu, il parlast a nos autrement, e trovissions en lui plus de
deduit que en cestui; mes cist est uns Gavains contrefez'.

The Third Fitt

Gawain does not admit the lady's claim that he should already have 'craued a cosse, bi his courtaysye'; but he does admit his duty, 'as a kny3t falle3', to kiss her when she commands it of him. His conception of 'cleanness' is not such as to demand a showdown on such an issue—if it were, there would hardly be room for three extended temptation scenes. So for the moment at least the crisis is postponed. The lady kisses Gawain and goes off. Gawain rises, goes 'bly>ely to masse', dines, and spends the rest of the day making merry with the two 'dyngne dame'.

The beginning of the following stanza returns us to the hunting-field, and so introduces the third phase of the day's action. This transition is one of the poem's sensitive points, for it is here that our conception of the relation between temptation and hunt is likely to be formed. We are by now in a position to see host and hostess working as a team, and also, perhaps, to see some relation between their respective activities. The equation between hunting and wooing is, of course, a well-established source of metaphors and conceits in courtly writing, both medieval and renaissance;[20] and the idea of Venus as huntress is common in medieval writing—as in this passage from the moral-allegorical *Pilgrimage of the Life of Man*:

> Thys lady doth euere espye,
> With huntys in hyr companye,
> Most perillous to hurte and wounde,
> Al pylgrymes to confounde.
> ffor ther ys hunte nor foster
> That chaceth ay the wylde deer,
> Nor other bestys that byth savage,
> That may be lykned to the rage
> Off Dame Venus: wherfor tak hede
> How gretly she ys to drede.
> And yiff thow kanst the trouthe espye,
> Venus ys sayd off venerye.[21]

[20] So Andreas Capellanus, in his *De Amore* (ed. E. Trojel, Havnia, 1892), speaks of the service of Venus as a kind of hunting (pp. 2 and 57). The conceit is familiar in Petrarch, Wyatt, Shakespeare, etc.

[21] Deguileville's *Pilgrimage of the Life of Man*, translated by Lydgate, ed. F. J. Furnivall, Part I, E.E.T.S. E.S. 77 (1899), ll. 8139–50.

The Third Fitt

It is possible, on the strength of passages such as this, to elaborate the parallelisms between hunt and temptation scenes, taking Gawain as the prey, and the lady as the huntsman bent on 'confounding' him; but I must confess that, with one exception (the death of the fox, to be discussed later), I find these detailed parallels rather unconvincing.[22] I cannot see the crucial distinction between the timid deer-Gawain of the first day and the aggressive boar-Gawain of the second: his behaviour on these two occasions does not seem to differ so extremely, or indeed in that way. And so far as any ground-metaphor is to be detected in the temptation scenes themselves (if that is relevant), it is one of fighting, not hunting—Gawain 'defending' himself (ll. 1282 and 1551), parrying the lady's advances (1777), etc.

It seems fairly obvious, anyway, that the prime effect of the juxtaposition of hunt and temptation is one, not of parallelism, but of *contrast*. This is best seen, perhaps, as a variation on the poet's favourite contrast between indoor and outdoor experience. Elsewhere in the poem (most picturesquely at the beginning of the fourth fitt) the outdoors is associated with winter hardship, the rigours of Gawain's quest, and contrasted with the desirable indoor world of festive well-being. True, the indoor world has its own problems; but it is only here in the third fitt that the world out-of-doors seems positively to be preferred. It is not that Gawain *ought* to be out exercising himself with his host—he deserves, as the host himself points out, to rest after his long journey. It is rather that he might be better off there:

> And ay þe lorde of þe londe is lent on his gamneʒ,
> To hunt in holteʒ and heþe at hyndeʒ barayne;
> Such a sowme he þer slowe bi þat þe sunne heldet,
> Of dos and of oþer dere, to deme were wonder. (1319–22)

---

[22] See especially H. L. Savage, 'The Significance of the Hunting Scenes in *SGGK*', *J.E.G.P.*, XXVII (1928), pp. 1–15.

'Venus dicitur a venandi' is written in the Stowe Ms. beside the last line quoted. Chaucer puns on 'venerie': see D. W. Robertson, *Preface to Chaucer* (Princeton, 1963), p. 253.

The effect of these lines, coming after the protracted, devious manoeuvrings of the bedroom scene, is idyllic—almost as the hunting scenes in Tolstoy are idyllic. They convey, that is, a strong sense of release, of escaping out of the toils of civilized living into a form of activity which—though governed by complex man-made conventions, and so far from 'natural'—is exhilarating and unproblematical:

> Þe lorde for blys abloy
> Ful oft con launce and lyȝt,
> And drof þat day wyth joy
> Thus to þe derk nyȝt. (1174–7)

This contrast is subtly reasserted in the poet's account of the exchange of winnings which follows the host's return from the hunting-field (ll. 1372–1401). The host brings back with him solid winnings—'schyree grece schorne vpon rybbes'—whose value is obvious to any experienced judge:

> 'Ȝe iwysse,' quoþ þat oþer wyȝe, 'here is wayth fayrest
> Þat I seȝ þis seuen ȝere in sesoun of wynter.' (1381–2)

But the value of the 'cheuicaunce' which Gawain offers in return is problematical:

> 'Hit is god,' quoþ þe god mon, 'grant mercy þerfore.
> Hit may be such, hit is þe better, and ȝe me breue wolde
> Where ȝe wan þis ilk wele bi wytte of yorseluen.' (1392–4)

What is a kiss worth? It depends who has given it. The problem belongs not in the hunting field but in the chamber. Indeed it is typical of Gawain's exchanges with the lady, where value ('pris', 'worchyp') is treated as a shifting, uncertain quantity: 'I am proude of þe prys þat ȝe put on me', 'Hit is þe worchyp of yourself, þat noȝt bot wel conneȝ', etc. Bercilak's reaction to the kiss is in the same chamber style—'Hit may be such, hit is þe better . . .'—and it contrasts sharply with the rich assured note of the hunt:

> here is wayth fayrest
> Þat I seȝ þis seuen ȝere in sesoun of wynter.

In the tricky indoor world of the castle, the scene of Gawain's trials, values are not so simple. The kisses are like merchandise ('cheuicaunce'), their value conditional upon the state of the market—a point which is made clear in Bercilak's comment on the third day:

> 'Bi Kryst,' quoþ þat oþer kny3t, '3e cach much sele
> In cheuisaunce of þis chaffer, 3if 3e hade goud chepe3.'
>
> (1938-9)

'You must be making a good profit trading in this merchandise —provided you got it at a favourable price'. There is a special irony in this in the context; but there is also an appropriate general comment—the comment of the returned huntsman on the complexities of life indoors.[23]

The first day ends with an account of the renewal of the exchange agreement—accompanied, as on the previous evening, by a ceremonial 'beverage'. As before, the covenant is made 'in bourde'; but as before it is to be understood as a real plighting of troth:

> Þay acorded of þe couenaunte3 byfore þe court alle;
> Þe beuerage wat3 bro3t forth in bourde at þat tyme,
> Þenne þay louelych le3ten leue at þe last,
> Vche burne to his bedde busked bylyue. (1408-11)

III

The poet's account of the events of the second day is almost the same length as his account of the first (276 lines to 286), but it is differently proportioned. The first and third phases, describing the boar-hunt, are somewhat longer than the corresponding passages about the deer-hunt; while the second, temptation, phase is distinctly shorter (92 lines to 140). I should like, nevertheless, to concentrate on this second phase here.

[23] D. W. Robertson, op. cit., pp. 263-4, points out that there is a 'good' hunt, presided over by Diana, as well as a 'bad' one, presided over by Venus, in classical and medieval tradition. The former represents virtuous activity, 'business' as against 'idleness', etc., and its quarry is often the hart (as in the case of Chaucer's Theseus). Robertson's discussion suggests a plausible moralization of the contrast between chamber and hunting-field in *SGGK*. But it is hard to see Gawain in his chamber as a type of idleness or vice. The hunt is good; but so are his reasons for staying at home.

The earlier part of the second temptation scene (up to the first of the two kisses, l. 1505) is linked by a simple but ingenious bit of invention to its predecessor. The lady tries to steal a march on 'oure luflych lede' (the poet is now outspokenly partisan) by misrepresenting the understanding which they had come to before parting on the previous day. On that occasion she had proposed, as a principle, that a courteous knight should 'crave a kiss' whenever the conversation presents him with the slightest opportunity to do so. Gawain, however, had not accepted this; and when he agreed to kiss her, it was on a different principle—that a knight should obey a lady's order and avoid displeasing her. From the lady's point of view, he did the right thing for the wrong reason; but on the present occasion she tries to get round this by simply assuming, from the start, that he did it for the right reason—on her principle. *If* you are Gawain, she says (with a casually threatening reminder of her former doubts), you should be kissing me, because we agreed, didn't we, that courteous knights always do that?

> '3et I kende yow of kyssyng,' quoþ þe clere þenne,
> 'Quere-so countenaunce is couþe quikly to clayme;
> Þat bicumes vche a kny3t þat cortaysy vses.' (1489-91)

The short dialogue which ensues (ll. 1492–1503) is an excellent specimen of the art of the temptation scenes. The poet does not allow conversation to become argument—because he is most interested precisely in those social and moral difficulties which are peculiar to conversation as against argument—but at the same time he contrives the to-and-fro of the reasoning with the utmost skill and economy. Gawain does not controvert the lady's 'principle'; he takes refuge in a gentlemanly caution:

> 'For þat durst I not do, lest I deuayed were;
> If I were werned, I were wrang, iwysse, 3if I profered.'
> 'Ma fay,' quoþ þe meré wyf, '3e may not be werned,
> 3e ar stif innoghe to constrayne wyth strenkþe, 3if yow lyke3,
> 3if any were so vilanous þat yow deuaye wolde.' (1493-7)

The lady uses two inconsistent arguments here. The first— '3e may not be *werned*'—speaks for itself, eloquently; but the second deserves comment. Here, as once in the previous scene ('3e ar welcum to my cors'), it may appear at first sight that the lady has resorted to a crudely provincial approach; but her words, as before, are less crude than they look. They involve, in fact, a quite subtle sophistry, which can be stated in the following syllogistic form: Anyone who refuses you is a villein (because only a villein could fail to appreciate your excellence); *but* it is legitimate to use force on a villein (*teste* Andreas Capellanus and others);[24] *therefore* it is legitimate for you to use force on anyone who refuses you. Gawain acknowledges the ingenuity of this point ('good is your speche'); but he does not trouble to argue it out. He simply enunciates a general principle which contradicts the lady's minor premiss ('þrete is vnþryuande . . .'), and reverts to his original position:

> 'I am at your comaundement, to kysse quen yow lyke3,
> 3e may lach quen yow lyst, and leue quen yow þynkke3,
>   in space.'
>   Þe lady loute3 adoun,
>   And comlyly kysses his face. (1501–5)

This takes us back to the conclusion of the last encounter, and marks the end of the discussion about kissing which began there. Though the problem is a somewhat academic one (of a kind with the courtly 'question d'amour'), the lady fails to win even a formal concession from Gawain. In the first part of their conversation on the previous day he had established himself as her 'servant'; and it is this comparatively non-committal role which has sustained him through the subsequent exchanges. He is indeed, as the lady later observes, 'coynt of his hetes'— cunning with his promises.

The kissing discussion is followed (as it was preceded) by a short passage of summary:

>   Much speche þay þer expoun
>   Of druryes greme and grace.

Then, at the beginning of the next stanza, the lady introduces a new topic. Her long speech (ll. 1508–34) is built on now-

[24] *De Amore*, ed. cit., Book I, Chap. XI ('De amore rusticorum'), p. 236.

familiar lines: 'since you are the famous Gawain, why have you not taught me some of your skill in love?' The lady seems to be running out of stratagems.²⁵ But her speech is interesting, nevertheless, since it provides her fullest version of what (for the purposes of the tests, at least) chivalry means to her. Gawain, she says, is young, vigorous, handsome, courteous and 'knightly'. It is surprising, therefore, that he has not spoken of love. For love is an essential part of knighthood:

> ... of alle cheualry to chose, þe chef þyng alosed˙
> Is þe lel layk of luf, þe lettrure of armes;
> For to telle of þis teuelyng of þis trwe kny3te3,
> Hit is þe tytelet token, and tyxt of her werkke3,
> How ledes for her lele luf hor lyue3 han auntered,
> Endured for her drury dulful stounde3,
> And after wenged with her walour and voyded her care,
> And bro3t blysse into boure with bountees hor awen. (1512–19)

Now the poet had nothing against the 'lel layk of luf', and he no doubt thought the avenging of a distressed mistress a perfectly good motive for knightly adventure. What the lady says is not so much wrong in itself as irrelevant and misleading. She plainly has no business to invoke 'loyal love' *here*, even though it is the 'chief thing' about chivalry; for, in the poet's system of values, no such love could possibly exist between a 'true knight' and his host's wife, and it is not for Gawain to teach her about it—'3e haf waled wel better'. It is worth noticing, though, that the lady's request is shown as springing, not from any rival 'system of values' (from Andreas Capellanus or wherever), but from a kind of honest misunderstanding. Her approach is a little tentative; almost—'you should be making love to me, shouldn't you? I have read ...'. The touch of bookishness is neatly conveyed in the comparison of a knight's 'works' with the works of an author: love is the 'chief thing' in the life of chivalry, just as the 'tytelet token' (the title or heading) and the 'tyxt' are the chief things in a book. It is no more than a comparison, of course; but it is enough—taken together with the somewhat

²⁵ Notice the rhetorical similarity between this speech and the speech with which the lady introduced the point about kissing (1297 ff.), especially the repetitions of 'so'.

literary character of the description of the knights suffering
'dulful stoundeȝ' for their mistresses—to suggest a second-
hand acquaintance, a reader away from the centre of things.
That, at any rate, is the impression which the lady creates—and
consciously, if her later reference to herself as a 'ȝonke þynk'
(a 'young thing') is anything to go by. But Gawain is not taken
in by her inviting modesty; and her attempts to portray herself
as a kind of medieval Catherine Morland provoke no more than
an equally modest reply (ll. 1535–48), at the end of which
Gawain takes refuge once more in his 'coynt hetes':

> I wolde yowre wylnyng worche at my myȝt,
> As I am hyȝly bihalden, and euermore wylle
> Be seruaunt to yourseluen, so saue me dryȝtyn. (1546–8)

The poet's attitude to the lady, here and elsewhere in the
temptation scenes, is somewhat ambivalent. In the present
scene, if not in its predecessor, he openly shares with the audience the knowledge that she is testing the hero. So at the beginning:

> Ful erly ho watȝ hym ate
> His mode for to remwe. (1474–5)

And at the end:

> Þus hym frayned þat fre, and fondet hym ofte,
> For to haf wonnen hym to woȝe, what-so scho þoȝt elleȝ.
>
> (1549–50)

Even so, though we know her purpose (in a general way, at
least), and can watch her calculating and manoeuvring as she
talks, the poet handles her 'real' feelings, as he does those of her
husband, with a certain generous vagueness. In the course of
the first scene he does indeed give a hint that she does not love
Gawain by saying that she 'behaved as if she did' ('ay þe lady
let lyk as hym loued mych', l. 1281); but in the second of the
passages quoted above he rather pointedly suggests that the
lady's thoughts were not entirely absorbed in her purpose of
leading Gawain into sin ('what-so scho þoȝt elleȝ');[26] and at the
beginning of the third temptation scene he goes further:

[26] I do not see how 'what-so scho þoȝt elleȝ' can 'hint' at 'some hidden
motive in her behaviour' (Gollancz's note to l. 1550). The hidden
motive is surely quite clearly stated in the preceding line-and-a-half.

The Third Fitt

Bot þe lady for luf let not to slepe,
Ne þe purpose to payre þat pyȝt in hir hert,
Bot ros hir vp radly. . . . (1733-5)

Gollancz glosses 'luf' in this passage 'pleasure in his company', on the grounds that the lady does not feel any *love* for Gawain, and compares the use of 'for luf' in l. 1086; but, even if this is what the poet intended (which I doubt), he can hardly have been unaware of the possible misunderstanding. He seems, in fact, to be cheating here, rather as he did over Bercilak's laughter in l. 909. Or perhaps one should say that he did not with absolute consistency imagine the lord and lady of Haut-desert as mere agents of Morgan le Fay—feeling no special interest in that side of the matter.

By the end of the second temptation scene the reader may well feel that Gawain and the lady have more or less talked themselves to a standstill. Certainly the sense of release attending the transition from chamber to hunting-field is nowhere stronger than here:

Þe lede with þe ladyeȝ layked alle day,
Bot þe lorde ouer þe londeȝ launced ful ofte,
Sweȝ his vncely swyn, þat swyngeȝ bi þe bonkkeȝ.[27] (1560-2)

The sense of violent physical motion in this ('launced', 'swyngeȝ') is sustained in what follows, and reaches a tremendous climax in the death of the boar: the hunter and his prey 'boþe vpon hepeȝ / In þe wyȝtest of þe water', the body of the animal swept away down the burn, and the lord marching home with its head carried before him in triumph. This 'huge head', presented as a seasonable though somewhat tactless gift to Gawain,

[27] Boar-hunts, like deer-hunts, are quite common in romances (see Tolkien and Gordon's note to l. 1412). An interesting new example has been provided by the publication of the Long Version of the First Continuation of Chrétien's *Perceval* in 1950. This contains— in the Carados section—a boar-hunt which was not to be found in the other versions (ll. 11975 ff.). Arthur and his companions come upon a 'sengler' or boar (cp. *SGGK* 1440, in its emended form), and chase it all day 'que li jors prist a anuitier' (cp. *SGGK* 1467-8). The boar takes refuge in a thicket, where he lies wallowing in a marsh (cp. the 'ker' or marshy thicket of *SGGK* 1421 and 1431).

The Third Fitt

brings us again to the exchange, fourth and last phase of each day's action.

The action here departs from that of the previous day in only one major particular. The two stanzas before allotted to this phase, one for fulfilment of the covenants and one for their renewal, are expanded to three by the addition of a stanza describing the supper intervening (ll. 1648–67). Since the previous supper was dismissed in two short lines (1400–1), there may seem no reason—beyond a love of 'manerly merþe' and poetic amplification—why it should be otherwise here. The stanza does allow the poet to further his temptation story a little, however:

> Such semblaunt to þat segge semly ho made
> Wyth stille stollen countenaunce, þat stalworth to plese,
> Þat all forwondered watȝ þe wyȝe, and wroth with himseluen,
> Bot he nolde not for his nurture nurne hir aȝayneȝ,
> Bot dalt with hir al in daynté. (1658–62)

There is nothing new in the exchanges themselves; but they are taking place for the first time in the presence of Bercilak, and this causes Gawain particular mortification: he is 'wroth with himseluen'. There is one factor in this situation which modern readers may not fully appreciate. Gawain is sitting at Bercilak's table as his guest. He is, we know, bound to him by positive obligations incurred in the formal plighting of troth; but he is also bound by the natural obligations incurred when he 'craved harbour' at Hautdesert. He has, in Malory's phrase, Bercilak's meat and drink in his body; and one function of the poet's scenes of dining, supping and drinking is to establish this fact in the reader's imagination—host and guest becoming 'fellows' as they feast together over Christmas. The sense of this fellowship runs right through the two central fitts of the poem. The exchange of winnings, for example, is, from this point of view, no more than a version of a gesture of fellowship well known to social anthropologists—the exchange of gifts. It serves, that is, to express and strengthen the natural bond between Gawain and Bercilak, as well as fulfilling their artificial covenants. Elsewhere, one may find traces of a still more primitive 'act of fraternization'—the shared or lent wife. This appears in its most conventional, civilized form in the seating arrangements for the feast on Christmas Day, when Bercilak concedes to Gawain his right to share his wife's dishes, and himself sits down with Morgan. It appears again when Bercilak, on the eve of the first hunt, promises to send his wife 'þat wyth yow schal sitte / And comfort yow with compayny'; and again on the present occasion, when Gawain sits at supper once more 'þe lady bisyde'.[28] With such things in mind, one should be able to follow the poet when he places the emphasis in his accounts of the tests, not only on the hero's 'cleanness', but also —and indeed primarily—on his 'trawþe' or loyalty; the point being not so much that he should not commit adultery (though that is taken for granted) as that he should not commit it with his host's wife. So when, in the third temptation scene, the lady gives up trying to seduce Gawain, she is not conceding defeat in the main battle—which, indeed, after a tactical withdrawal to better ground, she goes on to win. The main point is that Gawain should be *faithful*. As Bercilak says at the end of the second day:

> . . . I haf fraysted þe twys, and faythful I fynde þe.
> Now 'þrid tyme þrowe best' þenk on þe morne. (1679–80)

IV

The third day, New Year's Eve, is the last of Gawain's stay at the castle; but even if this were not so, the reader might suspect that it would prove critical. Things go by threes at Hautdesert;[29] and anyway the 'third time' traditionally has some-

[28] On exchanged gifts, shared wives, etc., see A. van Gennep, *Rites de Passage* (Paris, 1909), pp. 39 ff.

[29] All threes in the poem are connected with Hautdesert. There are none in the first fitt. The number first occurs in l. 763, where Gawain crosses himself three times and immediately sees the castle. There are three 'motes' on the first day of hunting and testing (1141); three cockcrows (1412) and three dead hounds (1443) on the second; three hounds catching the fox (1713), as well as three kisses, on the third. Notice that the poet—generally careful about times and dates—seems to treat the seven full days of Gawain's stay at Hautdesert (Christmas

thing special about it—as in Bercilak's proverbial 'þrid tyme þrowe best'. The poet fosters these suspicions, signalling unobtrusively to the reader from time to time as he deals with the first phase of the day's action, the fox-hunt. This starts in a perfectly ordinary way, with the host hearing Mass, eating a 'morsel', and setting out with men and dogs; but the account of these preparations is accompanied for the first time with a short but vivid description of the weather:

> Ferly fayre watȝ þe folde, for þe forst clenged;
> In rede rudede vpon rak rises þe sunne,
> And ful clere costeȝ þe clowdes of þe welkyn. (1694–6)

Here, as when the poet 'tarries' to describe the lady's dress and appearance at the beginning of the following temptation scene, again for the first time at such a point, the reason for the new amplification lies in its timing—held back until the beginning of the critical day, and producing, when it comes, expectancy, a sense of occasion.

Much the most important peculiarity of the third hunting scene, however, is its quarry, the fox. A lord hunting a fox is a familiar figure to modern readers—more so, indeed, than a lord hunting deer or boar; but the evidence clearly suggests that Bercilak's fox-hunt must have come as a surprise to the poem's contemporary audience. Deer and boar were considered 'noble game' and, as such, figure quite frequently in courtly romance, both French and English; but foxes were considered 'vermin', and fox-hunts are very rare indeed in the romances— if indeed there are any at all.[30] It must, therefore, have seemed odd that the author, after two conventional noble hunts, should resort to a 'foul fox' for his third and final quarry:

[30] See H. L. Savage, *The 'Gawain'-Poet*, pp. 33–35.

Day to New Year's Eve, inclusive) as two groups of three days: on the evening of St. John's Day (Dec. 27, the third day of the Christmas feast, see ll. 1020–3), Gawain says he has only 'bare þre dayeȝ' before Jan. 1. What has happened to Dec. 28? Gollancz thinks a line is missing after 1022 (note to 1020–3). See M. R. Watson, 'The Chronology of *SGGK*', *M.L.N.*, LXIV (1949), pp. 85–86.

The Third Fitt

Hunteres vnhardeled bi a holt syde,
Rocheres roungen bi rys for rurde of her hornes;
Summe fel in þe fute þer þe fox bade. . . . (1697–9)

'*The* fox' is worth noticing. There is nothing, so far as I can see, in the previous lines to suggest that Bercilak was out to find a fox; yet the fox is introduced (unlike the boar, ll. 1437–40) as if he were inevitable. This makes him particularly provoking. Why should it have to be a fox, of all animals? The reader has only to ask this question—in retrospect, at least—to see the answer. We learn from the poem itself, without resort to medieval animal lore, that the fox is a thief (1725), wily (1728 and 1905) and a shrew (1896); and we know that on the day of the fox-hunt Gawain cunningly and wrongfully keeps possession of what is Bercilak's by right—the girdle. The 'parallel' (though that is not a good word to describe the actual effect) is obvious—and that whether or not one sees similar parallels on the previous days. Indeed, it seems best to judge the cases separately. I myself cannot see that the second temptation scene differs from the first as the boar-hunt differs from the deer-hunt; but, where the fox-hunt and third temptation are concerned, I see that each differs from both its predecessors in the same sort of way.[31] Each involves a departure from the noble and exemplary conduct of the previous days. In each we recognize death as a terrifying thing which men and animals alike try to escape by every device in their power, regardless of dignity or duty.

The terror and the 'wiles' of the fox are vividly evoked in the first phase of the hunt: the fox dodging and 'tourneying' through the wood, doubling back, stopping to listen, jumping over a hedge to escape into the open, meeting the hounds and swerving back into the wood, making for the open once more and 'reeling in again':

And ȝe he lad hem bi lagmon, þe lorde and his meyny,
On þis maner bi þe mountes quyle myd-ouer-vnder. (1729–30)

Against this background of pursuit and desperate flight, the opening of the ensuing temptation scene takes on a special

---

[31] Savage, op. cit., pp. 35–37. Savage argues his distinction between a deer-like first temptation and a boar-like second on pp. 40–46.

poignancy and depth. Gawain is not, as before, sleeping soundly. He is restless and mutters in his sleep:

> In dreȝ droupyng of dreme draueled þat noble,
> As mon þat watȝ in mornyng of mony þro þoȝtes,
> How þat destiné schulde þat day dele hym his wyrde
> At þe grene chapel, when he þe gome metes,
> And bihoues his buffet abide withoute debate more.[32] (1750-4)

Gawain, like the fox, is afraid; and their common fear of death creates a context in which the figure of the lady, with her merry mantle, jewelled hair-net, naked throat and bare breast, assumes something of a symbolic value. She is like Dame Life, in the alliterative *Death and Life*:

> Of her druryes to deeme to dull be my witts;
> And the price of her perrye can no person tell;
> And the colour of her kirtle was caruen ffull lowe,
> Þat her blisfull breastes bearnes might behold;
> With a naked necke she neighed ther-till,
> Þat gaue light on the land as leames of the sunn.[33]

By her behaviour, too, Bercilak's lady represents life's cause—rather as Boethius' visitor, under similar circumstances, represents that of philosophy. She throws open a window, wakes Gawain from his nightmares with praise of the morning ('A! mon, how may þou slepe, / Þis morning is so clere?'), laughs, and kisses him. The 'wallande joye' which this inspires in the hero is as much *joie de vivre* as anything else; and the 'blis and bonchef' which follows is in the spirit of Bercilak's words on the previous evening:

> Make we mery quyl we may and mynne vpon joye,
> For þe lur may mon lach when-so mon lykeȝ. (1681-2)

At this point the poet is stacking the cards more than ever against his hero; and he makes it clear that Gawain is near to losing the game: 'Gret perile bitwene hem stod'. The crisis is

---

[32] Dante ascribes special powers of prophecy to dawn dreams in *Purgatorio*, IX, ll. 13-18; and Chauntecleer's warning dream comes 'in a dawenynge'. See *S.P.*, XLV (1948), pp. 50-59.

[33] Ed. I. Gollancz (Oxford, 1930), ll. 87-92.

The Third Fitt

not in fact a very real one for the reader, because the poet contents himself with a summary description; but the summary is important in itself, because it gives us, quite explicitly, the poet's understanding of the moral issues at stake between Gawain and the lady:

> For þat pryncece of pris depresed hym so þikke,
> Nurned hym so neȝe þe þred, þat nede hym bihoued
> Oþer lach þer hir luf, oþer lodly refuse.
> He cared for his cortaysye, lest craþayn he were,
> And more for his meschef, ȝif he schulde make synne
> And be traytor to þat tolke þat þat telde aȝt. (1770–5)

The meaning of this passage is quite clear, up to the last two lines. Gawain is faced with a choice of two evils. If he goes on refusing the lady's love, he must offend her ('*lodly* refuse'); and this would be a real evil, for Gawain *does* 'care for his courtesy'. He cares still more, however, for the 'mischief' he would incur were he to 'lach þer hir luf'—for by so doing he would, the poet says, 'make synne / And be traytor to þat tolke þat þat telde aȝt'. There are two ways of taking these words. Either the line 'And be traytor . . .' specifies the 'synne' (as if it were 'commit sin by being traitor . . .'), or it does not. I think that it does, and that the other reading involves two particularly mischievous errors: first, that the author was so preoccupied with chastity that he could use the word 'sin', without further ado, to mean 'sexual sin' or sin in the Sunday papers' sense; and second, that he did not regard treachery to the host as a sin, properly speaking, at all—or at least that he regarded it as 'taking second place'.[34] On such a view, the serious moral business of the poem is done once the hero has survived his so-called 'chastity test' (i.e. after l. 1800 or thereabouts); and his concealing the girdle is no more than a venial fault—a 'breach of the chivalric code', perhaps, but not 'synne'. I shall return to this point later.

[34] Introduction to Gollancz's edition, p. xxi, n. 1: 'Professor Hulbert . . . says that the test is for loyalty, not chastity. But ll. 1773–5 show that Gawain's chief fear is that he may sin against God, and his duty of loyalty to his host takes second place.' I agree with Professor Hulbert.

The Third Fitt

After the poet's summary, there follows a short bit of dialogue (ll. 1779–95) in which the lady makes her last attempt to
persuade Gawain to accept her love. Her appeal, by comparison
with the earlier scenes, is brief, simple, rather lyrical in tone,
drawing on the literary traditions of the slighted maiden's com-
plaint: 'I love you' ('Bifore alle þe wyȝeȝ in þe worlde wounded
in hert') 'and you should love me in return—unless you already
love another'. This elicits from Gawain his last, and, decisive,
refusal:

> Þe knyȝt sayde, 'Be sayn Jon,'
> And smeþely con he smyle,
> 'In fayth I welde riȝt non,
> Ne non wil welde þe quile.' (1788–91)

The movement of the short lines makes this sound abrupt; but
Gawain is obviously still trying to avoid refusing 'lodly'. The
reference to St. John, if it means anything, means that Gawain
is trying to live the life of celibacy for which that saint was
famous[35]—a convenient polite fiction which harmonizes well
with the suggestion of 'In fayth I welde riȝt non'. The claim in
the following line, however, is less grand: 'Ne non wil welde þe
quile'. This would be rude if there were not some specific and
recognizable reason why Gawain should not want a mistress
for the time being. The reason is, presumably, that he is on a
quest—a reason which he later adduces for not receiving love-
tokens (ll. 1836–8). There are good grounds, part pious, part
superstitious, for a knight to be abstinent while on a quest.[36]

[35] Oaths by St. John sometimes seem to have this kind of significance.
In the *Earl of Toulouse* a lady protests her innocence with the words,
'Be Seynte Iohn, / Hore was y neuyr none' (in French and Hale,
Middle English Metrical Romances, ll. 793–4). See also *Canterbury Tales*
III, 164–8. Both the other two saint-oaths in the poem have signifi-
cance. The porter swears by Peter, the porter of heaven (l. 813);
and Bercilak swears by Giles, the friend of a hind (l. 1644).

[36] See quotation from *Perlesvaus* above (p. 84). The mixture of piety
and superstition comes out well in the words of Malory's Lancelot:
'And as for to sey to take my pleasaunce with peramours, that woll I
refuse: in prencipall for drede of God, for knyghtes that bene adventures [adventurous] sholde nat be advoutrers nothir lecherous, for
than they be nat happy nother fortunate unto the werrys' (ed. Vinaver,
p. 270).

The Third Fitt

The lady, therefore, has to accept Gawain's declaration at its
face value; and this she does, with a faintly literary grace:

> 'Bot I am swared for soþe, þat sore me þinkkeʒ.
> Kysse me now comly, and I schal cach heþen,
> I may bot mourne vpon molde, as may þat much louyes.'
> Sykande ho sweʒe doun and semly hym kyssed. (1793–6)

This kiss, the second of the scene, marks the end of the lady's
'wowyng' (as Bercilak later describes it), but not of her testing.
Here, as at the end of the first temptation scene, she gets up
from the bed only to deliver a parting shot 'as ho stondes' (compare l. 1291). She asks for a keepsake—any kind of gift, a glove
would do. Her tone is friendly and informal, with a lot of sin-
gular pronouns ('þy . . . þi . . .þe'), as if confessing, confi-
dentially, to her failure; but it wins only one concession from
Gawain—a single 'thou', the only one he ever uses to the lady
(l. 1802). Otherwise his reply is much in the style of his earlier
refusals. In particular, there is the same polite, sophistical play
with values: nothing but the best is good enough to 'reward'
the lady (as if that were the point of a keepsake), and he, being
'an erande', has no 'menskful þingeʒ' with him. What he has
(taking up the lady's suggestion of a glove) is quite unworthy of
her—and even of him:

> Hit is not your honour to haf at þis tyme
> A gloue for a garysoun of Gawayneʒ gifteʒ. (1806–7)

The touch of self-esteem in the last phase is well-calculated:
the lady can hardly reject an argument which she herself has
used on more than one occasion.

The first part of the following stanza is devoted to the lady's
unaccepted offer of a rich gold ring with a precious stone in it.
This episode, besides 'leading up' in a general way to the offer
and acceptance of the girdle, seems designed specifically to
establish a point about Gawain's motives there. As we shall see,
the poet devotes a good deal of attention, once Gawain has
'fallen', to ensuring that the reader understands what, morally
speaking, he did and why he did it; and he insists, among other
things, that his hero was quite unmoved by the costliness and

beauty of the girdle. We are told this no less than three times in the fourth fitt, once by the poet (ll. 2037–40), once by the Green Knight (2367–8) and once by Gawain himself (2430–3). Gawain is not vain or covetous: he does not wear the lady's gift 'for wele' (2037, 2432). It seems clear, in retrospect at least, that the ring episode is designed to make the same point—to make sure in advance that the reader does not misunderstand the hero's motives. This explains the somewhat naïve stress on the costliness of the ring. It clears the ground. Anyone who refuses such a ring is immune from covetousness at least.

The importance of the scene's final episode—the turning-point of the poem—is marked from the outset. Up to this point in the castle scenes, the poet has been chary of any pointed allusion to the identity of the host; he has not, as it were, made any rhetorical capital out of it ('had Gawain but known . . .' etc.). So the occurrence of such an allusion, even though indirect, here in the description of the girdle which the lady produces from under her mantle, is doubly effective:

> Gered hit watȝ with grene sylke and with golde schaped. (1832)

The Green Knight's characteristic combination of green and gold, reappearing thus unexpectedly, creates a powerful sense of threat and complicity (almost as in some of Henry James' novels); but it does not alert the hero, who again replies in his old style of polite refusal, falling back into his defensive role of 'trwe seruaunt'. The lady ripostes, still in their best chamber manner, by drawing his attention to another problem of value ('pris'):

> 'Now forsake ȝe þis silke,' sayde þe burde þenne,
> 'For hit is symple in hitself? And so hit wel semeȝ.
> Lo! so hit is littel, and lasse hit is worþy;
> Bot who-so knew þe costes þat knit ar þerinne,
> He wolde hit prayse at more prys, parauenture.' (1846–50)

The casual tone is deceptive: the girdle is little and simple in itself, but it is perhaps ('parauenture') more valuable than it looks—for it has the power to protect its wearer from violent death.

It is a dramatic moment. After the subtle and elaborate manoeuvrings which have gone before, the lady suddenly shifts her ground and makes a direct appeal to a passion which, under the circumstances, must be stronger than sexual desire—the passion for life. The appeal goes home:

> Þen kest þe knyȝt, and hit come to his hert,
> Hit were a juel for þe jopardé þat hym iugged were. (1855-6)

Gawain first allows the lady to go on pressing him ('þulged with hir þrepe'), then accepts the gift and finally agrees not to reveal it to the host or anyone else 'for noȝte'. So, in order (as he thinks) to save his life, he incurs an obligation to the lady which is inconsistent with his obligations to her husband: he cannot now be true to both. However we take this, it plainly involves some falling off from the standards of 'truth' represented in the pentangle passage. The exemplary knight, the mirror of Christian chivalry—developed in that passage out of the more ordinary 'good Gawain' of the first fitt—gives way here, for the first time, to human weakness. There is a powerful and ominous note of finality (deriving in part from confused suggestions of the betrayal of Christ—by Judas with a kiss and by Peter three times before cockcrow) in the closing lines of the stanza:

> He þonkked hir oft ful swyþe,
> Ful þro with hert and þoȝt.
> Bi þat on þrynne syþe
> Ho hatȝ kyst þe knyȝt so toȝt. (1866-9)

What follows in the next stanza represents, I think, the poet's most significant departure from his carefully established pattern of action. On the two previous days both Gawain and Bercilak are said to hear Mass after rising (Gawain at ll. 1311 and 1558, Bercilak at ll. 1135 and 1414). On the third day Bercilak again hears Mass (l. 1690), but Gawain does not. Instead, once the lady has left him, he gets up and goes to Confession:

> Syþen cheuely to þe chapel choses he þe waye,
> Preuély aproched to a prest, and prayed hym þere
> Þat he wolde lyste his lyf and lern hym better
> How his sawle schulde be saued when he schuld seye heþen.

Þere he schrof hym schyrly and schewed his mysdedeȝ,
Of þe more and þe mynne, and merci besecheȝ,
And of absolucioun he on þe segge calles;
And he asoyled hym surely, and sette hym so clene
As domeȝday schulde haf ben diȝt on þe morn.[37] (1876-84)

The variation in the pattern seems very pointed; but its exact
significance is not so obvious. How does the little scene fit in?
What, in particular, is its relationship to the 'slip' or 'fall' which
precedes it?

One answer might be that there is no such relationship.
Gawain's fault, on this view, is essentially a breach of the
chivalric code. He has simply failed, for the moment, to live up
to the special standards of honourable conduct demanded of
him as a knight. Such failures may not, by Christian standards,
be 'synne' at all; or they may be no more than venial sin (which
is not obligatory matter for the confessional). So Gawain approaches his priest, not because he has just imperilled his
soul by agreeing to hide the girdle, but because he thinks
he is to die next morning. He simply takes a convenient opportunity to do what any Christian should do when in peril of
death. It is a routine visit.

This is a straightforward and in some ways attractive view of
the matter; but it seems to me to be open to two serious objections. For one thing, it flies in the face of the pentangle passage.
This passage definitely does not encourage the segregation of
'chivalric' from 'Christian' virtues; for it links them together,
emphatically, in a single code—courtesy and cleanness, fellowship and faith in the five wounds, each 'halched in oþer, þat
non ende hade'. This is an odd way of preparing Christian
readers to condone 'breaches of the chivalric code'. If things
are linked together in this way, such breaches are likely to

[37] All the editors print 'lyfte' in l. 1878, but the Ms. reading is
most probably 'lyste'. This makes better sense than 'lyfte'. In
Malory, Lancelot prays a hermit 'for seynte charité for to hyre hys
lyff' (ed. Vinaver, p. 896), where 'hyre hys lyff' ('hear his life') means
'hear his confession'. (Compare p. 891, where 'shew you my lyff'
means 'make my confession to you'.) 'Lyste' is common in M.E. as a
transitive verb ('listen to, hear'); so 'lyste his lyf' is a likely alliterative
equivalent for Malory's phrase.

involve more than meets the eye. It is true, of course, that they *may* be no more than venial (occasional bits of discourtesy, perhaps); but notice that the particular 'chivalric virtue' in question here, fidelity to the pledged word, shares its name with the whole Christian-chivalric complex to which it belongs—both are 'trawþe'. Are we to believe that Gawain's 'untrawþe' (narrow chivalric sense) involves no more than a marginal disturbance of his (broad sense) 'trawþe'? Surely not. If Gawain's integrity, his virtue, is 'trawþe' (and the poet chose the word), then 'untrawþe' is to be looked to. It is not, *prima facie* at least, a trivial matter.

I shall try to show later that this interim judgment is confirmed by the course of events in the fourth fitt. Here again the 'routine' view of Gawain's confession fails to take account of important passages—in particular, Gawain's own penitent self-analyses. However, these passages are best considered in their contexts; and I shall have for the moment to assume what they seem to me to prove: that Gawain's fault is a grave one, grave enough to be considered matter for the confessional.

But how, on such an assumption, is Gawain's confession to be understood? It is worth looking here at the way the scene is introduced. Gawain accepts the girdle, and, when the lady has gone, he

> gereʒ hym sone,
> Rises and riches hym in araye noble,
> Lays vp þe luf-lace þe lady hym raʒt,
> Hid hit ful holdely, þer he hit eft fonde.
> Syþen cheuely to þe chapel . . . etc. (1872–6)

The movement is swift (suggesting, surely, that the confession *has* something to do with the girdle), but there is time for one telling detail. Gawain 'lays up' the girdle, hides it 'faithfully' (in accordance with his promise to the lady) in a place where he may find it later. It is clear that he has no intention of giving it up, as a 'winning', to the lord. It is a 'jewel for his jeopardy', and he means to stick to it. This makes his subsequent confession look pretty hollow by any standards—and not least by those of the medieval church. Ever since the fourth Lateran

Council (1215) made it obligatory for every grown person to participate in the sacrament at least once a year, the church had conducted a formidable campaign to educate laymen in the theory and practice of Confession.[38] As a result of this campaign, any fourteenth-century audience would certainly have known that a 'right' or valid confession depended, not only on the fulfilment of the necessary external forms, but also on the presence in the penitent of a proper 'disposition'.[39] In the words of one standard fourteenth-century authority, this meant, first, that the penitent must be sorry for his sins ('doleat commissa'); second, that he must make restitution ('restituat ablata'); and third, that he must promise to sin no more ('promittat cessare').[40] The most important of these points for our present purposes is the second.

The doctrine that a man cannot be absolved if he does not (wherever possible) restore wrongfully acquired goods to their right owner is obviously one of great practical importance, and it has a regular place in medieval confessional theory. The prime authority is St. Augustine, who, in one of his letters, discussed the case of those who 'seek to have the punishment of their crime remitted, and at the same time keep possession of that for which the crime was committed'. This cannot be, says Augustine. 'Si enim res aliena, propter quam peccatum est, cum reddi possit, non redditur, non agitur poenitentia, sed fingitur: si autem veraciter agitur, non remittetur peccatum, nisi restituatur ablatum.'[41] Augustine's judgment became part of canon

---

[38] 'The correct use of the sacrament of penance is a theme which dominates or underlies most of the religious literature of the thirteenth and fourteenth centuries', W. A. Pantin, *The English Church in the Fourteenth Century* (Cambridge, 1955), p. 192. I have previously discussed Gawain's confession in 'The Two Confession Scenes in *SGGK*', *M.P.*, LVII (1959), pp. 73–79.

[39] See, for example, J. de Burgo, *Pupilla Oculi* (Paris, 1518), Part V, Chapter 2, Section A: 'Non enim sacerdos efficaciter absoluit, nisi reus sit in se debito modo dispositus ut sit capax absolutionis; quia sacramentum exterius est signum interioris absolutionis que nullo modo communicatur sine vera dispositione in mente interius absoluendi'.

[40] J. Bromyard, *Summa Praedicantium* (Venice, 1586), p. 119.

[41] 'For if another's property, on account of which sin has been

law; it was quoted by Peter Lombard in his *Sententiae* and by Aquinas in his *Summa*; and it appeared, in one form or another, in the fourteenth-century manuals.[42] The doctrine also figures very frequently in late medieval vernacular writing—in sermons, in the poetry of Hoccleve, Dunbar, etc., and above all in *Piers Plowman*, where it is one of Langland's recurrent themes.[43] It appears as late as Shakespeare's *Hamlet*—a remarkable case, for it shows that even a Protestant audience could be relied upon to see the point:

> (King).   But O, what form of prayer
> Can serve my turn? 'Forgive me my foul murder'?
> That cannot be, since I am still possessed
> Of those effects for which I did the murder,
> My crown, mine own ambition, and my queen.
> May one be pardoned and retain th'offence? (III, iii, 51–56)

This is precisely the question which St. Augustine had long ago answered in the negative: 'Non remittetur peccatum, nisi restituatur ablatum'.

It may be objected that Gawain's case is not covered by this rule, since he has not, at the time of his confession, had any opportunity to hand over the girdle to the host—indeed, the

[42] See Gratian's *Decretum*, Pars II, Causa XIV, Quaestio VI (Migne, *P.L.*, Vol. 187, col. 966); *Sententiae*, Book IV, Dist. XV, para. 7 (Migne, *P.L.*, Vol. 192, col. 877); *Summa Theologiae* II–II, Quaestio LXII ('De restitutione'), Art. II; de Burgo, op. cit., V, 5, A (quoted in text, below). As late as 1616, 'Non tollitur peccatum, nisi restituitur ablatum' is quoted as a proverb (under 'Restitution') by Thomas Draxe in his *Bibliotheca Scholastica Instructissima*.

[43] See *Middle English Sermons*, ed. W. O. Ross, E.E.T.S. O.S. 209 (1940), pp. 283–4 (with reference to Gratian); Hoccleve, *Jonathas and Fellicula*, ll. 617–26; Dunbar, 'Quhome to Sall I Complene My Wo?', ll. 61–64; *Piers Plowman* B. V. 232–9 and 276–85, XVII. 234–6, XIX. 389–93, etc. On restitution in *Piers*, see R. W. Frank, '*Piers Plowman*' and the Scheme of Salvation* (New Haven, 1957), pp. 106 f.

committed, is not returned when it can be returned, then the penance is not done, but feigned; but if it is really done, then the sin will not be remitted unless the carried-off property is restored.' Augustine's Letter to Macedonius, para. 20 (Migne, *Patrologia Latina*, Vol. 33, col. 662).

appropriate time for such payment has not yet come. But, as we have already seen, the poet is careful to make it clear that he has, from the start, no intention of honouring his promise. On the contrary, he firmly intends to 'retain th'offence'; and this is itself quite enough to invalidate any confession, according to contemporary opinion: 'Non dimittitur peccatum nisi restituatur ablatum, si restitui potest. . . . Oportet ergo ut de omnibus rebus iniuriose acquisitis fiat restitutio. Vel ad minus quam habeat firmum propositum restituendi si quid ab alio iniuriose ablatum est, antequam valeat satisfactio sacramentalis.'[44] I conclude, therefore, that Gawain's confession (always supposing it to relate somehow to the business of the girdle) must be seen as invalid—not a remedy, but a symptom of his fall from grace.

Throughout this last part of the third fitt—which on any reading, Christian or chivalric, shows us Gawain at his least admirable—the poet makes his points obliquely and sparely. He allows himself no moral comment at all when Gawain accepts the girdle on the lady's terms, and his treatment of the hero's confession is almost equally deadpan. Gawain, he says, confessed 'schyrly' ('completely')[45] to all his sins, great and small, and begged for mercy and absolution, which the priest granted:

> And he asoyled hym surely, and sette hym so clene·
> As domeȝday schulde haf ben diȝt on þe morn.

It is only in these last lines—and then perhaps only in retrospect—that a suggestion of comment is to be traced. Their

---

[44] 'The sin will not be remitted unless the carried-off property is restored, if it can be restored. . . . It is therefore necessary that restitution be made for all goods unjustly acquired. Or at least one should have a firm intention of making restitution, if something has been wrongfully carried off from another, for sacramental satisfaction to be valid.' De Burgo, op. cit., V, 5, A. On refinements of the doctrine of restitution, see art. 'Restitution' in *Dictionnaire de Théologie Catholique*, Vol. 13 (Paris, 1936), cols. 2466–501.

[45] Compare the use of 'scire' to describe complete, full confession in *Cursor Mundi*, ed. R. Morris, E.E.T.S. O.S. 57–99 (1874–92), l. 26609, and in the *Parlement of the Thre Ages*, ed. cit., l. 646.

ostensible purpose is to praise the priest: he gave Gawain secure absolution, and cleansed him as thoroughly as if the following day was to be the Day of Judgment itself. There is no question of the priest's *bona fides*, of course, but the poet's reference to Doomsday certainly does have, in its context, an odd effect. For one thing, it is less hypothetical than it looks: Gawain is to meet the Green Knight 'on þe morn' (New Year's Day), and, as we shall see in the next chapter, the idea that this encounter constitutes for him a kind of personal Doomsday is in various ways encouraged by the poet in the fourth fitt. Again, when the time for his judgment comes, Gawain does *not* find himself 'clene', despite the poet's assurance. The priest's absolution does not save him from bitter shame and remorse—any more than the lady's girdle saves him from the axe. It must be said again, though, that the poet does not stress these points at all here; and he ends the present phase of action in his most inscrutable style. Once his confession is done, Gawain joins the two ladies and makes merry with them 'as neuer he did bot þat daye, to þe derk nyȝt, / with blys'. The effect is most delicately balanced—as between hysteria, false confidence and heroism.

The continuation of the fox-hunt, which follows, is much shorter than the corresponding passages on the previous days—largely because the work on the carcase, elaborately described for the deer and the boar, is here compressed, with a fine scornful effect, into the two last lines of a wheel:

> And syþen þay tan Reynarde,
> And tyruen of his cote. (1920–1)

The only point I have to make about this passage has already been well made by H. L. Savage.[46] There is, as Savage points out, a close parallel between the death of the fox and the 'fall' of the hero. The fox, running with the hounds 'ryȝt at his heleȝ', suddenly comes upon Bercilak on horseback, across his path and with a drawn sword. He starts back, and, as he does so, falls victim to the hounds. So Gawain, after the lady's long and pressing pursuit, suddenly comes face-to-face with the prospect of the Green Knight's axe, and, as he tries to escape,

[46] Op. cit., p. 37.

falls victim at last to the lady. Cowardice, as he later confesses, leads him into covetousness (*sic*) and untruth. Both episodes seem designed to suggest the same paradox—that he who saves his life shall lose it (though it is hard to see what else the fox could have done). The parallel helps to define and fix the outlines, what one might call the *shape*, of Gawain's crisis in the reader's mind, pending more formal analysis in the next fitt.

The last section of the third fitt, to which I now come, is chiefly interesting because it contains some striking examples of the poet's oblique methods in this part of the poem—particularly his use of small dislocations in the established pattern of action. Thus, the 'pattern' for the lord's return from hunting is that he should come into the great hall, summon the household ('meyny'), and call Gawain and the ladies down from the private chambers for the exchange of winnings.[47] This time, however, he does not need to call. Gawain is already down in the hall—'fire vpon flet, þe freke þer-byside'—and meets him 'inmyddeȝ þe flore'. What is more, Gawain proposes that he, not the host as on previous occasions, should be the first to fulfil his promise:

> I schal fylle vpon fyrst oure forwardeȝ nouþe,
> Þat we spedly han spoken, þer spared watȝ no drynk. (1934-5)

The point of both these changes is, I take it, to suggest that Gawain has a bad conscience and wants to be done with the exchange as quickly as possible. This would also explain why, at the end of the same stanza, Gawain rather brusquely cuts short the host's bantering apologies for the inadequacy of his fox's skin:

> 'Inoȝ,' quoþ Sir Gawayn,
> 'I þonk yow, bi þe rode.' (1948-9)

One other novelty, still in the same stanza, deserves mention here—the introduction of a description of Gawain's dress. He meets his host in a blue 'bleaunt', a furred 'surkot' and a furred hood of the same colour ('of þat ilke'). The description, like those of the winter morning and the lady, is brief but pointed.

---

[47] See ll. 1368-76 and 1619-25.

The Third Fitt

For his one act of duplicity Gawain wears *blue*—the traditional colour of faithfulness, occurring here and nowhere else in the poem.[48]

The reader can if he wishes detect similar ironies in the last two stanzas of the fitt;[49] but he must also, certainly, appreciate the 'frenkysch fare', the real courtesy, of Gawain's leavetaking—first from the lord, then from the two ladies, and finally, best of all, from the 'meyny':

> Vche mon þat he mette, he made hem a þonke
> For his seruyse and his solace and his sere pyne,
> Þat þay wyth busynes had ben aboute hym to serue;
> And vche segge as soré to seuer with hym þere
> As þay hade wonde worþyly with þat wlonk euer. (1984–8)

Both the behaviour and (so far as one is allowed to see) the feelings of everyone involved here are exemplary—the ladies, with their 'cold sighings', ladylike, the men manly, everyone warmly courteous. Yet we know, after all, that the departing guest is both deceiver and deceived. It is an antinomy which the poet does not yet need to resolve. He has had it both ways with the lord and lady from the start; and he is equally content here to have it both ways with the hero. He leaves the third fitt, as he left the first, in suspense, stepping in again between us and the fiction:

> Let hym lyʒe þere stille,
> He hatʒ nere þat he soʒt;
> And ʒe wyl a whyle be stylle
> I schal telle yow how þay wroʒt. (1994–7)

---

[48] The meaning of blue was well known. Criseyde sends Troilus a 'blewe ryng' to assure him that she has not been false (*Troilus*, III, 885).

[49] E.g. when the host promises to furnish Gawain with a guide: 'Al þat euer I yow hyʒt halde schal I redé' (1970).

IV

THE FOURTH FITT

I

THE ACTION OF THE FOURTH FITT divides into three parts: the journey to the Green Chapel, the encounter with the Green Knight, and the return to Camelot. I shall discuss these in turn, beginning with the journey.

The fitt opens some time before dawn on New Year's Day. There is a snowstorm, and indoors the hero lies awake in his lamplit chamber, listening to the wind and the crowings of the cock:

> Þe werbelande wynde wapped fro þe hyȝe,
> And drof vche dale ful of dryftes ful grete.
> Þe leude lystened ful wel þat leȝ in his bedde,
> Þaȝ he lowkeȝ his liddeȝ, ful lyttel he slepes;
> Bi vch kok þat crue he knwe wel þe steuen. (2004–8)

This passage marks the limits, in one direction, of the poet's realism. Nowhere else does he go further in evoking what it would really feel like to be on a quest like Gawain's—wakefulness, a heightened sense of the hostility of the external world, a pressing awareness of time. The state of mind is wonderfully conveyed. Here as in his evocation of the corresponding bodily sensations ('Ner slayn wyth þe slete he sleped in his yrnes'), the poet gives much more than we expect, or normally get, from a romance—or indeed from any narrative genre before the novel. The solitary-earnest (mental, physical and moral) of his poem is not simply gestured at, with talk of fear, hardship and re-morse—it is entered into. Or entered into up to a point—for the realism is not unqualified by other interests. In the present passage the poet is interested, certainly, in what it would really feel like; but he is also interested in what it would look like—a very different matter—in the *picturesque* effect of a snowstorm before dawn, a chamber and a lamp. One must take account, too, of the touch of symbolism in the crowing cock. This bird is traditionally emblematic of spiritual alertness—waking men from the 'sleep' of the world. It is associated with the coming of the Last Judgment, and also (through the story of Peter denying Christ) with the oncoming of penance after sin.[1] These associations are in keeping, we shall see, with the poet's idea of the ensuing day as a day of judgment and penance for Gawain. The cock, like much else in this last and finest fitt, belongs not only in the literal but also in the symbolic action, and makes a striking and, it seems, effortlessly appropriate contribution to each.

Here and elsewhere, then, the poet enters into backstage experiences of hardship and fear, and makes us (up to a point) feel what they feel like. But it is characteristic of him that, having done so, he withdraws and, as it were, corrects the effect. Just as the nightmare on the morning of New Year's Eve gave way abruptly to the entry of the lady, so here Gawain's solitary fears are forgotten once he calls for his 'chamberlain' and starts donning his armour. There is no real continuity in either case: the Gawain who examines his armour for rust and praises Gryngolet's condition is not continuous with the Gawain who lies in bed listening to the cock. He *could be*, of course—it is not a question of implausibility; but he *isn't*. The poet goes, perhaps, as far as he could go with available techniques—to evoke 'what it would really feel like' being very much a matter of techniques.

When we turn to consider the arming itself (ll. 2013–43), the public, ceremonial action which follows the private vigil, we again need to think of technique—this time, the author's favourite technique of repetition-with-variation. Very obviously, the fourth fitt is here repeating the second, just as the third fitt so often repeats itself. First there are the 'cloþeʒ' (the doublet

---

[1] See Prudentius, *Hymnus ad Gallicinium* (Migne, *P.L.*, Vol. 59, cols. 775–85); and Ambrose, *Hexaemeron*, Book V, Chap. XXIV (Migne, *P.L.*, Vol. 14, cols. 240–1).

and 'capados' specified in ll. 571–3), then the 'oþer harnays', the body-armour (specified in ll. 574–85), then the coat-armour, with the pentangle embroidered on it, worn over the mail (compare l. 586), then the sword belted round the hips (compare ll. 588–9). This brings us, in the second fitt, to the end of a stanza and of the first stage of Gawain's preparations. Having belted on his sword, he goes off to hear Mass 'offred and honoured at þe heȝe auter' (593). In the fourth fitt, however, there is an extra item—the lady's girdle, which Gawain puts on after the sword, wrapping it twice round his waist over the 'ryol red cloþe' of the coat-armour.

In the poet's introduction of this new item, one thing is particularly noticeable—his efforts to bring it into juxtaposition with the pentangle. This was not altogether easy. It was the pentangle on the shield which was described at such length in the second fitt; but in the order of a knight's departure, which the poet is scrupulous to observe, the shield does not come until the very end—after he has mounted his horse, and therefore long after Gawain could reasonably be shown putting on the girdle. So the poet makes nothing of the shield on this occasion (it is just mentioned in l. 2061), and turns his attention to the coat-armour, which is also, as was customary, decorated with the 'conysaunce' of its bearer, the pentangle (l. 2026, cp. 637). Here he is able, with a little syntactic ingenuity, to bring the pentangle up against the girdle, despite the sword which, in the order of events, still comes between them:

> Whyle þe wlonkest wedes he warp on hymseluen—
> His cote wyth þe conysaunce of þe clere werkeȝ
> Ennurned vpon veluet, vertuus stoneȝ
> Aboute beten and bounden, enbrauded semeȝ,
> And fayre furred withinne wyth fayre pelures—
> Ȝet laft he not þe lace, þe ladieȝ gifte,
> Þat forgat not Gawayn for gode of hymseluen.
> Bi he hade belted þe bronde vpon his balȝe hauncheȝ,
> Þenn dressed he his drurye double hym aboute. (2025–33)

The pentangle, which occupied such a commanding position in the first arming scene, is here subordinated both rhetorically and grammatically ('whyle' has something like its modern concessive force) to the 'lace'. It is almost as if the latter has taken the pentangle's place:

> Þe gordel of þe grene silke þat gay wel bisemed,
> Vpon þat ryol red cloþe þat ryche watȝ to schewe. (2035-6)

In the first arming it was the pentangle that 'bisemed þe segge semlyly fayre', and the pentangle that was 'schapen . . . ryally wyth red golde vpon rede gowleȝ'. Gawain's colour-scheme has become more complicated: gold and green, not just gold, on red.

It is worth noticing how the poet sets out to direct our moral feelings at this point. He does not encourage any rigorous condemnation of the hero. Indeed it is here that he introduces the first of his three already-mentioned apologies:

> Bot wered not þis ilk wyȝe for wele þis gordel,
> For pryde of þe pendaunteȝ, þaȝ polyst þay were,
> And þaȝ þe glyterande golde glent vpon endeȝ,
> But for to sauen hymself, when suffer hym byhoued. (2037-40)

Gawain's motive for wearing the girdle (and, by inference, his motive for concealing it from the host) is at least not a contemptible one—churlish covetousness ('for wele') or womanish vanity ('for pryde').[2] He is concerned to 'sauen hymself', and this, the poet implies, is understandable enough—particularly when one recalls the unnerving character of the impending danger, 'to byde bale withoute dabate of bronde hym to were / oþer knyffe'. On the other hand, the poet does not adopt a merely indulgent attitude towards his hero, either here or anywhere else in the fourth fitt. Consider the lines already quoted:

> Ȝet laft he not þe lace, þe ladieȝ gifte,
> Þat forgat not Gawayn for gode of hymseluen.

The repetition 'ȝet laft not . . . þat forgat not' is obviously damaging—it asks to be delivered almost contemptuously—and

[2] A similar (equally unexpected) disavowal of covetousness is to be found in *Troilus and Criseyde*, III, 261, where Pandarus protests to Troilus about the purity of his motives: 'nevere I this for coveitise wroughte'.

so, a little less obviously, is the phrase 'for gode of hymseluen'. It suggests (as 'to sauen hymself', in its context, does not) the traditional idea of *amor sui*, the source of sin.[3] Such a suggestion implies, of course, an attitude quite distinct from that expressed in the ensuing apology; but the poet makes no attempt to reconcile these opposites. For the moment he simply leaves the reader with them: Gawain's conduct is 'understandable' and it is sinful. It is the business not of this passage but of the rest of the poem to articulate these two attitudes, to reconcile them as they should be reconciled, without either indulgence or rigour.

Once Gawain has donned the girdle he is ready, and he makes his way out into the castle court, where he finds his horse waiting:

> Thenne watȝ Gryngolet grayþe, þat gret watȝ and huge. (2047)

The first half of this line is almost identical with a half-line which occurs at the corresponding point in the first arming ('Bi þat watȝ Gryngolet grayth', l. 597); and this repetition serves to draw attention to another significant variation between the two scenes. On the first occasion Gawain, having donned his armour, hears Mass before going out to Gryngolet; on the present occasion he does not. The omission is striking. Gawain, as I have already noticed, is distinguished in the romances for his eagerness to hear Mass (the chief motive for his prayer on Christmas Eve); and the *Perlesvaus* says that he never left a 'hostel' without hearing Mass first, if he could.[4] It seems particularly odd that he should fail to do so on the day when he expects to meet his death. One's solution of this problem (as of some others) depends on one's reading of the confession scene. If Gawain's confession is taken as a 'routine' and valid one, then there seems no possible reason why it should not be capped by an equally routine receiving of the sacrament. The omission must, on this reading, be put down to a simple oversight. This is quite possible, of course; but I

---

[3] It may be compared with the damaging second half-line in Langland's comment on friars: 'Preched þe peple for profit of hemseluen' (B. Prol. 59).

[4] See above, Chap. 2, note 28.

would prefer to make sense of the poet's departure from his established pattern of action by seeing it as another indication of Gawain's current 'untruth'. As such, the hero's failure to go to Mass would belong with his failure to make restitution—perhaps as a consequence of it.[5]

The rest of the departure is briefly told. There is no occasion here for lingering over the shield, and the elaborate helmet is not even mentioned. After a further exchange of courtesies with members of the household, Gawain mounts his horse and, accompanied by the guide, rides off on the second phase of his winter journey. The occasion is marked by a burst of alliterative pyrotechnics—every lift alliterating over six whole lines:

> Þay boȝen bi bonkkeȝ þer boȝeȝ ar bare,
> Þay clomben bi clyffeȝ þer clengeȝ þe colde.
> Þe heuen watȝ vp halt, bot vgly þer-vnder;
> Mist muged on þe mor, malt on þe mounteȝ,
> Vch hille hade a hatte, a myst-hakel huge.
> Brokeȝ byled and breke bi bonkkeȝ aboute. (2077–82)

This is the outdoor winter vigorously reasserting itself—winter journey after winter feast, again. The conditions are very much the same as before, though intensified by the recent fall of snow.[6] The main difference to be noted here is that Gawain is not on this occasion 'leudleȝ'. He has a companion in the guide.

Sir Gawain is not rich in speaking parts. A list of the *dramatis personae* with speeches written for them would be a very short one: Arthur, Gawain, Bercilak (alias the Green Knight), his

---

[5] A right confession is a necessary preparation for communion. This is an important idea in *Cleanness* according to H. Bateson. See his edition of *Patience* (2nd ed., Manchester, 1918), Appendix I. Compare *Piers Plowman* B. XIX. 381 ff.

[6] The snow may have a symbolic value. In the Good Friday episode of Wolfram's *Parzival* it signifies the hero's state of sin (see M. Wynn, 'Scenery and Chivalrous Journeys in Wolfram's *Parzival*', *Spec.*, XXXVI (1961), pp. 405–8); and the same significance has been suggested for the snow in the bloodspots episode of Chrétien's *Perceval* (see D. C. Fowler, *Prowess and Charity* (Seattle, 1959), p. 44). It might be noted, too, that snow is associated with the eve of Judgment Day in, for example, *Cursor Mundi*, ll. 22689–92.

The Fourth Fitt

Wife, Porter of Hautdesert (ll. 813–14), Guide (ll. 2091–125 and 2140–51), Men of Camelot (ll. 674–83) and Men of Hautdesert (ll. 897–8 and 916–27). This means, in effect, that the guide is the only individual character outside the four principals who has anything significant to say. The chief reason why he enjoys this privilege is, of course, that he contributes materially to the testing of the hero by his frightening description of the Green Knight, coupled with his promise to keep quiet if Gawain will turn back. Gollancz went so far as to suggest that he might be seen as Bercilak, again in changed shape, continuing his tests in person; but this seems rather unlikely.[7] He is better taken, I think, simply as a member of Bercilak's household. Like the rest of the household he 'loves' Gawain (l. 2095, cp. 2468); but he also, like the 'segges' of the dinner scene, contributes to his difficulties. His account of the Green Knight may be hard to reconcile with what we learn later from Bercilak; but it weakens the effect of the scene if we conceive him as a liar or a conspirator. So far as Gawain himself is concerned, he is a misguided well-wisher who 'tests' not only his courage but also his courtesy (the problem of polite refusal, again). And that is the main point. The question of his 'real' thoughts or feelings is not, in this case, even raised, let alone answered.

Nevertheless, the guide's description of the Green Knight does contain some peculiar features. The Green Knight, he says, is bigger than any mortal man, and stronger than any knight of Arthur's house. He has long inhabited the Green Chapel ('He haȝ wonyd here ful ȝore', l. 2114); and the place is held perilous, for he loves fighting and kills everyone who passes by—knight, churl or priest—without mercy. No-one can stand up to his blows. The odd thing here is the way the Green Knight is presented as an ancient and well-known local hazard—when nearly everything else in the poem (notably Bercilak's own explanations at the end) suggests that he is simply a device, a 'wonder', contrived by Morgan le Fay on this one occasion to trouble Guinevere and the Round Table. Knights who take up a position by some path or road and stay there for years fighting everyone who comes by are, it is true,

[7] See Mabel Day's Introduction to his edition, p. xxxvi.

quite common in romances;[8] and it may seem natural enough that the guide should impute this well-known custom to the Green Knight in order to frighten the hero off. But the passage has more to it than that; and I think that we have to reckon again here with that association between the Green Knight and Death which was to be detected, sporadically, in the first fitt. This association comes out most clearly in the following lines from the guide's speech:

> Þer passes non bi þat place so proude in his armes
> Þat he ne dyngeȝ hym to deþe with dynt of his honde;
> For he is a mon methles, and mercy non vses,
> For be hit chorle oþer chaplayn þat bi þe chapel rydes,
> Monk oþer masseprest, oþer any mon elles,
> Hym þynk as queme hym to quelle as quyk go hymseluen.

(2104-9)

Notice that the list of the Green Knight's victims includes members of all the three estates of society—the knight 'proude in his armes', the churl, and the priest (chaplain, monk or mass-priest). It is at least unusual even for merciless killer-knights to be so indiscriminate.[9] Once more, as in the first fitt, the poet seems to ascribe to Gawain's adversary, momentarily, something of the inevitability and universality of Death itself; and again there is a parallel in Chaucer's *Pardoner's Tale*—in the taverner's description of the 'privee theef men clepeth Deeth / That in this contree al the peple sleeth'. Here as in *Sir Gawain* the universal executioner turns up eerily, in a warning speech, as the object of local superstitions and fears:

> The child seith sooth, for he hath slayn this yeer,
> Henne over a mile, withinne a greet village,
> Bothe man and womman, child, and hyne, and page;
> I trowe his habitacioun be there.
> To been avysed greet wysdom it were,
> Er that he dide a man a dishonour.[10]

---

[8] E.g. Aristor in *Perlesvaus*: 'Aristor est de si cruel maniere que chevaliers ne puet passer parmi ceste forest, se il l'encontre, que il nel voelle ocirre' (ed. cit., ll. 8742-4).

[9] Usually, like Aristor (note 8, above), they kill only knights.

[10] *C.T.*, VI, 686-91.

The effect of this Green Knight-Death analogy might be described by saying that it establishes Gawain's journey to death (for such it seems to be) as a type-case of man's Journey to Death. In this way it contributes to the cluster of eschatological motifs which, as I shall try to show, is to be detected, analogically, in the action of the fourth fitt. There is no question of the romance modulating into allegory: the poet does not at all prejudice the integrity of the genre in which he is writing. He simply makes the most of those occasions when the conventions of the genre allow him a coincidence, an analogy, with the motifs of the preachers and moralists. There is one such coincidence between the killer-knight of romance and the killer-Death of Christian homily; and another, more perfect, coincidence of the same sort comes his way a little later, in the 'desertion' of the guide. This arises quite naturally in the action of the romance. The guide makes his offer, which Gawain, as politely as he can, refuses. Whereupon the guide, shifting into an almost contemptuously familiar form of address ('þe'), gives him a few last directions and leaves him to his fate:

'Now fareȝ wel, on Godeȝ half, Gawayn þe noble!
For alle þe golde vpon grounde I nolde go wyth þe,
Ne bere þe felaȝschip þurȝ þis fryth on fote fyrre.'
Bi þat þe wyȝe in þe wod wendeȝ his brydel,
Hit þe hors with þe heleȝ as harde as he myȝt,
Lepeȝ hym ouer þe launde, and leueȝ þe knyȝt þere
al one. (2149–55)

Gawain is alone again at last (the bob, for once, contributes to the meaning as well as the movement of the stanza); and it is doubly appropriate that he should be so. As a knight of romance, he must face his final test alone; and as a man engaged on his Journey to Death, he must be deserted by his companions. The obvious analogue in homiletic writing is provided by *Everyman*, where Fellowship addresses the hero:

I wyll not a fote with the go;
But, and thou had taryed, I wolde not haue lefte the so.
And as now God spede the in thy iournaye,
For from the I wyll departe as fast as I maye.[11]

[11] *Everyman*, ed. Cawley, ll. 293–6.

Like Everyman, Gawain, 'summoned' from Camelot by the Green Knight (l. 1052), is now to face the Last Things, death and judgment; and he too can rely only on good deeds and the power of the sacraments to save him. Or so, at this point, the analogy might run—somewhat ominously for the hero.

II

I come now to the central episode of the fourth fitt—Gawain's encounter with the Green Knight in the valley of the Green Chapel (ll. 2160–2478). This is a long and obviously very important scene, and it will be convenient to consider it under three separate heads: first as a *recognition* scene, then as a *confession* scene and last as a *judgment* scene.

Aristotle says that the scene of recognition or 'discovery' is one of the most interesting and affecting parts of a tragedy; and the same can often be said of a romance. A familiar example is the Good Friday episode in Chrétien's *Perceval*, where the hero, after his mysterious visit to the Grail Castle, stays with the hermit and learns from him the identity of the Grail King and the nature of the Grail. The effect of such discoveries, coming after the mysteries and uncertainties of an Arthurian adventure, has been well described by one critic as a 'turning up of the houselights'.[12] This turning up of the lights is an interesting and, for the author, somewhat delicate business. Let us see how the *Gawain*-poet handles it in the present scene.

He opens dramatically, with what might be called a 'false discovery'. Gawain has been told by the guide to look for the Green Chapel on the left-hand side of the path when he gets down to the bottom of the valley; but when he gets there he cannot find it. Instead of whatever a Green Chapel might look like, there is merely a hollow mound or barrow with three holes in it:

> . . . nobot an olde caue,
> Or a creuisse of an olde cragge, he couþe hit noʒt deme
> with spelle. (2182–4)

The depreciating colloquial use of 'old' twice in these lines helps to convey the shock of surprise and disappointment

[12] D. C. Fowler, op. cit., p. 5.

which this first discovery occasions.[13] The Green Chapel is not
a real chapel at all—or not one of God's. So the 'Knight of the
Green Chapel', Gawain at once concludes, cannot be a real
knight either—he must be the Devil himself:

> Wel biseme3 þe wy3e wruxled in grene
> Dele here his deuocioun on þe deuele3 wyse.
> Now I fele hit is þe fende, in my fyue wytte3,
> Þat hat3 stoken me þis steuen to strye me here. (2191–4)

The idea is a plausible one. The fiend does sometimes wear
green; he does traditionally live in the 'strange countries' of the
North; and he does make contracts and appointments with men
in order to 'destroy' them.[14] On the other hand, *Sir Gawain* is a
romance, not an 'exemplum'; and the experienced reader is
likely to feel dissatisfied with Gawain's explanation. The true
discovery, one should feel, is yet to come—as it does, in its
proper place, after Gawain has received the Green Knight's
return blow and so 'achieved' his adventure.

Even here, though, the poet does not turn up the lights all
at once. The discovery is phased, divided into two stages. In the
first stage (Bercilak's speech to Gawain immediately after de-
livering the return blow, ll. 2338–68) Gawain learns what the
reader may be presumed to know already—that the Knight of
the Green Chapel is identical with the nameless host:

> For hit is my wede þat þou were3, þat ilke wouen girdel,
> Myn owen wyf hit þe weued, I wot wel for soþe.
> Now know I wel þy cosses, and þy costes als,
> And þe wowyng of my wyf: I wro3t hit myseluen. (2358–61)

This is for Gawain the crucial discovery, and we shall be concerned later with his reactions to it, which are immediate and
violent. But there is nothing particularly new in it for the reader.
His discovery comes later—in Bercilak's last speech, in fact

[13] On the poet's colloquial use of 'old', see above, Chap. 2, note 41.
[14] All three points come out in Chaucer's *Friar's Tale*: wearing green,
III, 1382 (see D. W. Robertson, 'Why the Devil Wears Green',
M.L.N., LXIX (1954), pp. 470–2); living in the north, III, 1413–16
(see Robinson's note—and compare *SGGK*, ll. 406–8 and 455);
making a contract, III, 1404–5.

(ll. 2444–70). By this time Gawain's first access of anger and
remorse is spent, and he is ready to leave for Camelot; but before he leaves he asks the Green Knight one more question:

> Bot on I wolde yow pray, displeses yow neuer:
> Syn ȝe be lorde of þe ȝonde londe þer I haf lent inne
> Wyth yow wyth worschyp—þe wyȝe hit yow ȝelde
> Þat vphaldeȝ þe heuen and on hyȝ sitteȝ—
> How norne ȝe yowre ryȝt nome, and þenne no more?
>
> (2439–43)

It will be remembered that in the first fitt Gawain asked his
challenger to 'telle me howe þou hattes' (l. 401), and that the
latter promised to reveal 'myn owen nome' (l. 408) and later
announced himself as 'þe Knyȝt of þe Grene Chapel'. But this
was a nickname or (in the old sense) a 'surname'; and Gawain is
now asking for more than that—for the real or 'ryȝt' name. This
distinction between nickname and 'right name' can be illustrated from Malory: 'He was called in the courte of kynge
Arthure Bewmaynes, but his ryght name is sir Gareth of
Orkeney'; 'There was a knyght that was called the Knyght with
the Strange Beste, and at that tyme hys ryght name was called
Pellynore'; 'Sir La Cote Male Tayle was called otherwyse be
ryght sir Brewne le Noyre'.[15] In each of these cases, as in *Sir
Gawain*, the nickname is a descriptive tag referring to some
characteristic feature or activity; whereas the 'right name' is
essentially the given name—though this will itself usually have
some descriptive appendage, as in 'Sir Gareth of Orkeney' or
'Sir Brewne le Noyre'. The nickname is by its very nature in-
formative ('Par le *sornon* connoist on l'ome' was what Perceval's
mother said); but it is the right name that counts in the end.
Nicknames come and go—and anyway they may, as in *Sir
Gawain*, tell you nothing which you do not know already. So
Gawain is not content to know his host and adversary simply
as the Knight of the Green Chapel. He wants to know his 'ryȝt
nome'—who he *really* is.[16]

[15] Ed. cit., pp. 350, 77, 476. Compare pp. 299 ('name of ryght'),
328, 329. ('Right name' is not always used in contrast to the chivalric
nickname. It may mean little more than just 'name'.)

[16] Compare the encounter between Lancelot and Perceval in Malory

The Fourth Fitt

The Green Knight tells him. His given name is Bercilak; his real 'home' is in the castle where Gawain spent Christmas; and the castle's name is Hautdesert.[17] Hence, not 'the Knight of the Green Chapel', but 'Bercilak de Hautdesert'. It is perhaps surprising how much this simple discovery of a name contributes to the 'turning up of the lights'. We feel that we are coming back rapidly to the world of everyday reality—the everyday reality of chivalry and romance, that is. The Green Knight, the nameless host, is known to his neighbours under a perfectly ordinary —if not actually familiar—knightly name:

> Bercilak de Hautdesert I hat in þis londe. (2445)

But this answer raises other questions. How did this Bercilak come to play the part of the Green Knight? And why? Here again the answers given are conventional and even—so far as the case allows—'realistic'. Morgan le Fay's hatred of Guinevere, Arthur and the Round Table is one of the données of romance—something which, though explanations are to be found in various French sources, is generally taken to need no explanation.[18] Hence she provides the poet with a final and

[17] 'Hautdesert' is commonly taken to be the name of the Green Chapel (e.g. by Tolkien and Gordon in their note to l. 2445), but this is almost certainly wrong. It would be very odd for both Bercilak's nickname *and* his right name to contain a reference to the Chapel. One would expect the latter to identify his real 'house and home' or ancestral dwelling-place (cf. 'Gareth of Orkeney', etc.); and that is plainly not the Chapel but the Castle. There is no reason why 'Hautdesert' should *not* refer to the Castle. At least two medieval English castles, one in Warwickshire, the other in Staffordshire, were called 'Beaudesert' (i.e. 'beautiful waste (land)'); so there is no need to go to Celtic 'disert' ('hermitage') to explain the second element. See *Place-Names of Warwickshire*, English Place-Name Society, Vol. XIII (1936), p. 199, and *Introduction to the Survey of English Place-Names*, E.P.N.S., Vol. I, Part I (1924), p. 115.

[18] On Morgan's hatred of Guinevere, etc., see L. A. Paton, *Studies in the Fairy Mythology of Arthurian Romance* (Boston, 1903), Chap. II.

(ed. cit., p. 829). Lancelot at first gives his name as 'Le Shyvalere Mafete' (his current nickname); but a little later Perceval asks his 'trewe name' (a variant of 'right name'), and Lancelot, having in the meantime discovered Perceval's identity, reveals it.

unquestionable answer to the reader's 'why?': 'Because Morgan wanted to humiliate the Knights of the Round Table and frighten Guinevere to death'. It is no more than one would expect from a woman who, in Malory's words, 'did never good but ill'. At the same time, economically, Morgan provides an answer to the other question, 'how?' It is true that we never discover how she could win Bercilak's consent to her schemes (though we would, I think, give Bercilak the benefit of the doubt on this); but we do discover how she managed the scheme itself. Here the poet shows an inclination to rationalize his wonders. He does not rest content, as he might have done, with the well-known fact of Morgan's magic powers. This time he does draw on the further explanations available to him in French tradition.[19] Morgan did not simply have her magic skills; she learnt them from Merlin, 'þat conable klerk'. They are a matter of 'koyntyse of clergye'—and this is, in the fourteenth century, at least a possible explanation of 'illusions' or 'appearances' such as the Green Knight and his returning head. A clerk *might* be able to produce such illusions—as we can see from Chaucer's *Franklin's Tale*, where a young clerk from the University of Orleans is able to do a similar trick: 'thurgh his magik, for a wyke or tweye, / It semed that alle the rokkes were aweye'. It is true that Chaucer treats such 'natural magic' with suspicion. He compares it with the work of jugglers or illusionists at feasts, speaks of it as 'a supersticious cursednesse' which 'hethen folk useden in thilke dayes', and asserts that it is no longer possible in modern times:

> . . . swich folye
> As in oure dayes is nat worth a flye,—
> For hooly chirches feith in oure bileve
> Ne suffreth noon illusioun us to greve.[20]

At the same time he probably thought that (given a non-contemporary setting) such learned magic provided the only reasonably plausible explanation available to him—a clerk might be able to do it that way, after all. It is in this spirit, I think, that one should take the *Gawain*-poet's stress on Mor-

---

[19] Paton, op. cit., p. 226.   [20] *C.T.*, V, 1131–4.

gan's 'koyntyse of clergye'—as another contribution to the turning-up of the lights. It leads on, in fact, to the last and most down-to-earth 'discovery' of all. This follows in the next stanza:

> Þat is ho þat is at home, þe auncian lady;
> Ho is euen þyn aunt, Arþureȝ half-suster,
> Þe duches doȝter of Tyntagelle, þat dere Vter after
> Hade Arþur vpon, þat aþel is nowþe.
> Perfore I eþe þe, haþel, to com to þy naunt. (2463-7)

Bercilak does not spare Gawain his last humiliating recognition: that his real adversary has been, not the Knight of the Green Chapel, or the Fiend, or even Bercilak de Hautdesert, but—most mundane of relations—his own aunt. 'Perfore I eþe þe, haþel, to com to þy naunt': it is not surprising that Gawain refuses the invitation and rides back to Camelot.

I want now to consider Gawain's encounter under my second head, as a *confession* scene. This means looking at that part of the episode, so far not touched on, which lies between Bercilak's two speeches of explanation; for this section (ll. 2369 ff.) is specially rich in penitential matter—indeed it follows closely the actual order of the confessional.

It is Bercilak's first discovery speech which sets things in motion here. He reveals that the exchange of winnings played a part in the test—indeed, almost *was* the test—and Gawain consequently realizes for the first time the significance of his failure on the third day. His reaction is strong:

> Þat oþer stif mon in study stod a gret whyle,
> So agreued for greme he gryed withinne;
> Alle þe blode of his brest blende in his face,
> Þat al he schrank for schome þat þe schalk talked. (2369-72)

Shame and mortification ('greme') may not be enough in itself to make up the contrition required by theologians in the sacrament of penance; but Gawain is clearly better 'disposed' here than he was during his formal confession to the priest at Hautdesert, where the poet failed to allow any expression of contrite feeling whatsoever. For what he evinces is at worst, one might say, the secular equivalent of contrition; and he may therefore claim to satisfy, in a sense, the first condition laid down by Bromyard for a proper 'disposition' ('quod doleat commissa'). In the same sense, he goes on to satisfy the second condition ('quod restituat ablata') when, in the following lines, he returns the girdle to its rightful owner:

> Þenne he kaȝt to þe knot, and þe kest lawseȝ,
> Brayde broþely þe belt to þe burne seluen. (2376–7)

The style of the gesture is quite unsacramental; yet what Gawain is doing here is something which he should have done and, again, did not do as part of his confession at Hautdesert. It is, in its way, an act of restitution (though a tardy one), coming as a response to the moral drawn by Bercilak in the previous stanza:

> Trwe mon trwe restore,
> Þenne þar mon drede no waþe. (2354–5)

'A true man must make faithful restitution—then he need fear no danger.'

The second 'act' of the confessional after 'contrition of heart' is 'confession of mouth'; and this stage too (or a secular equivalent of it) is easily recognized in the present case, when Gawain, after restoring the girdle, sets about analyzing his fault:

> For care of þy knokke cowardyse me taȝt
> To acorde me with couetyse, my kynde to forsake,
> Þat is larges and lewté þat longeȝ to knyȝteȝ.
> Now I am fawty and falce, and ferde haf ben euer
> Of trecherye and vntrawþe: boþe bityde sorȝe
>   and care!
> I biknowe you, knyȝt, here stylle,
> Al fawty is my fare. (2379–86)

'Biknowe' is, with 'shrive', the established equivalent for the loan-word 'confess' in Middle English;[21] and Gawain's speech does in fact deserve to be taken as a formal, considered con-

[21] This comes out clearly in the Green Knight's reply, where 'be-knowen' is parallel to 'confessed' (l. 2391). See also *Piers Plowman* B. V. 200 and X. 416, and *M.E.D.* under 'biknouen', 4.

fession, despite what might at first seem a passionate and haphazard piling-up of moral terms. The analysis turns quite specifically on three points and no more—both here and (the consistency is to be noted) in Gawain's two other brief confessional statements (ll. 2374–5 and 2506–9). The first point is *cowardice* (ll. 2374, 2379, 2508); the second is *covetousness* (ll. 2374, 2380, 2508), with its traditional opposite 'larges' (l. 2381);[22] the third is *untruth* (ll. 2383, 2509), otherwise called 'trecherye' (l. 2383), with its opposite 'lewté' (l. 2381). In the present passage, furthermore, these three moral ideas are carefully related one to another, articulated into a coherent account of the case as Gawain sees it. The method is essentially allegorical—as indeed one might expect, seeing that the combination of confessional self-analysis and allegorical technique is such a persistent feature of medieval thought and writing. The moral ideas are brought together as if they were people. Consider how easily the passage might be converted into the scenario for an episode in a Morality Play. The hero (Everyman, Mankind, Humanum Genus . . .) has been summoned by Death; but Cowardice promises that he can save him. He is persuaded by Cowardice's arguments and, against his better judgment, goes with him to where his former enemies, Covetousness and Untruth, are waiting to welcome him. He 'accords him' with them and joins their party, leaving his former friends, the virtues Largess and Lewty, to lament his defection. It is a coherent and largely persuasive version of what happened when Gawain agreed to accept the lady's girdle—particularly in the role of 'teacher' assigned to Cowardice. The only difficulty arises from the presence of Covetousness. It is not easy to think of Gawain as covetous: indeed, as we have seen, the poet several times goes out of his way to stress that he was not interested in the gold of the girdle, its workmanship, etc. Yet the fact is that 'covetise' does appear, not only here but also in both the other two confessional statements. I shall return to this difficulty later.

Gawain's speech ends, in the wheel, with a general con-

---

[22] See *Cursor Mundi* (Fairfax Ms.), ed. cit., l. 27404: 'Largesse gaine couaitise is sette'. In the *Castle of Perseverance*, Covetise fights against 'Lady Largyte'. This is a commonplace.

fession of guilt, a request for penance to be imposed, and a promise of future amendment:

> I biknowe yow, knyȝt, here stylle,
> Al fawty is my fare;
> Leteȝ me ouertake your wylle
> And efte I schal be ware. (2385–8)

The line 'Leteȝ me ouertake your wylle' could, as Tolkien and Gordon suggest, mean simply 'Let me win your goodwill'; but I would prefer, considering the context, to follow Gollancz here: '"Let me understand your will", *i.e.* what do you want me to do now? Gawain, having confessed, asks for penance'.[23] Gawain's confession is over, and in the following line he fulfils, though again in a secular style, the third and last condition of a proper disposition ('quod promittat cessare'). The time has therefore come for the last of his 'acts' as a penitent—making satisfaction by penance. The Green Knight's reply, with its explicit use of technical language ('confessed', 'penaunce'), makes it clear that the author understood the situation in this way:

> I halde hit hardily hole, þe harme þat I hade.
> Þou art confessed so clene, beknowen of þy mysses,
> And hatȝ þe penaunce apert of þe poynt of myn egge,
> I halde þe polysed of þat plyȝt, and pured as clene
> As þou hadeȝ neuer forfeted syþen þou watȝ fyrst borne.
>
> (2390–4)

Bercilak replies to Gawain's request for penance, then, by declaring that, so far as he is concerned, no penance is necessary, since Gawain has already made a clean confession and, what is more, received a wound in the neck. The idea that a contrite confession—besides being necessary in itself—counts towards a man's penance was generally accepted in the Middle Ages;[24]

---

[23] See the editors' notes to l. 2387. Doing penance is described as 'fulfilling the confessor's will and ordinance' in *Lancelot of the Laik*, ed. M. M. Gray, Scottish Text Society (Edinburgh, 1912), ll. 1420–1. See also *Cursor Mundi* (Fairfax Ms.), l. 26255, for a similar use of 'will'.

[24] See Aquinas, *Summa Theologiae*, III, Supplementum, Quaestio VI, Art. I ('per confessionis erubescentiam ... poena temporalis

and so, of course, was the idea that bodily mortification might serve to pay off whatever debt of satisfaction remained when the confession was over. Naturally, wounds do not figure in the penance-books among the normal forms of such mortification (hair-shirts, uncomfortable beds, beating of the breast, etc.); but Gawain's cut does admirably all the same. Not only is it physically painful; it is also (unlike a well-concealed hair-shirt) visible to all, and hence a source of mental as well as physical mortification. It is in fact, as Bercilak himself points out, an open or public penance—'penaunce apert'.[25] We may recall, too, that wounds were well-established in Christian tradition as symbols of sin, in part through allegorical readings of the parable of the Good Samaritan. A sinful man is a wounded man. So the cut can, rather like the green belt a little later, function as a 'syngne of surfet'—a symbol of, as well as a satisfaction for, the hero's act of untruth. We shall see in due course how the poet exploits this double symbolism of the wound and the belt in the last part of the poem.

The confession ends, as it should, with Bercilak's 'absolution':

> I halde þe polysed of þat plyȝt, and pured as clene
> As þou hadeȝ neuer forfeted syþen þou watȝ fyrst borne.

The use of 'polysed' to mean 'absolved', or more generally 'cleansed (of sin)', is paralleled in *Cleanness*:

> So if folk be defowled by unfre chaunce,
> Þat he be sulped in sawle, seche to schryfte,
> And he may polyce hym at þe prest, by penaunce taken,
> Wel bryȝter þen þe beryl oþer browden perles.[26]

[25] Public penance was still practised in the poet's time. See H. C. Lea, *History of Auricular Confession and Indulgences* (London, 1896), Chap. XVI.

[26] *Cleanness*, ed. R. J. Menner (New Haven, 1920), ll. 1129–32. Compare ll. 1068 and 1134.

---

expiatur'); also *Dictionnaire de Théologie Catholique*, Vol. 13, cols. 938, 954, 957. For a fourteenth-century English statement of the idea, see *The Book of Vices and Virtues*, ed. Francis, p. 46.

The poet does not allow Bercilak to use the proper clerical term 'assoil'; but it is clear that the term which he does allow him is one itself associated with the sacrament of penance—in the poet's mind, at least. Notice, too, that Bercilak's next words, 'pured as clene / As þou hadeʒ neuer forfeted syþen þou watʒ fyrst borne', are a variant on those used of the priest's absolution, at the end of the Hautdesert confession:

> And he asoyled hym surely, and sette hym so clene
> As domeʒday schulde haf ben diʒt on þe morn.[27] (1883–4)

What is the point of Gawain's second confession? How does it fit in? Two things at least seem fairly obvious. First, it is not a 'real' confession, since Bercilak, being a layman, has no power of absolution. Bercilak and Gawain are, as it were, playing at confession—though in very different spirits, Gawain seriously, Bercilak with laughter. They act it out between themselves, and God enters into the reckoning only insofar as Bercilak plays his part. For it is just Bercilak who stands to be satisfied by Gawain's contrite confession and penance: '*I halde* hit hardily hole, þe harme þat *I hade* . . . *I halde* þe polysed of þat plyʒt'. This being so, we should not expect his 'absolution' to mark a final closing of the accounts—in fact, so far as Gawain is concerned, we shall see that the account remains open, with a debit, to the very end of the poem. On the other hand, one should not neglect the fact that Bercilak *is* satisfied. Gawain's second confession is not 'real', but it is 'right'. He is contrite, he makes restitution, he resolves to sin no more. The play-acting is corrective: it makes good the imperfections of the confession at Hautdesert. For Gawain is only now at the point when he can appreciate both the full demands of 'trawþe' ("Trwe mon

---

[27] Compare Bercilak's formula with the following passages: 'I yow assoille . . . as clene and eek as cleer / As ye were born', *Pardoner's Tale*, *C.T.*, VI, 913–15; 'ʒee are als clene of syn, I plyghte, / Als þat day borne were ʒee', *Sege of Melayne*, ed. S. J. Herrtage, E.E.T.S. E.S. 35 (1880), ll. 908–9; 'Now I haue power and dignyte / For to asoyle þe as clene / As þou were houen off þe fount-ston', *Athelston*, ed. A. McI. Trounce, E.E.T.S. O.S. 224 (1951), ll. 676–8. It may well be that the *Gawain*-poet's other, Doomsday, formula represents a pointed departure from this more common birth/baptism type.

trwe restore') and his own failure to satisfy them. He can now see and feel what he could not before, and it is this which counts most for the reader in his scene with Bercilak. Of course, it is nonsense, theologically speaking, for a pretend, secular confession to 'make good' the inadequacies of a real, sacramental one; but here—as the reader will no doubt agree—it is necessary to remind oneself that even the confession at Hautdesert is not *really* real.

I should like now, third and lastly, to consider Gawain's encounter as a *judgment* scene. The main question here concerns the gravity of Gawain's fault; and the first thing to see is how Gawain and Bercilak differ in their estimates of this.

In the earlier part of the scene, up to the delivery of the return blow, Bercilak behaves very much as he did in the first fitt —he is 'proud' and censorious. He does, it is true, praise Gawain for turning up on time ('þou hatȝ tymed þi trauayl as truee mon schulde', l. 2241); but when Gawain shrinks away from the first blow, he reproves him 'with mony prowde wordeȝ'. The turn of the speech recalls both his own reproach to Arthur's household ('What, is þis Arþureȝ hous . . . þat al þe rous rennes of þurȝ ryalmes so mony?') and his wife's reproaches in the temptation scenes ('Sir, ȝif ȝe be Wawan, wonder me þynkkeȝ, / Wyȝe þat is so wel wrast alway to god'):

'Þou art not Gawayn,' quoþ þe gome, 'þat is so goud halden,
Þat neuer arȝed for no here by hylle ne be vale,
And now þou fles for ferde er þou fele harmeȝ!
Such cowardise of þat knyȝt cowþe I neuer here.' (2270–3)

The cowardice which 'taught' Gawain to accept and conceal the life-saving girdle, here teaches him to mistrust it; and Bercilak does not spare him the recognition of his falling-off.

After both the second and the third blows, however, Bercilak speaks 'merrily' (ll. 2295 and 2336); and his behaviour throughout the rest of the scene is that of the genial host, not the hostile challenger. Accordingly his final judgment, when it comes (at the end of his first 'discovery' speech), differs entirely in spirit from his earlier reproaches. He speaks of the hero as

The Fourth Fitt

On þe fautlest freke þat euer on fote ȝede;
As perle bi þe quite pese is of prys more,
So is Gawayn, in god fayth, bi oþer gay knyȝteȝ.
Bot here yow lakked a lyttel, sir, and lewté yow wonted;
Bot þat watȝ for no wylyde werke, ne wowyng nauþer,
Bot for ȝe lufed your lyf; þe lasse I yow blame. (2363–8)

Gawain is not, as the poet claimed in the pentangle passage, 'faultless' *absolutely*, like refined gold or a perfect pearl; but he is so *relatively*, in comparison with other men ('bi oþer gay knyȝteȝ'). He is even—as Bercilak somewhat illogically puts it—'quite the most faultless man that ever trod ground'.[28] It is true that he failed 'a little' in loyalty; but his reasons for doing so extenuate the fault. He was not interested in the fine workmanship of the girdle (the 'wylyde werke'), nor did he want it as a token of the lady's love ('wowyng'). His sole motive was to save his life, and that—as the poet has himself already suggested in the parallel passage, ll. 2037–42—was understandable: 'þe lasse I yow blame'.

The contrast between this passage and Gawain's confession—which, be it noted, follows immediately after—hardly needs emphasis. The double or two-sided judgment, already implicit, as we have seen, in the arming episode earlier in the fitt, is here wrought up to a pitch and presented to the reader in its most challenging form. Gawain and Bercilak are at odds both in their analysis of the moral facts of the case and in their assessment of its upshot and significance.

Let me take the 'facts of the case' first. Gawain's analysis, as we have seen, involves three terms, cowardice, covetousness and untruth; whereas Bercilak's involves only one, untruth (lack of 'lewté'). There is no doubt, here or anywhere else in the poem, about the untruth—everyone agrees that Gawain *was* false; but what about the cowardice and the covetousness? Some moral theology is useful here. Gawain's sin is a 'sin of passion' (as against a 'sin of ignorance' or a 'sin of malice'): that is to say it was 'caused' by fear, one of the passions of the soul.

[28] On emphatic expressions of the type 'on þe fautlest freke', see Mustanoja's *Middle English Syntax*, Part I, pp. 297–9. They should not be equated with more moderate expressions like 'one of the best men'.

Gawain made off with the girdle because he was afraid of death. Now such sins may or may not be serious; but the fact that they are caused by passion rather than malice is admitted by the theologians as an alleviating consideration—more or less so according to the strength of the passion. For passion diminishes sin, according to Aquinas, insofar as it diminishes the voluntary character of an action: 'passio minuit peccatum, inquantum minuit voluntarium'.[29] So Bercilak is right: the fact that Gawain's sin was caused by his fear of death rather than by some weaker passion (love for the lady, perhaps) or by malice does diminish his sin—'þe lasse I yow blame'. Yet Gawain is right too when he accuses himself of cowardice, and identifies this as the source of his sin ('cowardyse me taȝt . . .'). For passions, insofar as they are governable by reason and the will, are themselves good or evil—evil where they run counter to the order of reason. So fear, insofar as it is not 'involuntary', and where, in Aquinas' words, it 'flees things which reason says should be borne', is morally blameworthy—'cowardice', in fact.[30] The term is applicable to Gawain's case because his fear of death led him to incur spiritual evils in order to escape bodily ones—and so to prefer the greater evil to the less, which is again reason. Thus the single passion, fear, gives valid occasion both for extenuation ('love of life') and for blame ('cowardice').

The 'contradiction' over covetousness is less easily resolved. We have seen that the poet goes out of his way to stress what in any case seems obvious, namely that Gawain had no interest in the costliness or fine workmanship of the girdle; yet he has Gawain confess—and on three occasions—to 'covetise'. This is something of a crux of interpretation, which I myself would solve, tentatively, as follows.[31] There are two ways of looking at

[29] *Summa Theologiae* I–II, Quaestio LXXVII, Art. VI ('Utrum peccatum allevietur propter passionem'). Aquinas' discussion of the passion 'timor' is to be found in I–II, Qq. XLI–XLIV.

[30] Aquinas' discussion of the vice 'timor' (his Latin does not distinguish between 'fear' and 'cowardice') is to be found in II–II, Q. CXXV.

[31] I here abandon the explanation put forward in my article, pp. 78–79.

a moral act—'objectively' as an external action ('actus exterior'), and 'subjectively' as an internal act of the will ('actus interior voluntatis').[32] Now the object of the external action may not coincide with the end proposed by the will—as, in Aquinas' Aristotelian example, when a man steals in order to fornicate. Such an act, says Aquinas, is theft 'materially' (i.e. with respect to its object as an external action) and fornication 'formally' (i.e. with respect to its end as an internal act of the will). Both specifications are valid, though the 'formal' specification is more important: 'he who steals in order to fornicate is more fornicator than thief'. So with Gawain's action, perhaps. He stole in order to save his life; and that is obviously not an act of covetousness with respect to the end proposed by the will. But it *is* an act of covetousness with respect to its object as an external action; for so considered, 'materially' or 'objectively', it is simply a kind of theft—withholding what rightfully belongs to another. And all kinds of theft, including this kind, fall under 'covetise', as the manuals agree:

> alkin taking wrangewisly
> And alle halding wiþ trecchry.[33]

I would argue, therefore, that so far as the facts of the case are concerned there is no real contradiction between Gawain's confession and Bercilak's judgment. Both their accounts are incomplete; but each is perfectly valid as far as it goes. Both Gawain and Bercilak, in fact, lay their emphasis on those points which harmonize with their own particular assessment of the upshot of the adventure. And it is here that the real disagreement is to be found. For Bercilak the adventure demonstrates

[32] *Summa Theologiae* I–II, Q. XVIII, Art. VI.

[33] *Cursor Mundi* (Fairfax), ed. cit., ll. 27844–5. Compare *Handlyng Synne*, ed. Furnivall, ll. 5343–8; and *Ancrene Riwle*, trans. M. B. Salu (London, 1955), p. 93: 'withholding what has been promised, found, or borrowed, . . . is not this a species of covetousness and a kind of theft?' D. F. Hills, in his article 'Gawain's Fault in *SGGK*', *R.E.S.*, N.S. XIV (1963), pp. 124–31, suggests that 'covetise' should be taken in an extended, Augustinian sense (= inordinate love of anything other than God). I give my reasons for rejecting this in a letter in the same journal, N.S. XV (1964), p. 56.

man's possibilities for good; for Gawain it demonstrates his possibilities for evil. Where one sees 'grete trauþe' (l. 2470), the other sees 'þe faut and þe fayntyse of þe flesche crabbed' (l. 2435).

It will be convenient at this point to reconsider Bercilak's judgment in a wider context, as one aspect of his conduct of the return match. How, generally, does he treat the hero in this last part of the poem? Better, clearly, than either Gawain or the reader had reason to expect. When Gawain first undertook the beheading match, he granted his adversary the right to deliver a return blow—provided only that he could survive to do so; and once he had survived, there was every reason to think that he would claim his right. One good blow, he said, deserves another. The action of the middle fitts, therefore, takes place under the threat of imminent death; and the guide does no more than confirm existing fears when he says that the Green Knight is 'a mon methles, and mercy non vses'. Yet, as it turns out, Gawain 'gets the grace of his life' (see l. 2480). Indeed the Green Knight is doubly merciful. In the first place, he waives his original unconditional right to behead the hero, and claims no more than a conditional right—the right to punish Gawain for a failure in the exchange test. What is more, he exercises even this limited right with mercy and moderation ('meth'). True, it is—on these new terms—no more than Gawain's due that he should be spared on the first two strikes. That is simple justice, or 'ryȝt' (l. 2346). But Bercilak could fairly have axed him on the third strike; for on the third day, though Gawain continued to resist the lady, he failed miserably at the exchange—which is, after all, Bercilak's chief concern. Yet he receives no more than a skin-wound:

> Þaȝ he homered heterly, hurt hym no more,
> Bot snyrt hym on þat on syde, þat seuered þe hyde. (2311–12)

It would be wrong, however, to see Bercilak too exclusively as a merciful, merry or permissive character, either as adversary or as judge. There is a danger here of weakening the poem's narrative tensions and trivializing its moral attitudes. We must feel, surely, that Bercilak *might* have killed Gawain if things had gone worse at the castle, just as we must feel that he *could* have done so (despite the lady's 'magic' girdle). Otherwise the story becomes merely dull—not an 'outtrage awenture of Arthureʒ wondereʒ' at all. Bercilak is not merciless like Shylock, out for his pound of flesh; but this does not mean that he cares nothing for justice, his own rights and the hero's deserts. He does after all exercise his right to deliver the return blow; and if the hero survives, it is because he has deserved—if not thoroughly deserved —to do so. Like Shakespeare in the *Merchant of Venice*, the *Gawain*-poet makes room for justice as well as mercy in his judgment scene.

The ideal of the just-and-merciful is a familiar one, but its place in the last part of *Sir Gawain* will excuse, perhaps, a few general comments on it here. People who exercise any kind of authority over others must, it is generally agreed, try to *reconcile* justice and mercy, 'tempering', 'clothing' or 'seasoning' the one virtue with the other. The most obvious case, and one very frequently treated in medieval didactic writing, is that of the justiciar—the king, the magistrate, etc. The ideal for such people is neatly expressed in the Latin verses quoted by Langland ('pietas' is 'mercy'):

> O qui iura regis Christi specialia regis,
> Hoc quod agas melius, iustus es, esto pius!
> Nudum ius a te vestiri vult pietate.[34]

The same double obligation rests on confessors and spiritual counsellors. They too must inspire both fear and hope. Justice requires that they bring the penitent face to face with his sins and with the pains of hell; mercy requires that they hold out the prospect of God's forgiveness. Like the Good Samaritan, they pour both soothing oil and biting wine into the wound of sin, 'inspiring hope of pardon in the penitent and fear of punishment in the sinner'.[35] And in each individual case they must

---

[34] *Piers Plowman* B. Prol. 133–5. See *Proverbs* 20. 28: 'Misericordia et veritas custodiunt regem'.

[35] Image and quotation from Bede's Commentary on *Luke* 10. 34, in Migne, *P.L.*, Vol. 92, col. 469. Compare *Ancrene Wisse*, ed. J. R. R. Tolkien, E.E.T.S. 249 (1962), p. 220.

so temper the mixture that the penitent neither despairs before
God's justice nor presumes on his mercy: 'Hope and fear must
always be mingled. . . . Let no man separate these two, one
from another, for as Saint Gregory says: "Hope without fear
grows rankly into presumption. Fear without hope degenerates
into despair." '36

The authority of both judge and confessor is, of course, held
to derive from God; and it is in the last resort because God himself is just and merciful that they must be so too. In this as in
other respects they are 'types' of God. Mercy, as Portia says,

> is an attribute to God himself;
> And earthly power doth then show likest God's
> When mercy seasons justice.

The key text for this idea of God's mercy and justice was Psalm
85. 10: 'Mercy and truth are met together; righteousness and
peace have kissed each other'. This text gave rise, first in Jewish
and then in Christian exegesis, to the tradition of the Four
Daughters of God.37 It became customary to handle the problem of God's mercy and justice in the form of an allegorical
debate, in which, usually, Mercy and Peace were set against
and finally reconciled with Truth and Righteousness. The wide
currency of such a fable illustrates the medieval preoccupation
with this particular moral problem. How can anyone be both
merciful *and* just? The problem touches God both as redeemer
and as judge; and Miss Traver, in her study of the subject,
shows that the Four Daughters motif was applied to both cases.
Most commonly it was applied to the redemption; but it could
also—and very naturally—be applied to God's judgments:
either the 'particular judgment' of the individual soul after
death (as in Deguileville's *Pèlerinage de l'Âme* and the English
Castle of Perseverance), or the 'general judgment' at the end of
time (as in the *Processus Belial*).

Most readers of *Sir Gawain* will agree that the Bercilak of the

---

36 *Ancrene Riwle*, trans. Salu, p. 147. Compare *Cursor Mundi*,
ll. 27304–7, and the speech of John the Baptist in the *Ludus Coventriae*,
ed. K. S. Block, E.E.T.S. E.S. 120 (1922), pp. 229–30.

37 See H. Traver, *The Four Daughters of God* (Bryn Mawr, 1907).

fourth fitt is a particularly, even strangely, powerful and impressive figure, and that his handling of the hero, both in the return match and after, feels somehow *exemplary*. The purpose of my digression is to identify one source of this strength. Bercilak is, though not in a literal or institutional sense, both a confessor and a judge in this part of the poem; and his conduct of affairs is such as to satisfy our feeling for what is desirable in such persons. The dubious blend of earnest and game which marks his behaviour in the first fitt gives place here to a final, authoritatively tempered, blend of justice and mercy. It is not only that he pours both oil and wine into Gawain's wound—it is that he pours them, we feel, in just the right proportions. If the mercy of his final judgment is more evident than its strict justice, this is because Gawain is disposed more to despair than to presumption. Bercilak tempers the wind to the shorn lamb; and in this moderation or 'meth', as in other things, he resembles a good judge or a good confessor. He also—though more remotely—resembles their prototype, the God of Judgment.

Earlier in this chapter I pointed out certain 'eschatological motifs' in the first or 'journey' part of the fourth fitt—the crowing of the cock and (perhaps) the snowy weather, the guide's description of the Green Knight and his desertion of the hero. Such details, I suggested, helped to establish Gawain's journey as a 'type-case' of man's journey towards Death and Judgment. I would like now to draw attention to one or two points in which the present encounter scene fulfils the expectations so created—analogies, again, between the romance and Christian myth, between Bercilak's judgment and God's.

The first point is that Gawain is brought face to face with an assessor who knows his unspoken secrets:

> Now know I wel þy cosses, and þy costes als,
> And þe wowyng of my wyf: I wroȝt hit myseluen. (2360–1)

This knowledge is quite adequately explained by the plot: there is nothing mysterious or supernatural about it. Yet it does invest the Green Knight with a special authority and grandeur. He is both less and more than an ordinary confessor: he does not command the power of the keys; but his judgment on Gawain is *final*, in the sense that there is not possibly any new information which could disturb it. It has a share, as it were, in the finality of the fiction itself. So Bercilak figures, like the Minos of Dante's Inferno, as an infallible 'conoscitor delle peccata'. Like Minos, he has no theological credentials; but he is a 'type' or poetic surrogate of the all-seeing God of Judgment.

The second point is that Gawain suffers in Bercilak's presence because he has not 'made restitution'. It is one of the recurring themes of medieval didactic writers that failure to make restitution has dangerous consequences on the Last Day. This theme—which arises naturally out of the general late-medieval concern with restitution—can be illustrated from the poets. Dunbar has a stanza (somewhat clumsily constructed) on the subject:

> O! quha sall weild the wrang possessioun,
> Or the gold gatherit with oppressioun,
> Quhen the angell blawis his bugill sture,
> Quhilk vnrestorit helpis no confessioun?[38]

Langland, too, dwells on the subject more than once in *Piers Plowman*, notably in the speech of Repentance to Covetise in Passus V:

> Thow art an vnkynde creature, I can þe nouȝte assoille,
> Til þow make restitucioun and rekne with hem alle,
> And sithen þat resoun rolle it in þe regystre of heuene,
> That þow hast made vche man good, I may þe nouȝte assoille;
> *Non dimittitur peccatum donec restituatur ablatum, etc.*
> For alle þat haue of þi good, haue god my trouthe!
> Ben holden at þe heighe dome to helpe þe to restitue.
> And who so leueth nouȝte þis be soth, loke in þe sauter glose,
> In *miserere mei deus*, where I mene treuthe,
> *Ecce enim veritatem dilexisti, etc.*[39]

[38] 'Quhome to Sall I Complene My Wo?' (No. XXI in the Scottish Text Society edition of Dunbar's works), ll. 61–64. 'Quhilk vnrestorit' is an absolute expression, referring to the 'wrang possessioun' and the 'gold': 'If ill-gotten goods are not restored, confession gives no protection'. 'Restore' has its technical sense: see note 41, below.

[39] B. V. 276–83. Compare V. 472–8 and XX. 287–91. The biblical text is *Psalms* 51. 6.

I have quoted this at length for its association of restitution with judgment and 'truth'. The God of Judgment ('at þe heighe dome') loves truth, or 'veritas'; and to be judged 'true', a man must make restitution. The same set of ideas reappears later, in the speech of Conscience to the dreamer in Passus XIX. Christ, says Conscience,

> wil come atte laste
> And rewarde hym riȝte wel þat *reddit quod debet*—
> Payeth parfitly as pure trewthe wolde.
> And what persone payeth it nouȝt, punysshen he þinketh,
> And demen hem at domes daye, bothe quikke & ded.[40]

Restitution, judgment, truth—when we see the ideas linked together in this way, we should find it easier to understand why the *Gawain*-poet introduced the rather technical matter of restitution into his truth-test romance. We should also see new significance in the moral which Bercilak draws for Gawain from the outcome of the test: 'Trwe mon trwe restore, / Þenne þar mon drede no waþe'. The immediate reference is to the danger of the Green Knight's axe (compare the use of 'waþe' in l. 488); but the generalization makes the axe no more than a typical case—typical of the dangers attending any failure to 'restore'. 'Restore' is the usual word in Middle English for 'to make restitution' (as in the passage from Dunbar),[41] and it therefore is reasonable to suppose that a medieval audience would be reminded of preachers' warnings about the consequences of 'wrong possession' on the Last Day—the danger of God's wrath. Here again, then, I would see an analogy between Bercilak's judgment and God's.

My third and last point in this connection concerns the shame ('schome', 'greme', 'gref') which Gawain suffers when his

---

[40] B. XIX. 187–91. Langland's 'redde quod debes' includes the idea of restitution, though it is not confined to that. See Frank, *'Piers Plowman' and the Scheme of Salvation*, pp. 106–9.

[41] Here is one very clear example: 'Restore also with-owte anny dilacion þe goodes þat þou oweyst oþur holdes aȝeyns conciens. For leue me who-so listes, I shall sey pleynly þe trowthe, with-owten restitucion iff it be in þi poure to restore, þou shalt not be forȝeven,' *Middle English Sermons*, ed. Ross, pp. 283–4.

secret untruth is publicly spoken of. The idea of the Last Day as a day of secret things made manifest is of course a commonplace; and so too is the idea that the manifesting of such secrets (sins not blotted out by penance) will cause great shame to sinners. In the words of Chaucer's Parson: 'Men sholden eek remembren hem of the shame that is to come at the day of doom to hem that been nat penitent and shryven in this present lyf. For alle the creatures in hevene, in erthe, and in helle shullen seen apertly al that they hyden in this world.'[42] The analogy with the end of *Sir Gawain* is clear enough—the hero's hidden and unshriven sin made manifest, to his shame, in the belt and the wound, first before Bercilak and later before the court of Arthur. 'Non may hyden his harme'. So far as the return to court is concerned, it may be noted here that John Mirk, in his sermon for Advent, has an interesting comparison between a man at the Judgment and a knight returning wounded from an expedition: 'For ryght as a knyght scheweth þe wondys þat he haþe yn batayle, yn moche comendyng to hym; ryght so all þe synnys þat a man hath schryuen hym of, and taken hys penans for, schull be þer yschewet yn moch honowre to hym, and moche confucyon to þe fende. And þose þat haue not schryuen hom, hit schall be schowet to all þe world yn gret confusyon and schenschyp'.[43]

Before going on to consider Gawain's return to Camelot, however, I should like to look a little more closely at the nature of his 'confusyon and schenschyp' in the present scene. For a rather tricky problem has been raised here. Are Gawain's reactions—his shame, remorse, anger—exemplary, like Bercilak's? Or are they—to some degree, at least—extravagant and overwrought?

The case for accepting Gawain's behaviour without reservation has a strong foundation in traditional moral thinking. Men

[42] *C.T.*, X, 1063–4.
[43] *Festial*, ed. Erbe, p. 2. A true confession is, as one authority puts it, 'confusionis prohibitiva'. 'The trouthe is schameles ate ende', according to a 'proverb' quoted by John Gower, 'Bot what thing that is troutheles / It mai noght wel be schameles' (*Confessio Amantis*, VII, 1964–6). This special connection between shame and untruth is well illustrated in Gawain's case.

may legitimately hope as well as fear, when their judge is merciful as well as just; but everyone agrees that it is a particularly dangerous thing for sinners to be *lenient* with themselves. Despair is a sin, but so is presumption. Forgiveness and absolution belong to confessors and Gods, and it is not for sinners to usurp their privilege—not until after a decent interval, at least. People, in fact, should not be too ready to forgive themselves—least of all *heroes*. These feelings are so strong that most readers are prepared to accept a considerable degree of 'exaggeration' in the first responses of a penitent person: indeed, where a hero of epic, romance or tragedy is concerned, we may even be said to *demand* such exaggeration. Hence, in the present case, we may recognize a degree of extravagance in Gawain's assessment of his failure, and still feel that he is reacting just as he should—grandly. As Bercilak is right to temper justice with mercy, so Gawain is right not to. The behaviour of each is exemplary, because each fulfils the demands of his particular role—a matter, again, of 'decorum'.

This account of the matter seems to me basically right; but it cannot be left without some qualification. I would say that the poet does want us to feel that his hero is now on the right road, but not that he has reached the end of it. There is, after all, more of the poem yet to come. Gawain's wound, literally and metaphorically, is still open and bleeding, and the remorse which makes him shrink and flush is like a pain. The poet allows us to see not only contrition here, but also mortification and revulsion and wounded pride. Consider, for example, this passage from Gawain's last speech to Bercilak:

'Bot your gordel' quoþ Gawayn 'God yow forȝelde!
Þat wyl I welde wyth good wylle, not for þe wynne golde,
Ne þe saynt, ne þe sylk, ne þe syde pendaundes,
For wele ne for worchyp, ne for þe wlonk werkkeȝ,
Bot in syngne of my surfet I schal se hit ofte,
When I ride in renoun, remorde to myseluen
Þe faut and þe fayntyse of þe flesche crabbed,
How tender hit is to entyse teches of fylþe.' (2429–36)

The general tone and tenor of the passage are unexceptionable. Gawain is already somewhat calmer and more controlled than he was, and his acceptance of the girdle as a 'syngne of surfet' is no extravagant gesture. Yet the defensive opening is a little strained, and so, surely, are the references to the 'filth' of the 'flesh':

> Þe faut and þe fayntyse of þe flesche crabbed,
> How tender hit is to entyse teches of fylþe.

In Middle as in Modern English the word 'flesh' could be used in the Pauline sense, with reference to man's fallen nature, the source of all sin. In this sense it was contrasted with 'spirit'. More commonly, though, the Flesh was contrasted with the World and the Devil, as the source of a particular kind of sin— the 'sins of the flesh', sloth, gluttony and above all lechery. Similarly, 'filth' could in Middle English refer to any kind of sinfulness; but it more usually referred to bodily, particularly sexual, sin.[44] What is more, when the words were combined (as they often were) in the phrase 'filth of the flesh', the reference was always, so far as I know, to bodily sin—as in this striking passage from *Cursor Mundi*, where the author is moralizing on Solomon's sinful loves:

> Bot hard it es, þe wird o sin
> Þat yarked was til Adam kin!
> Þe sorful wark him ane he wroght,
> Þat all his sede wit sorou soght,
> Man for to fall in filth o fless
> Thoru forme kind þat es sa nesse.
> Ouerpassed has þat caitiue kind
> And mad King Salamon al blind.[45]

Observations phrased like this seem more appropriate to Solomon's case than to Gawain's. Gawain's sin does indeed, like all other sins, arise out of his fallen nature, his 'flesh' in the

---

[44] 'Filth' refers particularly to sexual impurity in *SGGK*, l. 1013, and in *Cleanness*, ll. 251 and 574. But the three uses at the beginning of *Cleanness* (ll. 6, 14, 31) seem more general.

[45] *Cursor Mundi* (Cotton Ms.), ed. cit., ll. 8981–8 (compare 'nesse' with the *Gawain*-poet's 'tender'). See also *Cleanness*, ll. 202 and 547 (referring to the vices of the 'sons of God'). Cf. 'sordes carnis' in the Vulgate, *I Peter* 3. 21.

Pauline sense; and it does, as a sin of passion or infirmity, illustrate specifically the weakness or 'tenderness' of that nature (as distinct from its ignorance or malice, that is). But it is not a 'sin of the flesh' in the ordinary sense, medieval or modern, for Gawain has not—conspicuously not—failed in cleanness. So the language which he uses, even though it is technically justifiable, can hardly fail to seem a little inappropriate; and its peculiar sensual timbre ('flesche . . . tender . . . entyse . . . teches . . . fylþe') creates an effect of emotional disturbance, as of barely-controlled revulsion. I find it impossible to read aloud l. 2436, in particular, without feeling something of this.

These considerations have some bearing on the rather more substantial critical problem presented by Gawain's attack on women earlier in the same speech (ll. 2414–28). It has more than once been pointed out that the theme of this passage, the wiles of women, is commonplace, and that the list of Old Testament examples (Adam, Solomon, Sampson, David) is traditional.[46] But why does the poet draw on just these conventional elements (which do not, after all, belong properly to the tradition of romance) at just this point? One must recall, first, that he is involved in a fictional demonstration of the possibilities and limits of human goodness. This in itself lends point to the catalogue of humbled heroes—Adam the perfect man, Solomon the wise, Sampson the strong, David the holy. The moral is that of Chaucer's Parson: 'Ful ofte tyme I rede that no man truste in his owene perfeccioun, but he be stronger than Sampson, and hoolier than David, and wiser than Salomon'.[47] It is particularly noteworthy that Solomon, who has previously figured as patron of the pentangle, emblem of Gawain's perfect truth, should reappear here, after the hero's failure, as an example of the im-

[46] See R. W. King, 'A Note on *SGGK*, 2414 ff.', *M.L.R.*, XXIX (1934), pp. 435–6; and A. C. Friend, 'Sampson, David, and Salomon in the *Parson's Tale*', *M.P.*, XLVI (1948–9), pp. 117–21. Two further examples, from the Vulgate romances, may be mentioned here: *Queste del Saint Graal*, ed. A. Pauphilet (Paris, 1949), p. 125, and *Mort le Roi Artu*, ed. cit., p. 70.

[47] *C.T.*, X, 1955. Quoted in this connection by R. H. Green, 'Gawain's Shield and the Quest for Perfection', *E.L.H.*, XXIX (1962), p. 131. The author's discussion of Solomon (130 f.) is especially valuable.

perfection of fallen man—a doctrine with which he was particularly associated in the Middle Ages, both as type and as teacher:

> Salamon to vs seyþ and kalleþ
> 'Seuene tymes on a day þe ryȝtwys man falleþ'.[48]

However, Gawain refers to Solomon and the rest not as famous sinners but as great men beguiled by women; and it is here that the difficulty arises. For it is not clear that the Old Testament examples, so considered, provide him with quite the parallel—or the excuse—that he claims to find in them. It is true that he was, as he now knows, deceived by the two ladies of the castle (though he does not yet know of the older lady's leading role); but he was also deceived by Bercilak, towards whom, strikingly enough, he shows no hostility at all. What is more, he did not 'use' Bercilak's wife (see l. 2426): his was not, as we have seen, a sin of the flesh in the ordinary Middle English sense. If his adventure proves of women that one should 'luf hom wel, and leue hem not', then surely it proves the same of men too. Once more, what was said appropriately of Solomon in *Cursor Mundi* is said inappropriately of Gawain here:

> Now Salamon I red of here,
> Þat neuer had o wisdom pere,
> Sin womman has þir suiken sua,
> Qua mai o þam be seker? qua? . . .
> Blisced, I sai, for-þi es he
> Þat dos him noght in hir pouste.[49]

There are two critical possibilities here, both of them interesting. Either the poet was driven slightly off course by the prevailing wind of medieval anti-feminism; or, as I prefer to think, he was making some allowance, here as in the next stanza, for the immediate impact of Gawain's discoveries on his equanimity and judgment. The impression of a man struggling to control himself is very strong in lines such as the following:

[48] *Handlyng Synne*, ed. cit., ll. 11405–6. The reference is to *Proverbs* 24. 16.

[49] *Cursor Mundi*, ed. cit., ll. 9007–10 and 9015–16. The passage immediately follows references to Adam, Sampson and David (9001–6).

comaundeӡ me to þat cortays, your comlych fere,
Boþe þat on and þat oþer, myn honoured ladyeӡ,
Þat þus hor knyӡt wyth hor kest han koyntly bigyled.
Bot hit is no ferly þaӡ a fole madde,
And þurӡ wyles of wymmen be wonen to sorӡe. (2411–15)

There is a sense of passionate revulsion in these lines which
—whether we like to assign it dramatically to the hero, bio-
graphically to the poet, or historically to the Middle Ages itself
—represents a departure from the true course of the poem. For
Sir Gawain is concerned with women's wiles no more than it is
with chastity: each has a place, but a very subordinate one.

By the end of the encounter scene Gawain has taken the decisive steps in his spiritual restoration: he has faced up to his
fault, and made his peace, by penitence and restitution, with
the Green Knight. But for him, as for Spenser's perjured hero
in Book I of the *Faerie Queene*, the 'disease of grieued conscience' is not easily cured. His condition when he parts from
Bercilak is comparable to that of the Red Cross·Knight when he
first enters the House of Holiness and hears the teaching of
Fidelia and Speranza:

> The faithfull knight now grew in litle space,
> By hearing her, and by her sisters lore,
> To such perfection of all heauenly grace,
> That wretched world he gan for to abhore,
> And mortall life gan loath, as thing forlore,
> Greeu'd with remembrance of his wicked wayes,
> And prickt with anguish of his sinnes so sore,
> That he desirde to end his wretched dayes:
> So much the dart of sinfull guilt the soule dismayes. (I, x, 21)

This condition is good, but it is not (despite echoes from the
end of Chaucer's *Troilus*) final. The 'loathing' and the 'anguish'
are indeed *morbid* symptoms which disappear when, through
the ministrations of Patience and Repentance, the hero's conscience is finally 'cured':

> Whom thus recouer'd by wise Patience,
> And trew Repentance, they to Vna brought:
> Who ioyous of his cured conscience,

Him dearely kist, and fairely eke besought
Himselfe to chearish, and consuming thought
To put away out of his carefull brest. (I, x, 29)

It will be obvious that Bercilak, though he offers Gawain comfort and hope, never brings him to the point of 'putting away
consuming thought'.

III

The last two stanzas of *Sir Gawain* are among its finest things.
It would not be easy to find better examples of the poet's characteristic creative power—his ability to draw out latent significances from the conventional world of romance, without
violating its fictional integrity or allowing a too palpable moral
design to intrude upon it. Gawain returns to Camelot, tells the
story of his adventures, and takes his place once more among
the brotherhood of Arthur's knights. It is all solidly natural and
orthodox. There are no wild symbolic inventions such as the
voyage of the Grail heroes to Sarras at the end of the *Queste del
Saint Graal*. Yet the action, even in some of its most matter-of-
fact details, is as richly significant, in its own way, as anything
in the *Queste*.

Consider the healing of Gawain's wound:

Ofte he herbered in house, and ofte al þeroute,
And mony aventure in vale, and venquyst ofte,
Þat I ne tyȝt at þis tyme in tale to remene.
Þe hurt watȝ hole þat he hade hent in his nek. (2481-4)

The journey home is a long one, and it is perfectly natural that
Gawain's flesh-wound should heal before he gets back to
Camelot. There is no question of a magical healing such as
Perceval enjoys in the *Queste* when the wound that he has in-
flicted upon himself in remorse heals up in the presence of a
supernatural counsellor.[50] Yet Gawain's wound is, like Perceval's, symbolic satisfaction for a sin; and the healing of it has,
though much more discreetly, a like symbolic value. What is
involved in both cases is the commonplace medieval idea that

[50] *Queste del Saint Graal*, ed. cit., p. 115,

after true penance sin 'heals up' like a healthy wound: 'Diex en est poissans; car si tost com uns hom vient a veraie confession, ia tant n'iert cargiés de viel pechié que diex nel regart; & si tost com il l'aura regardé ia puis ni covendra autre mire ne autre medicine ne lier autre emplastre; ains est la plaie saine & nete si tost com il l'a regardée'.[51] Langland has this same image in his discussion of penance in Passus XIV of *Piers Plowman*:

> Ac satisfaccioun seketh oute þe rote and bothe sleeth and voideth,
> And as it neuere had ybe to nouȝt bryngeth dedly synne,
> Þat it neuere eft is seen ne sore, but semeth a wounde yheled.[52]

So when Gawain arrives at Camelot 'al in sounde', with no more than a scar (a 'nirt in þe nek') on his body, it is a sign that he has survived his adventure spiritually as well as physically. The symbolism is elegant, unobtrusive and eminently natural.

Much the same may be said of the symbolism of the belt, though this is rather more explicit:

> Þe hurt watȝ hole þat he hade hent in his nek,
> And þe blykkande belt he bere þeraboute
> Abelef as a bauderyk bounden bi his syde,
> Loken vnder his lyfte arme, þe lace, with a knot,
> In tokenyng he watȝ tane in tech of a faute. (2484-8)

'Tokens' carried or worn about the person are among the stock-in-trade of medieval romancers. These tokens—ranging from a lady's sleeve to a bloody shirt—have a variety of possible functions; but often, as here, they are connected in some way

---

[51] 'In this God is all-powerful; for as soon as a man comes to true confession, he shall never be so laden with long-standing sin but God will look favourably upon him; and as soon as he has looked upon him there is no need for any other doctor or medicine or binding of plaster; for the wound is healthy and clean as soon as he has looked at it.' *Vulgate Romances*, ed. Sommer, Vol. III, pp. 221-2.

[52] B. XIV. 94-96. According to the *Cursor Mundi*, clean-shriven sins will cause no more shame in heaven 'Þan if þou cummen o batel ware / Wit wondes þat þou þar had tan, / And þou war heleid o þam ilkan' (ed. cit., ll. 23502-4). Compare the passage from Mirk's *Festial* quoted above; and see No. 178 in Carleton Brown's *Religious Lyrics of the XVth Century* (Oxford, 1939), especially the last verse.

with a sin of the wearer. Such 'signs of penitence' may, in more didactic romances, conform to actual penitential practice: the knight may, that is, wear one of the 'arms of shrift' sanctioned by the contemporary church—most commonly a hair-shirt. Or he may wear some quite eccentric article, as the story dictates, such as the severed head which Malory's Gawain carries back to Camelot hung about his neck or the enchanted serpent wrapped round Carados' arm in the *Perceval* Continuation. In either case one may make a further distinction. Either the token is worn strictly as a *penance*—as a physical trial or mortification to the wearer; or it is worn as a *reminder*, something which will force the wearer to think on his past misdeeds. These two functions are obviously not mutually exclusive, but the distinction is worth making. Gawain's green belt is clearly, in a general way, a 'sign of penitence'; but it is not, like the wound, strictly a penance for his sin. The Green Knight inflicts the wound as a 'penaunce apert', but he offers the belt simply as a reminder:

> And I gif þe, sir, þe gurdel þat is golde-hemmed;
> For hit is grene as my goune, Sir Gawayn, ȝe maye
> Þenk vpon þis ilke þrepe, þer þou forth þryngeȝ
> Among prynces of prys, and þis a pure token
> Of þe chaunce of þe grene chapel at cheualrous knyȝteȝ. (2395–9)

It is in this spirit that Gawain accepts and adopts the gift, too— not as a penance but as a 'syngne of my surfet' which will remind him in after days of 'þe faut and þe fayntyse of þe flesche crabbed'. The belt bears little resemblance to any of the accepted medieval 'arms of shrift' (though there is some suggestion of the penitential halter about it),[53] but it is well adapted to serve as a reminder of the Adventure of the Green Chapel, both because it played a crucial part in the adventure and because its

[53] Compare the paraphrase of *Nahum* 3. 5–6 in the *Ancrene Riwle*, trans. Salu, p. 143: 'You would not uncover yourself to the priest in Confession, but I will show your iniquity all naked before all nations and your shameful sins to all kingdoms . . . and I will tie all your shamefulness about your own neck as is done to the thief when he is taken to be judged, and thus with all that shame you shall go forth'.

colours, green and gold, are those of Gawain's adversary ('hit is grene as my goune').

This distinction between the significance of the wound and that of the belt is of some importance in grasping the 'symbolic action' of the last part of the poem. By the time Gawain has reached Camelot his wound is healed, but the belt is still on his back. His penance (the wound) is done and his sin (the wound again, symbolically) is atoned for and forgiven; but the memory of it (the belt) is still with him—indeed it will be with him for the rest of his life: 'I mot nedeȝ hit were wyle I may last'. Obviously the poet did not want this ever-after ending formula to suggest that his hero was to die in a state of mortal sin.

By the time Gawain reaches Camelot, then, he has atoned for his sin, but he still carries the burden of memory and knowledge which his adventure has imposed upon him. The rest of the poem is devoted to coming to terms with this burden— with the memory of Gawain's failure and the fresh realization of the sinfulness of man which that failure provokes. The poet's method here is the same as in the encounter scene—the juxtaposing of two contrasted points of view. In the encounter scene the hero faced his adversary; in the present scene he is turned towards the other point of the poem's basic triangle, the court. Having come to terms with his judge, he now must come to terms with his companions. That the poet should think this right and proper as the last stage of the adventure is in itself a significant thing. His poem is a comedy; and this means, among other things, that it ends with the reincorporation of the hero into his society. There is no question here either of a tragic death or of a mysterious departure to unknown lands; nor is the return to court in any way—as it is in the romances of the Grail-quest—a confession of failure. The poet follows, in fact, the old orthodox conception of an Arthurian adventure as a closed circuit which begins and ends at Camelot. In romances of this sort, the court at Camelot provides the hero with a peer-group which he respects and to which he is content to belong. Hence, in the words of a critic of Chrétien de Troyes, 'l'importance capital qu'il faut attribuer aux rentrées du héros à cette court, de la répercussion que les exploits du héros ont dans l'opinion de la société'.[54] Let us look first at the conduct of the returned hero, and then at its 'repercussions' in the court.

It is one of the most familiar conventions of Arthurian romance that the hero of the hour should make a report on his adventures when he gets back to Camelot. The *Gawain*-poet adapts this convention to his purposes by treating Gawain's report as a kind of public confession of guilt:

> Þe kyng kysseȝ þe knyȝt, and þe whene alce,
> And syþen mony syker knyȝt þat soȝt hym to haylce,
> Of his fare þat hym frayned; and ferlyly he telles,
> Biknoweȝ alle þe costes of care þat he hade. . . . (2492–5)

The romantic lay and the moral tale are nicely balanced here. 'Ferlyly he telles' suggests a story of wonders ('ferlies'); 'biknoweȝ', as we have seen, suggests a confession; and 'costes of care' is ambiguous—it could mean 'hardships', as Tolkien and Gordon suggest, or it could mean 'sinful ways'.[55] Gawain's report is, in fact, both a story of wonders *and* a confession. He tells first how he survived the return blow ('Þe chaunce of þe chapel'); then how the knight entertained him over Christmas ('þe chere of þe knyȝt') and how the lady made love to him; and finally ('at þe last') how he came to accept the belt and so receive the neck-wound. The order of the report, in the poet's summary, is worth noticing. The fact that Gawain leaves the matter of the belt until the end, contrary to the natural order of his story, may suggest either an understandable reluctance to mention it (in which case 'at þe last' is faintly comic) or a determination to make it as prominent as possible. The poet seems to encourage the more favourable view. Gawain *is* reluctant, of course; but he is as ready to face up to his fault at Camelot as he was at the Green Chapel:

---

[54] R. R. Bezzola, *Le Sens de l'Aventure et de l'Amour* (Paris 1947).

[55] Compare the lines in *Cursor Mundi* describing David's reaction to Nathan's judgment on his sins: 'Quen Dauid knew his cost of care / Him rewed neuer þing sa sare' (ed. cit., ll. 7963–4). For 'costes' meaning sins confessed to a priest, see the same poem, ll. 25748 and 26093.

He tened quen he schulde telle,
He groned for gref and grame;
Þe blod in his face con melle,
When he hit schulde schewe, for schame. (2501-4)

The sequence in the last three lines of this wheel—groaning in grief and mortification, blushing, shame—recalls, line for line, the poet's account of Gawain's first reactions to Bercilak's judgment:

So *agreued* for *greme* he *gryed* withinne;
Alle þe *blode* of his brest *blende in his face*,
Þat al he schrank for *schome* þat þe schalk talked. (2370-2)

In this way Gawain's public confession at Camelot is linked with his private confession at the Green Chapel. His awareness of his guilt has not yet lost its bitterness and intensity. A similar link is to be observed in Gawain's last speech, at the beginning of the next stanza. Here the poet—with a characteristic overlapping between two stanzas—gives us the last part of Gawain's report, which he has already summarized *in toto*, over again in direct speech. But whereas the poet, like Bercilak, speaks in his summary only of the hero's 'vnleuté' or untruth, he allows Gawain, in the direct speech, to reiterate his characteristic three-term account of the case:

Þis is þe laþe and þe losse þat I laȝt haue
Of *couardise* and *couetyse* þat I haf caȝt þare;
Þis is þe token of *vntrawþe* þat I am tan inne. (2507-9)

It is clear from all this that there is no question of the hero 'putting away consuming thought' the moment he sets foot in Camelot. We do not see him, in Spenser's phrase, 'cherish himself'—not even in the very last words which he speaks in the poem:

Þis is þe token of vntrawþe þat I am tan inne,
And I mot nedeȝ hit were wyle I may last;
For non may hyden his harme bot vnhap ne may hit,
For þer hit oneȝ is tachched twynne wil hit neuer. (2509-12)

It is vexing that this final, and presumably significant, *sententia* of Gawain's should be so obscure and controversial. I would translate it as follows: 'No-one can conceal his guilt without misfortune betiding; for where it once gets a hold it will never let go'. The alliterative phrase 'hide one's harm' is recorded in the Middle English *Romance of the Rose* (l. 2395) in the sense 'conceal one's affliction', but this hardly suits the context here. The poet seems to be using 'harm' in another, fairly common, Middle English sense—'guilt' or 'sin'.[56] He may, in fact, have composed the whole line with the first part of *Proverbs* 28. 13 in mind, in which case 'harm' would correspond to the Latin 'scelera': 'Qui abscondit scelera sua non dirigetur; qui autem confessus fuerit et reliquerit ea, misericordiam consequetur'— 'He that covereth his sins shall not prosper: but whoso confesseth and forsaketh them shall have mercy'.[57] This parallel suggests that Gawain is referring in l. 2511 to the guilty act which, having been concealed or 'covered' at Hautdesert, led to his present humiliation or 'vnhap'. The experience has taught him not to cover things up (least of all belts) in future. But what about the following line? This cannot mean that a sinful act, once concealed, becomes inexpiable. That would be bad theology, and anyway it would be quite untrue to the author's view of Gawain's case at the end of the poem. I think that there is a real muddle here. When Gawain talks about 'harm' in this passage he is thinking, among other things, about the belt—explaining why he has to wear it for the rest of his life. Now the belt, as we have seen, clearly stands at the end of the poem for the memory of his sin. It is this memory which will 'never let go' of the hero while he lives, surely; and it is this which constitutes his 'vnhap'. So the 'harm' of l. 2512 (the attached belt) is not really the same as the 'harm' of l. 2511 (the hidden belt): one is the memory of sin, the other is the sin itself.

[56] Not recorded in the *O.E.D.*, but well attested in the poems of the Cotton Nero Manuscript. In *Pearl*, ll. 676 and 725, 'harmleȝ' means innocent or sinless; and 'Dame Penance', the third Beatitude, is rendered 'Thay ar happen also þat for her harme wepes' in *Patience*, l. 17.

[57] This text, naturally enough, was quoted by writers on Confession. See Gregory's *Moralia*, Book VIII, Chap. XX (Migne, *P.L.*, Vol. 75, col. 822), and Bromyard's *Summa Praedicantium* (Venice, 1586), Chap. VI ('Confessio').

This rather obscure shift of meaning may be taken as a sign of the author's unwillingness to press his theological point home. In strictly theological terms, Gawain is still in a state of sin at the end of the poem—for he has made no sacramental atonement. However, although the poet is, as I have tried to show, genuinely concerned with the right use of the sacrament of penance and genuinely aware that 'he that covereth his sins shall not prosper', his imagination—like that of most decent men in his time, Langland for example—is wedded to the second part of the text: 'but whoso confesseth and forsaketh them shall have mercy'.

To get a clearer view of this prevailing 'comic mercy' (if the analogy of 'tragic justice' warrants that phrase), we must look, finally, at the behaviour and attitudes of the court. There are two passages to notice here, of which the first and less important concerns the reception of the hero:

> Þer wakned wele in þat wone when wyst þe grete
> Þat gode Gawayn watȝ commen, gayn hit hym poȝt.
> Þe kyng kysseȝ þe knyȝt, and þe whene alce,
> And syþen mony syker knyȝt þat soȝt hym to haylce. (2490-3)

This passage contains the last of the poet's many references to the hero's name; and it is worth noticing that the precise form of the reference—'gode Gawayn'—is matched only once elsewhere, and then in the poet's very first reference to the hero:

> There gode Gawan watȝ grayþed Gwenore bisyde.[58] (109)

The poet's love of these circular effects is well known. He liked beginning and ending a poem with the same line (*Pearl*, *Patience* and, in effect, *Sir Gawain* itself); and in *Patience*, ll. 37-38, he links the last of the Beatitudes with the first:

> For in þe tyxte þere þyse two arn in teme layde,
> Hit arn fettled in on forme, þe forme and þe laste.

The poet probably regarded this 'fettling' as a peculiar privilege of the artist (for in life 'þe forme to þe fynisment foldeȝ ful

[58] The hero is called 'Gawayn þe gode' in ll. 1110 and 1926, and 'Gawayn þe god mon' in l. 1179; but this is not quite the same thing.

selden'); but he did not practise it for its decorative effect only.
The expression 'good Gawain' has a familiar, affectionate ring;
so it is appropriate that it should be used only when the hero is
among his 'cort-fereȝ'—as if it represented their way of talking
about him. Hence the effect as of reported speech in the present
lines:

> when wyst þe grete
> Þat gode Gawayn watȝ commen, gayn hit hym poȝt.

Gawain is reassuming his everyday social identity. Just as
the Knight of the Green Chapel is normally Sir Bercilak de
Hautdesert, so the hero is normally good Sir Gawain of Camelot—the Gawain of the first fitt.

The second passage about the court concerns their reactions
to Gawain's report, or confession. This passage—the last part
of the poem before the Brutus epilogue—must be quoted in
full:

> Þe kyng comforteȝ þe knyȝt, and alle þe court als
> Laȝen loude þerat, and luflyly acorden
> Þat lordes and ladis þat longed to þe Table,
> Vche burne of þe broþerhede, a bauderyk schulde haue,
> A bende abelef hym aboute of a bryȝt grene,
> And þat, for sake of þat segge, in swete to were.
> For þat watȝ acorded þe renoun of þe Rounde Table,
> And he honoured þat hit hade euermore after,
> As hit is breued in þe best boke of romaunce. (2513–21)

There is a similarity between the behaviour of the court here
and that of Bercilak in the encounter scene: both in their
different ways 'comfort' the hero. And this similarity is pointed,
as so often, by a verbal parallel. When Gawain has finished his
confession at the Green Chapel, the Green Knight laughs before replying:

> Thenn loȝe þat oþer leude and luflyly sayde. . . . (2389)

So here, after Gawain's renewed confession:

> Þe kyng comforteȝ þe knyȝt, and alle þe court als
> Laȝen loude þerat, and luflyly acorden. . . .

Both adversary and companions 'laugh', and both, in the second half-line, respond 'luflyly' to the hero's self-reproaches. The poet uses 'lufly' (one of his favourite words) in a double sense here: it has both an active sense ('loving' or 'affectionate') and a passive one '(lovable' or 'admirable', so 'graceful', 'courteous'). The responses of Bercilak and the court both express their love and admiration for the hero ('oure luflych lede', as the poet called him) and reflect their own grace and courtesy. It is quite wrong, I think, to suppose that either is being crass or unperceptive.[59] It is true that the court, unlike Bercilak, makes no comment on Gawain's act of untruth; but then it is not for them to do so. The court is involved in the case neither as injured party nor as judge: there is plainly no call for them to pour 'biting wine' into the wound. Their part is, like Spenser's Una, to 'rejoice' and to 'cherish' the returned knight.

The court's adoption of Gawain's belt can in part be understood in a similar fashion. Unlike the pentangle, the belt is not, so far as the poem is concerned, a 'natural' symbol.[60] It does not, that is, have any particular symbolic value on the strength simply of its intrinsic natural properties. So while the pentangle is necessarily a token of 'trawþe' and could not possibly, in the poet's view, be otherwise, the belt is a token of untruth only because it happened to play the part it did in Gawain's adventure—and is therefore, like all non-natural signs, open *ad placitum* to any other significance that people might choose to ascribe to it. This is why it makes sense for the court simply to agree ('acorden' . . . 'acorded') to adopt the belt not as a shameful 'token of vntrawþe' but as an honourable emblem of the 'renoun of þe Rounde Table'. The new meaning is just as legitimate as the old; and the communal action serves to give permanent symbolic expression to the court's feelings on the occasion—like stamping a medal or renaming a street. However, the new meaning does not in this case entirely supersede the old; and the poem's final tableau—all the lords and ladies of the Round Table wearing their green baldrics 'for sake of þat

[59] For a moderate version of this view, see R. H. Green, art. cit., pp. 138–9.
[60] See Appendix One.

segge'—has a distinctly ambiguous effect. Clearly the Green Knight has not succeeded in his attempt to overthrow 'þe reuel and þe renoun of þe Rounde Table'; yet by breaking down Gawain's 'truth' he has demonstrated that no-one, not even a knight of Arthur's court, can justly claim the pentangle as his emblem. The adventure has, in fact, established a strong *a fortiori* proof of the old doctrine of original sin; for 'if gold rust, what shall iron do?' It is this doctrine, I think, which lies behind the poet's presentation of his last, ambiguous tableau. The knights and ladies share the baldric with Gawain as a sign both of their corporate renown and of their common humanity.

V

CONCLUSION

I

Sir Gawain is a poem about a test, or rather a series of tests. One could say that every story inevitably tests its hero in some sense—brings out some quality in him or at least requires him to exercise some mental or physical faculty. But this is obviously not what we mean by a 'test'. A test-story must have an air of calculation about it. We must feel that the hero is subjected to difficulties *contrived* in such a way as to try him out. In a test-story proper, this contriving is ascribed to some character within the story itself—whom we may call, according to his motives, either 'tester' or 'adversary'. Bercilak in *Sir Gawain*, Walter in the *Clerk's Tale*, the Duke in *Measure for Measure*, God in the story of the sacrifice of Isaac, all play this part. However, there are other stories of a rather similar sort which have no tester. Chaucer's *Franklin's Tale* is a familiar example. Certainly Dorigen is subjected to a contrived test in this poem; but it is not Aurelius, the technical 'adversary', who does the contriving. It is rather the author, whose chief purpose seems to be to demonstrate his heroine's peculiar virtues in the most striking way possible.

Medieval authors had a particular fondness for such tests and demonstrations. They liked to take an unusually noble and virtuous hero, and subject him to unusually severe strains. It was a kind of moral laboratory work, designed to establish the potentialities of human goodness. The result is often naïve and sophisticated at once. The author will take some traditional story, commonly of folk origin (a rash promise, a disguised

Conclusion

return or a fairy mistress), and work it up into an elaborate
test of loyalty, obedience or whatever, often obscuring the
motivation in the process. Chaucer's *Clerk's Tale* shows that
even the best medieval authors were ready to sacrifice some
credibility of behaviour in order to make the test really severe;
for the point of this kind of story is lost if the reader does not
feel that the hero has been subjected to something approaching
an ultimate test of the virtue for which he stands. I think that
the *Gawain*-poet would have accepted this. He certainly screws
his tests up as tight as he can make them.

There are two basic kinds of test-situation, both of which
have a place in *Sir Gawain*. The less problematical kind is that
in which some virtue comes into conflict with some deep but
fundamentally ignoble passion. Such a conflict—represented
in the *Gawain*-poet's outer, beheading test—is rather too simple
in itself; and medieval poets attempt to work it up in various
ways. They may make the issue more doubtful by weakening
the virtue's case somewhat and strengthening the passion's.
The *Gawain*-poet's folk-tale beheading test turned on a straight
conflict between fidelity to the pledged word and love of life,
like the classical story of Regulus and the Carthaginians. He
tightened it up by exploiting the traditional Christmas setting
of Arthurian adventure, allowing the pledge to partake of the
festive character of the season. Regulus swears a solemn oath
to the Carthaginians and it is plainly his duty to honour it;
but Gawain's oath to the Green Knight is not entirely solemn,
and this casts a shadow of doubt across his obligations. If he chose
to ignore them he would have some sort of a case: the affair was,
after all, no more than a Christmas game or 'cavelacioun'. The
poet does in fact allow something like this view to be voiced in
his poem, by the 'segges' of Arthur's court (ll. 674–83); but the
hero himself never entertains it for a moment—any more than
he entertains the cruder arguments of the guide in the last fitt.
There is a high-mindedness here that is typical of courtly test-
stories. The poet is aware of low arguments; but (except in one
crucial instance) he either ascribes them to unheroic people or
else leaves them out altogether, sometimes rather pointedly.

The more problematical kind of test-situation—represented

161

in the inner, exchange-of-winnings part of *Sir Gawain*—involves conflict between a virtue and some other virtue or virtuous passion. A well-known example is the Bible story of the sacrifice of Isaac, in which the tester (God) contrives to involve the hero in a conflict between obedience and love. The popular story of Griselda (as in the *Clerk's Tale*) involves a similar conflict, with Walter playing God's part. A less cruel example of the same sort is the *Franklin's Tale*, where fidelity to the pledged word conflicts with fidelity to husband. This kind of Cornelian situation is very common in Arthurian romance. *Perlesvaus*, to give just one example, has a story of how Gawain, having sworn to do whatever a damsel next tells him to do, is ordered on the morning of a tournament to disgrace himself by fighting like a coward.[1] Such a conflict between a knight's passion for honour and his fidelity to his sworn word appealed to the casuistical spirit of medieval Christian and courtly thinking alike. It posed a question or 'demande' for the reader to puzzle over.

The exchange-of-winnings part of *Sir Gawain* involves, in fact, both these two kinds of conflict, interwoven in such a way as to yield an unusually close and subtle moral texture. Gawain is indeed here subjected to one of the most complex and elaborately contrived test-situations in all medieval literature. Up to the moment when the lady offers him her magic girdle, the dominant issue is the 'problematical' conflict between two knightly virtues—*courtesy* which requires that he should respond to the lady's advances, and *truth* which requires that he should be loyal to the host:

> He cared for his cortaysye, lest craþayn he were,
> And more for his meschef, ȝif he schulde make synne
> And be traytor to þat tolke þat þat telde aȝt. (1773–5)

The conflict is particularly critical because the exchange agreement is, even more than the beheading agreement, easily mistaken for a mere Christmas game; and Gawain has no idea that he is being tested. He is led to think of the whole episode as little more than a diversion, thoughtfully provided by his host

---

[1] *Perlesvaus*, ed. cit., ll. 6836 ff.

to take his mind off a forthcoming test—part of the festive interlude between his two winter journeys. There is also, all the
time, the more straightforward conflict between virtue and
passion, 'cleanness' and sexual desire; but this is subordinated
to the conflict between truth and courtesy. The poet, that is,
makes us feel that Gawain is drawn towards the lady *primarily*
by his sense of what is due to her, and held back *primarily* by his
sense of what is due to her husband. The sexual issue is certainly there; but the poet is inclined to play it down in favour of
the nobler and more problematical conflict. However, in the
short but crucial passage following the offer of the girdle, these
priorities are reversed; for here it is a conflict between virtue
and passion which takes pride of place. The courtesy–truth conflict is still kept up (Gawain feels it would be churlish to go on
refusing the lady's offers); but it is love of life, not courtesy,
which leads at last to the crucial concession.

It is clear that the *Gawain*-poet devoted a large part of his
conscious attention to such matters. He conceives a superlatively virtuous hero, 'as golde pured, voyded of vche vylany,
wyth vertueȝ ennourned', and exercises all his ingenuity to subject that hero to a series of superlatively difficult tests—like
Chaucer's Walter, who 'tempts' Griselda 'to the outtreste preeve
of hir corage'. The situations are certainly contrived with great
ingenuity and executed with great skill and delicacy; but the
basic conception is so far quite naïve—a superlative hero, a
superlative test. Nor is this way of thinking confined to the basic
conception. It spills over into the fictional world of the poem.
Here almost everything is, like the hero and his predicaments,
superlative in its kind. The Green Knight is 'on þe most on þe
molde on mesure hyghe', the Green Chapel is 'þe corsedest
kyrk þat euer I com inne', the walls of Hautdesert are 'enbaned
vnder þe abataylment in þe best lawe', Gawain's 'vrisoun' is
'bounden wyth þe best gemmeȝ', the lady is 'þe fayrest . . . of
alle oþer', the boar is 'on þe sellokest swyn', and so on. This
constant stream of superlatives is, I suppose, characteristic of
romance; but it can hardly fail to weary the reader a little, even
where, as here, it has a kind of source in the poet's basic conception of his theme.

Conclusion

I have suggested that the extreme or superlative test-story is a kind of moral experiment designed to establish some truth about human nature; but this perhaps gives too flattering an impression of the case. The test-story resembles an experiment insofar as it is contrived, set up and controlled towards a particular end; but the end is not really experimental or, in critical language, 'exploratory'. The author is more like an instructor demonstrating something he himself already knows than an experimenter finding out something new. Chaucer does not allow Walter to devise his 'outtreste preeve' in order himself to explore what happens when a superlatively patient person is subjected to such treatment. The story is not so much an experiment in patience as a demonstration of it—an instructive and striking demonstration (as striking as possible) of what patience is and what it can stand.

Another way of putting this is to say that the conduct of the hero is never, in a conventional test-story, seriously in doubt. Such test-stories always end happily, at least in the sense that the hero's virtue is thoroughly vindicated. Regulus may be executed on his return to Carthage, but he has proved his surpassing truth. We expect such a man, in such a story, to conquer ignoble passions. This is the simpler kind of test-story, of course; but the outcome of the more problematical kind is just as predictable, if rather more complicated. What usually happens is this. The hero, caught in some impossible predicament where he cannot conceivably reconcile his various obligations, perseveres with the course of conduct dictated by whichever obligation the author regards as 'higher' (very often, in courtly literature, fidelity to the pledged word, for 'trouthe is the hyeste thyng that man may kepe', as Arveragus says). This demonstrates in a striking way his dedication to some important virtue. Then, when the demonstration is sufficient—often more than sufficient—to convince everyone concerned, the tester suddenly relents, releases the hero from his higher obligation and allows him to fulfil the lower. This moment of release is an important feature of many test-stories. The angel releases Abraham ('lay not thine hand upon the lad'), Aurelius releases Dorigen ('I yow relesse, madame'), the Damsel, on the last day of the tourna-

Conclusion

ment in *Perlesvaus*, releases Gawain ('I want you to be as good today as you have ever been'), Walter releases Griselda ('This is ynogh, Grisilde myn'). A more modern example is the moment under the giant horse-chestnut tree in *Jane Eyre* where Rochester, having tried Jane's love by pretending for many weeks that he means to marry Miss Ingram, reveals his true intentions—a 'moment of release' very like the one at the end of the *Clerk's Tale*.

The case of Rochester and Jane Eyre is valuable because it shows clearly how remote such test-stories are from the 'real' world of the modern novel. For even in the passionate and poetic world of Charlotte Brontë, the episode of Rochester's test seems out of place. Rochester is a dark, romantic, wilful man—but how can even he have subjected the woman he loves to such an ordeal? ('I wished to render you as madly in love with me as I was with you'!) Jane is a most resilient heroine—but how can even she have stood for it? ('You have a curious, designing mind, Mr. Rochester.') Despite all Charlotte Brontë can do, the behaviour of tester and heroine alike is implausible; and the whole episode remains in the mind as a piece of dream-work— one of the fantasies which the author spins round the person of her hero.

The truth is that such stories belong, essentially, to the fantasy-world of myth and folk-tale;[2] and they are truly at home only in those literary forms which are still close to myth and folk-tale—the 'exemplum', the saint's legend, the romance, etc. It is only here that the demonstration can proceed untroubled by questions of plausibility—Why does the tester behave like that? How can the hero behave like that? We do not question the motives of the Damsel in *Perlesvaus*, any more than we question God's in the story of Abraham and Isaac; and the French Gawain's obedience is just as plausible, in its own way, as Abraham's. But when high romance (courtly or hagiographic) begins to give ground before lower, more realistic forms of presentation, cracks appear in the façade, and the conduct of both

[2] For a survey of test motifs in folk-tale, see Stith Thompson, *Motif-Index of Folk-Literature*, Revised Ed. (Copenhagen, 1955–8), Section H.

tester and hero begins to present problems. The most instructive example of this is Chaucer's *Clerk's Tale*.

Chaucer was well aware of his tester problem (why did he do it?), and he makes several attempts to paper over that crack, without ever really hiding it. He acknowledges that Walter's behaviour is 'cruel' and 'wicked'; but he suggests, as he is bound to do, that it is not as inexplicable as it may seem. Such cases are not unknown, he says (l. 449): married men can never restrain themselves with a patient wife (ll. 622–3), lords are by nature wilful and obstinate (l. 581), and anyway there are always people who, like Walter, 'kan nat stynte of hire entencion' (l. 703). These observations hardly meet the case; and the tale would have broken down had not Chaucer been more successful with his other and more important problem—the problem of the heroine (how could she do it?). He obviously cannot entertain the idea that her behaviour was in any way wicked or unnatural; but once the tale is done he accommodates doubts about its plausibility by making two interesting concessions, the first borrowed from Petrarch:

> This storie is seyd, nat for that wyves sholde
> Folwen Grisilde as in humylitee,
> For it were inportable, though they wolde;
> But for that every wight, in his degree,
> Sholde be constant in adversitee
> As was Grisilde . . .
> For, sith a womman was so pacient
> Unto a mortal man, wel moore us oghte
> Receyven al in gree that God us sent.[3]

The third line here seems to mean both that women could not and that they should not tolerate behaviour such as Walter's. In ordinary human terms the story is unbearable as well as impossible; and it must therefore be understood in an allegorical, or better an *a fortiori*, fashion. It teaches us how to bear the adversities that *God* inflicts on us—and so is really no more difficult to accept than the Abraham and Isaac story.

[3] *C.T.*, IV, 1142–7, 1149–51.

Conclusion

Having reproduced this argument from Petrarch, Chaucer goes on to make a different concession of his own:

> But o word, lordynges, herkneth er I go:
> It were ful harde to fynde now-a-dayes
> In al a toun Grisildis thre or two;
> For if that they were put to swiche assayes,
> The gold of hem hath now so badde alayes
> With bras, that thogh the coyne be fair at ye,
> It wolde rather breste a-two than plye.[4]

These lines and those which follow have an ironic, dramatic point, of course—the Clerk is tilting at the Wife of Bath; but they also testify, I think, to Chaucer's sense that superlative test-stories are not quite at home, as they stand, in the lower, more realistic world of the Canterbury pilgrimage. Griselda's absolute patience is a thing of former ages (the 'whilom' of l. 64 of the Tale), not of 'now-a-dayes'. Griselda lived in an age of gold; we live in an age of brass. This is a gracious way of accommodating folk-tale material to the demands of a latter-day audience—more gracious than Petrarch's moralizing application to things divine. It obviously attracted Chaucer's follower Hoccleve, who, after telling the story of Regulus, concludes in the same vein:

> He held it bette his oth for to obserue
> And dye in honur, as þat a knyght oghte,
> Than by periurie his lif for to preserue;
> Of suche vnknyghtly trikkes he nat roghte.
> I trowe now-a-dayes, thogh men soghte,
> His heir ful hard were in þis lond to fynde;
> Men list not so ferforth to trouthe hem bynde.[5]

The example of Chaucer shows, I think, that by the later Middle Ages at least, intelligent and imaginative authors were no longer content to tell the old stories of superlative heroes and tests quite straight—or rather, perhaps, were no longer able to tell them quite straight. Such stories were still thought

---

[4] *C.T.*, IV, 1163–9.

[5] *The Regement of Princes*, ed. F. J. Furnivall, E.E.T.S. E.S. 72 (1897), ll. 2283–9. Cp. *Ywain and Gawain*, ed. A. B. Friedman and N. T. Harrington, E.E.T.S. 254 (1964), ll. 33–40.

fascinating and instructive; but they were not quite viable, as they stood, in the latter-day, or 'nowaday', world. Prevailing modes of literary presentation no longer favoured the extreme, exemplary case; and authors who were drawn to treat such cases at all seriously faced a challenge which was something more than just technical. Let me now consider briefly how the *Gawain*-poet met this challenge and solved his two main problems—the problem of the tester and the problem of the hero. First, the tester.

Chaucer's Walter may well be descended, in the tradition of the story, from an other-world visitant or supernatural lover; but so far as the *Clerk's Tale* is concerned he is just a Marquis of Saluce. The original fairy-tale has been transposed into a latter-day mode which excludes the supernatural. Walter may correspond to God in the Petrarchan moralization; but he must stand or fall as a human character—as Chaucer would, I think, have been the first to claim. The case of *Sir Gawain* is rather different. The *Gawain*-poet is quite as ready as Chaucer to 'transpose' his fairy-tale—indeed, as I shall suggest in a moment, his transposition is in one important particular more thorough-going than Chaucer's—but he could hardly exclude the supernatural altogether, even if he wanted to. Magic of some kind is built in to the story of the beheading game, rather as it is built in to the story of Dorigen's rash promise. The motives of the tester might be humanized, but his methods could hardly be naturalized.

The poet's solution to this problem (a solution which he may or may not have inherited from his sources) is to *split* the tester, and apportion the part out between two characters—Bercilak de Hautdesert and Morgan le Fay. The function of Morgan is to take care of the older, less interesting, and in part untransposable aspects of the tester's role. She is important largely because she frees the poet's hand for other matters by explaining both the method and the motive of the test. Since magic and malice were her two conspicuous attributes in tradition, the poet could allow himself to bottle up in her person all the magic and malice implicit in his old story. Once this is done, he no longer has to worry about his tester's magic methods, as

Conclusion

Chaucer did in the *Franklin's Tale*. Nor does he have to worry, like Chaucer in the *Clerk's Tale*, about his tester's motives. His extreme test is, like most such tests, cruel and even wicked, from an ordinary, honest, human point of view (the point of view from which Chaucer judges Walter); but then Morgan is notoriously cruel and wicked. So he keeps his poem steady by allowing it to have one foot firmly, though not too obtrusively, planted in the old world of 'faery'.

Morgan and Bercilak inhabit the same castle; yet they hardly belong to the same world. Bercilak, unlike the 'olde auncian wyf', is very much a fourteenth-century, Chaucerian creation. He is as much Gawain's tester as Morgan, and he plays his part in the first fitt with gusto; but he is no magician, and the poet is careful to dissociate him from Morgan's malicious purposes. Having satisfied in the person of Morgan the less congenial demands of the folk-tale, the poet is free to create a second, richly human and naturalistic tester—as Walter might have been, had he not carried the responsibility for his actions. It should be pointed out in fairness to Chaucer, though, that this freedom has its price. Bercilak is a brilliant, modern creation, and his relation with Gawain is splendidly convincing; but his relation with Morgan, so far as it can be made out at all, seems quite eccentric and unlikely. It is hard to think of such a character either sharing Morgan's malice or submitting to her magic.

Where the test-hero is concerned, however, the poet does undoubtedly bring off a transposition bolder and more radical than anything Chaucer attempted in his test-poems. The basic fact here is a very simple one: Gawain does not entirely pass his complex test. This is a very unusual feature indeed in a one-story lay. In long romances, where more than one hero undergoes a given test (e.g. the Grail test, or the beheading test in *Fled Bricrend*) or where many heroes undergo many tests, failures are not uncommon; but in such cases the failure of one hero is always, I think, offset by the success of another. In *Sir Gawain* there is no such offset. The poet subjects a superlative hero to a superlative test, and he cracks. There is no suggestion that any other knight could have done better. On the contrary, the reader must surely be meant to feel that if Gawain, the mirror of truth, fails to be true, then no-one else can hope to be. As Guinevere (mistakenly) says of Lancelot in the French *Mort Artu*: 'Ha! Dex, qui esprovera mes loiauté en nul chevalier ne en nul home, quant desloiauté s'est herbergiée el meilleur de touz les bons?'[6] It is an *a fortiori* argument significantly unlike Petrarch's argument from the Griselda story. The adventure of the Green Chapel is, in a way, a demonstration of what virtue is and what it can stand—but not in the same way as the Griselda story. For Gawain, unlike Griselda, has something in common, despite his 'great truth', with the latter-day ladies of whom the Clerk speaks:

> if that they were put to swiche assayes,
> The gold of hem hath now so badde alayes
> With bras, that thogh the coyne be fair at ye,
> It wolde rather breste a-two than plye.

However slight Gawain's breach of truth may at first seem to us, we must recognize in it the poet's crucial concession (if that is the right word) to the demands of reality, as these demands were understood by orthodox, imaginative men in the fourteenth century. It is crucial, because without it all the other realistic elements in the poem would be essentially pointless.

Gawain is subjected to a complex and difficult test—difficult, but not impossible. The problematic conflict between the virtues in the inner test is very tricky, but even here the dilemma is not impossible: the hero is not *obliged*, like Chaucer's Dorigen, to do wrong in order to do right. Indeed, he survives this part of the test, reconciling the virtues in 'clene cortays carp'. What he does eventually succumb to is a plain, everyday conflict between virtue and ignoble passion. The poet is not interested in impossible situations. The pentangle represents an ideal of reconciled virtues which can be attained—or rather, could be attained if it were not for the 'badde alayes' in man's fallen nature. There is nothing intrinsically impossible about it. The

[6] 'Ah, God! who will ever find loyalty in any knight or in any man, when disloyalty has found lodging in the best of all good men?' *La Mort le Roi Artu*, ed. cit., p. 32. Guinevere is referring to Lancelot's supposed infidelity with the Maid of Escalot.

fact that Gawain 'brestes a-two' does *not* prove, as is sometimes suggested, that there is some internal contradiction in the courtly-Christian ideal which he represents; nor does it prove merely that life sometimes makes irreconcilable demands even on the best of men. What it does prove is that Gawain—even Gawain—is a sinner like everyone else. This is important because the doctrine of the sinfulness of man is one of the chief sources of medieval literary realism; and its presence in the *Gawain*-poet's imagination goes a long way towards explaining why his work is richer and more profound than the *Clerk's Tale* or the *Franklin's Tale*.

II

So far I have been considering *Sir Gawain* as a story about a superlative hero subjected to, and partly failing, a superlative test. I should like now to turn away from the story, and take up an idea which I have so far only touched on. The idea is that there are two distinct 'modes' to be detected in the poem—an older 'romantic' mode (associated with the superlative hero and the superlative test) and a newer 'realistic' mode (associated with the partial failure in the test). The general distinction I have in mind here is not at all unfamiliar; but it will be convenient at this point to quote an extended statement of it by Dr. Johnson, from one of his *Rambler* essays: 'In the romances formerly written, every transaction and sentiment was so remote from all that passes among men, that the reader was in very little danger of making any applications to himself; the virtues and crimes were equally beyond his sphere of activity; and he amused himself with heroes and with traitors, deliverers and persecutors, as with beings of another species, whose actions were regulated upon motives of their own, and who had neither faults nor excellences in common with himself. But when an adventurer is levelled with the rest of the world, and acts in such scenes of the universal drama, as may be the lot of any other man; young spectators fix their eyes upon him with closer attention, and hope, by observing his behaviour and success, to regulate their own practices, when they shall be engaged in the like part. For this reason these familiar histories may, perhaps, be made of greater use than the solemnities of professed morality.'⁷ We have already seen how, in the story of *Sir Gawain*, the hero is in part 'levelled with the rest of the world' and 'acts in such scenes of the universal drama, as may be the lot of any other man'. Let us now see how far the hero's environment, the 'world' of the poem, is affected by this same levelling. I shall restrict my discussion to three topics—time, space and the marvellous.

'The romances formerly written' were set in a remote and vaguely-imagined past. Their typical opening was 'Once upon a time'. Chaucer's Wife of Bath, rather surprisingly, provides a good literary example of this:

> In th'olde dayes of the Kyng Arthour,
> Of which that Britons speken greet honour,
> Al was this land fulfild of fayerye.
> The elf-queene, with hir joly compaignye,
> Daunced ful ofte in many a grene mede.
> This was the olde opinion, as I rede;
> I speke of manye hundred yeres ago.⁸

Here, of course, the 'olde dayes of the Kyng Arthour' are not in any sense historical. They represent, simply, a far-off time, many hundred years ago, when Britain was 'al fulfild of fayerye' —unlike the Britain of 'nowadays' where, as the Wife goes on to point out in a fine comic passage, the friars have taken over from the elves: 'But now kan no man se none elves mo.'

The two opening stanzas of *Sir Gawain*, though they set the poem in the same period, create a quite different impression. For one thing the author, drawing on the tradition of Geoffrey of Monmouth, places Arthur in his historical context—as one of a line of rulers running from Aeneas through Romulus and Brutus to the 'Bretaygne kynges'. Of course Aeneas, Romulus and Brutus are, from a modern historical point of view, little better than the elf-queen; but it is necessary to realize that the

---

⁷ The passage comes from *Rambler* No. 4 (March 31, 1750). Johnson did not have medieval literature in mind.

⁸ *C.T.*, III, 857–63.

'legendary history of Britain' was not yet recognized as legendary in the *Gawain*-poet's day. There was still general confidence
in Geoffrey's veracity, even among the Latin chroniclers; and
an official map of about 1360 marks Dartmouth as the place
where 'Brutus landed with his Trojans'.[9] So we may be fairly
sure that the contents of the poet's prologue would have im-
pressed an educated contemporary audience as sober historical
fact, and that the poet himself understood them as such.
Notice that he does not, like the Wife of Bath, distinguish
Arthur's day from the present as a specially fairy time. He says
that Britain has always, ever since Brutus founded it, been an
unstable, adventurous, warlike country, and that it has always
been more favourable than any other country to marvels
('ferlyes'):

> Mo ferlyes on þis folde han fallen here oft
> Þen in any oþer þat I wot, syn þat ilk tyme. (23–24)

The 'outtrage awenture' of the Green Chapel, then, is typical
not only of 'Arthureȝ wondereȝ' but of all the wonders of
Britain. It is a characteristic episode in the history of a country where such adventures are not at all uncommon. The
author reasserts this claim very clearly at the end of his work:

> Þus in Arthurus day þis aunter bitidde,
> Þe Brutus bokeȝ þerof beres wyttenesse.
> Syþen Brutus, þe bolde burne, boȝed hider fyrst,
> After þe segge and þe asaute watȝ sesed at Troye,
> iwysse,
> Mony auntereȝ here-biforne
> Haf fallen suche er þis. (2522–8)

The claim is not very convincing perhaps; but it suggests the
poet's determination not to let his story escape into the never-
never land of 'Once upon a time'. This is one manifestation of
his 'levelling' realism.

No reader of *Sir Gawain* can fail to notice, however, that this

---

[9] See L. Keeler, *Geoffrey of Monmouth and the Late Latin Chroniclers,
1300–1500* (Berkeley, 1946), and *The Map of Great Britain, circa A.D.
1360, known as the Gough Map*, facsimile with introduction by E. J. S.
Parsons (Oxford, 1958).

particular kind of realism, this sense of historical time, is entirely confined to the prologue and the little epilogue. The first
two stanzas of the poem do indeed place the world of the poem
in a firm historical context; but once the poet has plunged into
that world, with the words 'Þis kyng lay at Camylot vpon Krystmasse' at the beginning of the next stanza, we lose all sense of
historical time. The point is not so much that the things and
people do not seem to *belong* to the past (one expects medieval
writers to be anachronists), as that they do not seem to *have* any
past, or any future either. The only object in the world of the
poem to have any real history is the pentangle ('a syngne Þat
Salamon set sumquyle'); and the only person to have any real
history is Morgan ('ho hatȝ dalt drwry ful dere sumtyme').
Otherwise people and things exist only insofar as they participate in the immediate here-and-now of the adventure. When the
Beowulf-poet describes the arming of his hero, he allows both
the past (the history of the equipment) and the future (the
impending plunge into the mere) to penetrate his immediate
present; but when the *Gawain*-poet describes the arming of
Gawain, he confines himself entirely to the here-and-now (except in the pentangle-digression, for which he apologizes). He
neither anticipates the future nor reflects on the past. Indeed
the equipment has, effectively, no past to reflect on—it is all
either new or recently renovated ('for Þat note ryched'). But
this is not the main point; for even when things are old and must
have a history, the poet makes nothing of it. The Green Chapel
is as much an ancient barrow as the Dragon's Mound in *Beowulf*; but the *Gawain*-poet does not, like the Old English poet,
explore the history of the place. He does not even respect its
antiquity:

> Hit hade a hole on Þe ende and on ayÞer syde,
> And ouergrowen with gresse in glodes aywhere,
> And al watȝ holȝ inwith, nobot an olde caue,
> Or a creuisse of an olde cragge, he coupe hit noȝt deme
> with spelle. (2180–4)

It is worth recalling here that the word 'old' occurs only four
times in *Sir Gawain*, that all four uses are colloquial, and that

Conclusion

three of them (including the two in the passage just quoted) are depreciatory.[10]

The truth is that, in the body of his poem, the *Gawain*-poet transfers his whole attention from 'linear time or the time of history' to 'cyclic time or the time of nature'.[11] What counts, outside prologue and epilogue, is time of year and time of day. The here-and-now may be outside 'linear time', but it is firmly inside this 'cyclic time'. We almost always know what time of year it is (every stage but one of the adventure is precisely datable), and we almost always know, at least approximately, what time of day it is (though this may require some knowledge of medieval meal-times and service-times). The account of the passing seasons, the plotting of the days of the Christmas feast at Hautdesert, the careful synchronizing of the events of the last three days—these are familiar examples of the poet's art; but such things, though characteristic of *Sir Gawain*, are not characteristic of romance. In romance, as Auerbach has pointed out, intervals such as the *Gawain*-poet's ten months from January to November are typically left 'empty': 'nothing seems to have happened or at least we are told nothing about it'.[12] Again, it is unlike a romance-writer to date every stage of an adventure. References to All Souls' Day or Easter are common enough; but such references rarely amount to a complete or systematic calendar of events. They occur sporadically, as either the story or some convention may require, in company with many quite unspecific indications of time ('on a day' or 'after many weeks'). And much the same is true of the time of day. Specific indications are not uncommon ('towards noon', etc.); but I do not know of any case in the romances where the events of a day are plotted as carefully as are the hunts and temptations in *Sir Gawain*. I have already

[10] See above, Chap. 2, note 41.

[11] M. W. Bloomfield, '*SGGK*: An Appraisal', *P.M.L.A.*, LXXVI (1961), p. 18. This article is a valuable guide to *Gawain* criticism.

[12]. E. Auerbach, *Mimesis: The Representation of Reality in Western Literature*, trans. W. Trask (New York, 1957), p. 113. Auerbach's discussion of romance in this chapter ('The Knight Sets Forth') is notable.

suggested that the poet may here be drawing on the technical tradition of fabliau-comedy rather than romance.

Treatment of 'cyclic time', like treatment of 'linear time', plays an important part in determining what one may call the 'mode of reality' of a fiction. We call the *Winter's Tale* a romance partly because it is a play in which time can 'slide o'er sixteen years, and leave the growth untried of that wide gap'. A romance is, among other things, a story in which we do not call such wide gaps to account, any more than we ask the date or the time of day; and our lack of concern for such matters is intimately connected with a lack of concern for certain more fundamental matters of human probability (e.g. whether Hermione could really have brought herself to lie low for so long). Similarly, one might say that a story which fills intervals and dates events is thereby committed, in the logic of the imagination, to a roughly corresponding degree of probability or realism in other matters. Of course, not all stories obey this kind of logic, even approximately; but I would say that *Sir Gawain* does. There is certainly a rough correspondence between the treatment of time and the treatment of space in this poem.

The geography of Arthurian romance is, like its history and its chronology, notoriously irresponsible. The Logres of Chrétien de Troyes, for example, makes as little sense geographically as it does historically: Auerbach points out that the hero of *Yvain* makes his 'vague and legendary' journey from Carduel to Broceliande in Brittany without any sea-crossing. One has only to compare such journeys with Gawain's journey from Camelot to Hautdesert to appreciate the strangely mixed character of the latter. The first part of the journey, from Camelot through Logres into North Wales, is in itself pure romance; for Camelot, Logres and North Wales ('Norgales') are all stock romantic places, and there is nothing in the poet's description— up to l. 697—to suggest real geography. The reader has no more sense of direction than the hero: 'Mony wylsum way he rode'. By contrast, the geography of the second stage is both real and (for a reader who will identify with the original audience) familiar. The journey takes on a direction when

Conclusion

Gawain 'holds' the islands of Anglesey on his left hand; and for a time he is no longer wandering 'wylsum ways', in a state of typical romantic disorientation, but riding purposefully east along the coast road, across the Dee and into the Wirral. Once past the Wirral, however, he plunges back into the 'contrayeʒ straunge' of romance, with their ogres, trolls and dragons; and the journey ends as it began—Hautdesert being no more a 'real place' than Camelot.

It is of some importance that the *Gawain*-poet should (like Malory) show an inclination to map events realistically; for mapping events, like calendaring them, creates 'realistic' expectations in the reader. A hero who passes through one's home town on the way to an adventure is—to put it baldly—rather less likely to succeed in it than one who does not. However majestic his passage, it will 'level' him a little and perhaps prepare us—as in *Sir Gawain*—for the discovery that he is not entirely exempt from our own more ignoble passions. So the down-to-earth geography of Gawain's passage from North Wales through the Wirral is not just an arbitrary bit of realism. Like the realistic time-scheme, it is linked, in the logic of the imagination, with the author's conception of his hero's partial failure.

It must be said, however, that the correspondence between map and calendar in *Sir Gawain* is imperfect. The calendar is fully realistic, but the map is not: it would, if drawn for an end-paper, look very like one of those curious medieval maps where reality is blended with fantasy. We would have to enter 'Wirral' in one place and 'woodwoses' in another. I would say, though, that this curious blend is in fact more typical of the *Gawain*-world than is the neatly realistic time-scheme. For that world is surely characterized, not so much by a single, solid, all-inclusive mode of reality, as by a complex and sometimes problematical combination of rival modes. Much of the poem's peculiar fascination and many of its peculiar problems arise from the fact that it is, in this sense, a 'transitional' poem. The rival modes coexist and, sometimes, compete. Once we discover that the poet's North Wales is not the 'Norgales' of the French romances—'the scene of numerous events which required no specific localization', according to Vinaver[13]—but the real North Wales which lies between Anglesey and the Wirral, we may well begin to wonder where Camelot was, and why the hero rode from there (N.W.?) into Wales.

The chief source of such problems in *Sir Gawain* is the marvellous. The poet, as we have seen, safeguards his basic marvels —the ability of Bercilak to shift his shape and survive the beheading stroke—by referring them to the traditional magic arts of Morgan. They are not—could not be—open to question, despite Arthur's jokes. But what of the marvellous elsewhere in the poem? A number of miscellaneous difficulties arise here. When Gawain reaches the Green Chapel, for example, he is decked out like a savage with talismans of every description. His helmet is circled with diamonds, which 'keep the bones and the members whole'; his coat-armour is set with 'virtuous stones'; his shield bears the image of Mary on one side and the magic pentangle on the other; and he carries round his waist a magic life-saving belt. Gawain himself obviously believes in this sort of thing (he has even sacrificed his loyalty for the sake of the belt); yet the poet blithely assumes, and we assume with him, that the Green Knight can have no difficulty in cutting off his head, if he so wishes; and he never bothers to justify this assumption by explaining, say, that Gawain forfeited the protection of Mary and the pentangle when he trespassed against truth, or that the lady tricked him over the belt. We may be left with the impression that the dominant mode is realistic here (though not realistic enough to make the hero look ridiculous); but this is certainly not always the case. The sudden appearance of the castle after Gawain has crossed himself thrice on Christmas Eve is a genuine, potent marvel—whether divine or magical; and the dominant mode here is undoubtedly romantic (though not romantic enough to exclude the suggestion that

---

[13] *Works of Sir Thomas Malory*, p. 1333 (note to 127.23). Note the comment which follows: 'Malory's tendency to localize the story and to refer the place-names he found in his source to real places is noticeable throughout . . . and it has the effect, which he no doubt desired to achieve, of transferring the action from the vague fairyland of romance to a precise and familiar geographical setting.'

Gawain needed good luck to hit on the main road up to the castle gate: 'he *ful chauncely* hat3 chosen to þe chef gate').

The cumulative effect is to create in the reader a degree of uncertainty about the rules or laws governing the *Gawain*-world. In the *Queste del Saint Graal*, or in *Emma*, we know pretty well what is possible and what is not; but in *Sir Gawain* we can never be quite sure. One critic will entertain the possibility that the guide is Bercilak shape-shifting again; another will dismiss it out of hand. One critic will entertain the possibility that Arthur is restrained by magic from striking at the Green Knight; another will dismiss it out of hand. The fact that some of these disputes can be settled by reference to the text does not alter the fact that they would never arise but for a very real uncertainty in the world of the poem itself—an uncertainty of boundary between the natural and the marvellous, the 'familiar' and the 'remote'.

III

The terms 'romantic' and 'realistic', used so crudely in the last section, are essentially relative or comparative terms. The *Gawain*-poet's handling of time of year, for example, shows up as 'realistic' when we compare it with the usual practice of romance-writers; but by comparison with the practice of Fielding or Jane Austen it is 'romantic'. Where Fielding and Jane Austen give us the day of the week, and often the day of the month as well, using an almanac to work the scheme out, the *Gawain*-poet is content with a reference to a feast-day (New Year's Day, All Saints' Day, St. John's Day, etc.). There is no mention of any month or day of the week in his work; and he never, of course, makes any attempt to relate cyclic time to linear, historical time in the manner of an almanac (by telling us that Christmas Day fell on a Tuesday that year, and the like). In this and in every other respect his 'realism' is a relative thing—like that of Jane Austen herself, and indeed of all writers. This being so, it may be useful to try to plot the position of *Sir Gawain*, however roughly, on a quite general romantic-realistic scale, and so pin the shifting terms down somewhat.

Conclusion

I adopt for this purpose the scale of five 'fictional modes' presented by Northrop Frye in his *Anatomy of Criticism*.[14] In Frye's scale, fictions are classified according to the hero's power of action, which 'may be greater than ours, less, or roughly the same. Thus:

1. If superior in *kind* both to other men and to the environment of other men, the hero is a divine being, and the story about him will be a *myth* in the common sense of a story about a god. . . .

2. If superior in *degree* to other men and to his environment, the hero is the typical hero of *romance*, whose actions are marvellous but who is himself identified as a human being. The hero of romance moves in a world in which the ordinary laws of nature are slightly suspended: prodigies of courage and endurance, unnatural to us, are natural to him, and enchanted weapons, talking animals, terrifying ogres and witches, and talismans of miraculous power violate no rule of probability once the postulates of romance have been established. . . .

3. If superior in degree to other men but not to his natural environment, the hero is a leader. He has authority, passions, and powers of expression far greater than ours, but what he does is subject both to social criticism and to the order of nature. This is the hero of the *high mimetic* mode, of most epic and tragedy, and is primarily the kind of hero that Aristotle had in mind.

4. If superior neither to other men nor to his environment, the hero is one of us: we respond to a sense of his common humanity, and demand from the poet the same canons of probability that we find in our own experience. This gives us the hero of the *low mimetic* mode, of most comedy and of realistic fiction. . . .

5. If inferior in power or intelligence to ourselves, so that we have the sense of looking down on a scene of bondage, frustration, or absurdity, the hero belongs to the *ironic mode*. . . .'

Such—somewhat abbreviated—are Frye's basic definitions of his five modes. The argument which follows cannot be summarized here; but two points must be noticed. Frye argues

[14] *Anatomy of Criticism* (Princeton, 1957), pp. 33–52.

that 'European fiction, during the last fifteen centuries, has
steadily moved its centre of gravity down the list', that is,
through myth (pre-medieval), romance (medieval), high mimetic (renaissance) and low mimetic (eighteenth and nineteenth
centuries), down to ironic (twentieth century). But, he says, no
one mode will have exclusive rights either in a given period or in
a given individual work, 'for while one mode constitutes the
underlying tonality of a work of fiction, any or all of the other
four may be simultaneously present. Much of our sense of the
subtlety of great literature comes from this modal counterpoint'.

R. S. Loomis believes that the *Gawain*-poet's beheading
game story was originally myth—the story of a young sun-god
beheading and superseding an old one.[15] If this is so, we must
say that the story is, in *Sir Gawain* itself, pretty thoroughly
transposed or, in Frye's language, 'displaced' from its original
mode; for it is difficult (though not, of course, impossible) to see
the hero as a god, or to interpret his actions mythologically.
Certainly the poem *as a whole* does not make sense, is not coherent, in the mode of myth, whatever may be true of individual
episodes in it. The prevailing romantic, or non-realistic, mode
so far as this poem is concerned is plainly the mode of romance
itself, the second of Frye's five. Indeed, this is the mode which,
as Frye's historical hypothesis leads us to expect, 'constitutes
the underlying tonality' of the poem. For the poem is *primarily*
a romance, at least in the sense that most readers respond
to it *first* as the story of a 'superior' though not supernatural
hero, capable of prodigies of courage and endurance, who survives a series of extreme tests in a superlative world where the
ordinary laws of nature are slightly suspended. There is a great
deal in the poem which makes sense at this level. We can see
Bercilak and Morgan, for example, as the traditional antagon-
ists of the romance hero—'the black king and queen', Spenser's
Archimago and Duessa—or we can see the guide as the traditional low-minded servant of romance (like Spenser's 'fearful'
dwarf), whose function it is, in Frye's words, to 'call attention

---

[15] See *Celtic Myth and Arthurian Romance* (New York, 1927), *passim*.

181

to realistic aspects of life, like fear in the presence of danger, which threaten the unity of the romantic mood'.[16]

If it is agreed that the primary, or 'underlying', mode of *Sir Gawain* is romance, we should then go on to identify the lower or more realistic mode which enters into counterpoint with it. Surprisingly enough, the 'high mimetic' mode, although it is romance's immediate neighbour on the realistic side, does not count for much here. Indeed, to read Frye's discussion of this classical and renaissance mode is to realise how little *Sir Gawain* and poems like it have in common, from this point of view, with the characteristic work of those ages. The main point is that the hero of the romance does not figure as a 'leader'— the chief term in Frye's definition of high mimetic. He is of course a superior man, both morally and socially, a noble knight of the Round Table; but he is not a *great* man, as, say, Shakespeare's Antony is great. He is not a head of his society but a member of it, although a conspicuous one; and it is because his death would not involve his society in catastrophe that he is free, unlike Arthur, to offer himself as its representative. He offers himself, in fact, both because he *is* a romance hero and because he is *not* a high mimetic hero or 'leader'. The low-minded 'segges' of Camelot fail to see this:

> Warloker to haf wroȝt had more wyt bene,
> And haf dyȝt ȝonder dere a duk to haue worþed;
> A lowande leder of ledeȝ in londe hym wel semeȝ;
> And so had better haf ben þen britned to noȝt. (677–80)

There is nothing of what Frye calls the 'hamartia of leadership' in *Sir Gawain*, because the hero is both more romantic and more realistic than the Aristotelian great man. He is a hero of romance who is also 'one of us'. The poet's realism, in fact, properly belongs not to the high mimetic but to the fourth or 'low mimetic' mode, the mode characterized by a sense of the hero's 'common humanity'.

To suggest that the fundamental 'modal counterpoint' of *Sir Gawain* is built up out of the second and fourth of Frye's modes, with little trace of the third, need not imply, historically,

[16] Op. cit., pp. 196–7.

that a poet writing in the age of romance was able somehow to overleap the renaissance and anticipate the 'familiar histories' of the age of Johnson. Certainly the realism of *Sir Gawain* has more in common with low mimetic realistic fiction than with the epics and tragedies of the renaissance; and in that sense the poet anticipates the eighteenth century. His hero succumbs secretively to a base passion, and his fall, so far from shaking kingdoms, shakes only himself. It is what we would call a 'personal experience', and it lacks the grandeur and public significance which attach to the doings of renaissance heroes like Antony. By it Gawain is 'levelled with the rest of the world', scaled down to become 'one of us'; and we 'respond to a sense of his common humanity' almost as if we were reading a novel. Even so, there is no occasion to regard the poet's low mimetic realism as a mysterious pre-echo of the eighteenth century; for it has a plain contemporary source, in medieval thinking about the nature of man.

It should be obvious that any religion which teaches that all men are sinners will be, potentially at least, destructive of the distinctions on which Frye's scale is based. It will still leave room for stories in the mythic mode—canonical stories featuring the all-powerful, all-virtuous god himself—but otherwise it will tend, insofar as it makes itself felt imaginatively (an important proviso), to encourage a low mimetic sense of community between hero and audience, levelling down the heroes of the romantic and high mimetic modes (as well as levelling up the heroes of the ironic mode). There are, it is true, many ways by which, even in strongly Christian periods, the mind can escape these consequences—by simply ignoring 'doctrine', by inventing displaced Christ-figures like Galahad, by dwelling on saints, etc. But the *Gawain*-poet does not take any of these ways. He assigns to his hero a part in the 'universal drama' of sin and penance, death and judgment, and so accepts Christianity as a source of realistic awareness of human character and motive.

It is here, if anywhere, that I may hope to justify my preoccupation with the sacrament of penance in previous chapters. The cultural consequences of the penance campaign in the thirteenth and fourteenth centuries have not yet been thoroughly studied, so far as I know, but they must have been far-reaching. The Church over many years devoted a large part of its formidable propaganda machine to the task of teaching people how and what to confess. The hundreds of treatises, poems and sermons on this subject—not to mention innumerable sessions of private instruction in the confessional itself—can hardly have passed unheeded. For the first time a whole community was being taught to analyze its feelings and actions systematically—to become aware, not just of the general fact of human sinfulness, but of the many subtle workings of the soul in particular situations, 'How tender hit is to entyse teches of fylþe'. Hence all the moral allegories and the moral 'pictures' (the Tree of the Virtues, the 'branches' of the seven deadly sins, etc.). Such things were the models of a new moral psychology. The *Gawain*-poet's moral 'picture' of the pentangle, or his picture of the hero poised between Discourtesy and Untruth, or his allegory of Cowardice introducing the hero to Covetousness and Untruth—these are all typical literary products of this new awareness. They are schematic or diagrammatic in character; but the point of the scheme in each case is to convey something of the complexity and difficulty of the moral life.

I suggest, therefore, that penitential thinking is a likely source of what Frye calls 'low mimetic' realism in later medieval literature; and that it is the probable prime source of such realism in *Sir Gawain*. The poem is both a lay of marvels and a moral tale; its hero is both a superior romantic figure, capable of prodigies of courage and endurance, and an Everyman figure, 'one of us'. This is the basic 'modal counterpoint' which gives rise to much of our sense of the subtlety of the poem. It is not simply a matter of setting the hero up as a romantic figure at the beginning and cutting him down to Christian low-mimetic size towards the end. Something like this does indeed happen in the *action* of the poem; but in the *world* of the poem the two modes are present together more or less continuously from start to finish. Gawain's encounter with the Green Knight in the first fitt can be seen both as the encounter of a hero of romance with his magic adversary (the primary romantic mode) and as the encounter of an Everyman with Death the Summoner (the low mimetic, Christian mode). The counterpoint here is essentially the same as that which we find, after the hero's fall, in the scene of his second encounter with the Knight at the Green Chapel, where we can see Gawain either as a hero keeping his tryst or as a man facing his judgment.

IV

We cannot, finally, properly appreciate *Sir Gawain*, either as lay or as moral tale, without keeping a grasp on the rather obvious fact that it is a *comic* poem—by which I mean not so much a poem full of fun and games (though it is that), as a poem which ends happily, with the hero reincorporated into his society (to borrow another formulation from Frye). It is particularly important to appreciate that the poem is just as much a comedy, in this sense, at the moral level as at any other. Morally it is, one might say, a comic version of *Everyman*. Of course *Everyman* is itself a comedy inasmuch as its hero's confrontation with sin, death and judgment ends happily, thanks to his penance and God's mercy: the play, as Dante says, 'brings its matter to a prosperous end' with the salvation of the hero. But *Sir Gawain* goes one better than this, comically speaking; for its version of the Everyman experience is such that the hero can survive it bodily as well as spiritually, returning from it with honour and being reincorporated into his society—a more human kind of happy ending. Gawain faces Death, but he does not experience it, any more than he experiences Judgment. What he does experience is rather a kind of analogue of these Last Things. In particular, the mercy which allows him to rejoin his human society is an analogue of the mercy which allows Everyman to join the heavenly society. In each case the judge's mercy is associated with the hero's penance; but whereas Everyman's penance is the condition of holy dying, Gawain's is the condition of his return to social living—a necessary preparation for his reincorporation.[17]

[17] See van Gennep's discussion of penance and 'reaggregation' in his *Rites de Passage*, p. 137.

Conclusion

Another way of putting this is to say that the action of *Every-man*, like that of *Pilgrim's Progress*, is linear and final—'from this world to that which is to come'—whereas the action of *Sir Gawain* is circular and repeatable. It embodies, in however romantic a mode, a familiar *cycle* of personal experience—that recurrent cycle of self-discovery and self-acceptance of which Christian eschatology is the mythic projection or 'final' form. To some extent the poet presents this cycle of experience in terms of the appropriate Christian ritual—the ritual of Penance —just as he projects it in terms of the appropriate Christian myth—the myth of Judgment. But Bercilak is not literally a Confessor any more than he is literally a Judge; and the poem invites us to see the peculiarly Christian cycle of righteousness, sin, penance and absolution in a generously wide human context. Hence, the fact that Gawain receives no sacramental absolution is immaterial, for in this context sacramental absolution is barely distinguishable from Bercilak's lay imitation of it: both are equally (in no derogatory sense) ritual gestures of reincorporation. Dogmas do not matter here: Bercilak can be God, priest, man and superego, all at once and without incon-sistency. What does matter is the fundamental cycle of ex-perience, and this must in the last analysis be stated quite ab-stractly, however bald the statement may sound—as a cycle of social living, alienation, self-discovery, desolation, recovery and restoration. This, or something like it, is the abstract comic form of the poem.

APPENDIX ONE

Hit is a syngne þat Salamon set sumquyle
In bytoknyng of trawþe, bi tytle þat hit habbeʒ,
For hit is a figure þat haldeʒ fyue poynteʒ,
And vche lyne vmbelappeʒ and loukeʒ in oþer,
And ayquere hit is endeleʒ. (625–9)

The pentangle passage involves all three branches of the medieval 'trivium'. I have said in the text that it forms part of a *rhetorical* description, and that it is *logical* (syllogistic) in structure. I want to show here that it establishes its major premiss—that the pentangle is a sign of truth—with an argument drawn from speculative *grammar*.

The philosophical or speculative grammarians (as distinct from the ordinary practical grammarians) of the fourteenth century were much concerned with the theory of signs. Their speculations on this subject (based largely on Aristotle) were chiefly devoted to linguistic signs, but not exclusively so: they involved, to some extent, a *general* theory of signs. According to this theory, most human signs—words and hunting-calls, for example, but not groans—have their origin in an act of 'impositio'. In every such case, that is, there must have been someone—the 'impositor'—who first established the sign as a sign by 'imposing it on', or assigning it to, a thing (or, more correctly, a mental concept of a thing). In doing so, the wise old 'impositor' may have been 'guided by the nature of things'—that is, he may have attributed a given meaning to a given sign on the strength of some natural similarity between sign and thing-signified (Aquinas' 'ratio similitudinis'). This is known as 'impositio secundum naturam'. Or he may have made a quite arbitrary attribution without any such similarity to guide him, in which case the signification depends on custom and consent (Aquinas' 'ratio institutionis'). This is known as 'impositio ad placitum', 'impositio iuxta arbitrium humanae voluntatis', etc.[1]

---

[1] For the ideas discussed in this paragraph, see especially the first chapter of Aristotle's *De Interpretatione* (*Peri Hermeneias*) and the

Appendix One

In the case of the pentangle, the 'impostor' is Solomon. He is the wise and authoritative ancient who established or 'set' this particular 'syngne'. (It may be noted that the verb 'set' is used elsewhere—by Ælfric, for example—precisely like the Latin 'imponere' in its technical, semantic sense, *O.E.D.*, 'set' 30.) However, the sign does not rest on his authority alone, since this is a case of 'impositio secundum naturam'. The relation between the moral concept truth and the geometrical figure is not merely arbitrary, like the relation between that concept and the various *verbal* signs which denote it ('truth', 'veritas', 'loiauté', etc.); it is *natural*, because, as Solomon was the first to see, the pentangle is of its nature *like* truth—or so the poet claims. Both are fivefold, interlocking, 'endless'. The pentangle is a kind of geometrical 'picture' of truth, in fact, and so has a natural right or 'title' to its signification.[2]

The poet's use of the word 'title' here has not been fully understood (Tolkien and Gordon gloss it 'symbolism'). The notion of a sign having a right or title to its signification is too popular and metaphorical for the scholastic grammarians themselves; but there are at least two similar uses of 'title' in Middle English—both referring to verbal signs. Educated opinion in the Middle Ages generally regarded words as arbitrary or conventional signs. On this point, as on others, Aquinas agrees with Saussure and his successors: 'nec voces naturaliter significant, sed ex institutione humana'. But it was possible to argue that many words did have a qualified 'title' to their signification insofar as they could be shown, by 'etymology', to describe, or at least say something not too inappropriate about, their referents. So etymologists such as Isidore of Seville set out to prove that a grove, for example, had a special *claim* to be called 'lucus' because of its

[2] The four sciences of the 'quadrivium', which included geometry, were commonly justified on the ground that they helped readers to understand the nature of 'things' in the Bible and so grasp their (natural) allegorical significance. The *Gawain*-poet's geometrical analysis of the pentangle is a good non-biblical example of this.

---

commentaries of Boethius and Aquinas upon it: Boethius, *Commentarii in Librum Aristotelis 'Peri Hermeneias'*, ed. C. Meiser (Lipsiae, 1877), Book I, Chap. I; Aquinas, *In Libros 'Peri Hermeneias' Expositio*, ed. R. M. Spiazzi (Turin, 1955), Book I, Lectio II. Also C. Thurot, *Notices et Extraits de Divers Manuscrits Latins pour Servir à l'Histoire des Doctrines Grammaticales au Moyen Âge* (Paris, 1868), pp. 122 ff., and R. G. Godfrey, 'The Language Theory of Thomas of Erfurt', *S.P.*, LVII (1960), pp. 22–29.

natural properties ('non lucendo').[3] It is in this way that the word 'title' is used (of the referent, not of the sign as in *Sir Gawain*) in my two English examples. The author of *Cursor Mundi* says that St. Peter had a *title* to his name ('tu es Petrus, et super hanc petram ...'):

> His nam es giuen til him o ded
> And titel of his might o med.[4]

And Hoccleve, in a flattering passage, says that Humphrey of Gloucester was *entitled* to his name ('Humphrey' = 'homme ferai' ='I shall make a man'):

> Bataillous Mars in his natiuitee
> Vnto þat name of verray specialtee
> Titled him, makynge him therby promesse
> Þat strecche he sholde into hy worthynesse.[5]

There is in *Sir Gawain* an interesting contrast between the pentangle, so considered as a naturally 'entitled' sign, and the green girdle which the hero later adopts in its place, as a 'token of vntrawþe'. The latter has no natural title to any particular moral signification: Gawain institutes it as a sign of untruth for purely personal reasons. This is 'impositio ad placitum'. Hence it is open for the court to decide that it should be instituted a second time—as a sign of the 'renoun of þe Rounde Table'. Their significance runs counter to Gawain's; but this is always possible with an arbitrary sign: 'potest significare oppositum suae significationis'.

[3] See Isidore's discussion of etymology in *Etymologiae*, Book I, Chap. XXIX. Medieval etymology is best regarded not as a historical science but as a method of 'motivating' as many words as possible. See Saussure's section on 'L'arbitraire absolu et l'arbitraire relatif' in his *Cours de Linguistique Générale*, 4th Ed. (Paris, 1949), pp. 180–4.

[4] Ed. cit., ll. 20873–4; quoted in *O.E.D.* under 'title', 6.

[5] *Dialogue with a Friend*, ll. 592–5. In *Hoccleve's Minor Poems*, ed. F. J. Furnivall, E.E.T.S. E.S. 61 (1892). Malory uses 'right' very much as Hoccleve and the others use 'title' in a passage about the Round Table: 'Merlyon made the Rounde Table in tokenyng of rowndnes of the worlde, for men sholde by the Rounde Table undirstonde the rowndenes signyfyed by ryght', ed. cit., p. 906.

APPENDIX TWO

Alle þe iles of Anglesay on lyft half he haldeȝ,
And fareȝ ouer þe fordeȝ by þe forlondeȝ,
Ouer at þe Holy Hede, til he hade eft bonk
In þe wyldrenesse of Wyrale. (698–701)

In a recent discussion of this puzzling passage J. McN. Dodgson,
taking 'þe Holy Hede' in apposition to 'þe fordeȝ by þe forlondeȝ',
understands it to refer to some 'ford of the Dee estuary at the very
mouth, at the forelands, the seaward extremities of the land, from
Point of Air in Flintshire to the northwest corner of the Wirral
peninsula'.[1] This he identifies as the legendary crossing-place of
William, Constable of Chester, who, according to Henry Bradshaw's
Life of Saint Werburge (*c.* 1500), made a miraculous crossing from
Hilbre into Wales to rescue the Earl of Chester. Such a legendary
ford, he suggests, might have been thought more appropriate for a
romance hero than the usual crossing. Mr. Dodgson interprets 'þe
Holy Hede' as a riddling version of '(West) Kirby', the name of a
village in the Wirral at the eastern end of the supposed crossing.
'Caer Gybi', the Welsh name of Holyhead in Anglesey, appears in
medieval English records in forms such as 'Kaerkeby'. Hence, 'if the
poet knew West Kirby as *Kerkeby* and Holyhead as *Kaerkeby*, etc.,
then *þe Holy Hede* could be a periphrasis for *Kerkeby* (West Kirby)
by a fancied analogy with the place-name Holyhead for *Kaerkeby*
(Caer Gybi)'.

The only positive alternative to this elaborate hypothesis, so far
as I know, is to follow R. W. Chambers and Gollancz in supposing
that 'ouer at þe Holy Hede' contains a reference to the cult of St.
Winifred, and points to a crossing near her cult centre, Holywell in
Flintshire.[2] In my discussion of Gawain's journey I have adopted

[1] 'Sir Gawain's Arrival in Wirral', in *Early English and Norse
Studies Presented to Hugh Smith*, ed. A. Brown and P. Foote (London,
1963), pp. 19–25.
[2] See R. W. Chambers' note '*SGGK*, Lines 697–702', *M.L.R.*, II
(1907), p. 167, and Gollancz's note to *SGGK* l. 700. Chambers says

this explanation in preference to Mr. Dodgson's, though it is admittedly open to two serious objections. Firstly, there is no evidence that Holywell was ever known as 'Holyhead'. E. Davies, in his *Flintshire Place-Names* (Cardiff, 1959), records only 'Holywell' forms—from as early as 1093. Secondly, there seems to be no known medieval record of any crossing, real or legendary, from the Welsh bank near Holywell over to the Wirral. Gollancz's note refers to 'remains of a ford or ferry' still to be seen 'near Holywell Station and also at Gayton in Wirral', and there is indeed evidence, dating from 1840, of a ferry running between Gayton and Flintshire; but I do not know of any medieval evidence for such a ferry.[3] Nor have I been able to find any reference to a ford at that spot. Dodgson is right, so far as I know, when he says that the lowest identified ford across the Dee is the one at Shotwick, a good deal higher up the estuary.

Neither of these objections is quite decisive, however. One need not necessarily look to find a town-name in the poet's reference to the Holy Head. 'Ouer at þe Holy Hede' could have been a colloquial phrase referring directly (not *via* a supposed town-name 'Holyhead') to a crossing-place near where Winifred was beheaded. The form of the phrase—it is not 'ouer at Holy Hede'—is at least consistent with this supposition. Again, one need not suppose that such a crossing-place must have been in sufficiently regular and general use for it to figure in the records. Indeed, regular and general use is rather unlikely, for, as a writer in *Notes and Queries* has observed, 'few people would ever need to cross from the County of Flint to the Wirral because, as the poet tells us, the Wirral was a wilderness'.[4] The same writer goes on to suggest that the poet may have been thinking of some small local ford, used mainly by farmers and country people. This is certainly a possibility—a local ford, running from the Flintshire coast near Holywell, and known to the poet and his original audience as the crossing 'ouer at þe Holy Hede'. Today the estuary is some four miles across by Holywell, and it may have been a little broader in the fourteenth century; but silting had already begun

[3] See S. Lewis, *Topographical Dictionary of England* (London, 1840), under Gayton. Dodgson refers to a mention, in 1357, of ferries at Caldy and Burton; but neither of these can be relevant.

[4] 'G.P.J.', 'The Author of *GGK*', *N. and Q.*, 201 (1956), pp. 53-54.

---

that Gawain and Gryngolet could have swum across the narrowed channel at low tide; but the poet's phrase suggests an established crossing-place.

Appendix Two

before 1400, and the sands of Dee could already have permitted surprisingly long crossings at low tide, at least to local people. It may be pointed out that in 1403, during Owen Glendower's revolt, four Wirral men, two from Puddington and two from the neighbouring village of Burton, were commissioned by the Prince of Wales to 'seize all grain, etc., in the hundred of Wirral, sold to the Welsh, who, the Prince had heard, entered by night and day by certain fords *ultra aquam de Dee*, and carried thence a great quantity of grain, etc.'. Since Burton and Puddington are both some distance below Shotwick, this document may be taken to imply that there *were* fords, otherwise unrecorded, across the estuary below Shotwick ford—a fact which makes one hesitate to rule out a ford near Holywell.[5]

There are a number of possible reasons why the poet should have picked upon such a relatively obscure crossing-place in preference to Shotwick. He may simply have thought it more adventurous and so more appropriate to a knight errant; he may have wished his hero to cross the Dee at the first opportunity and so display a noble eagerness to get into the 'strange countries' of the North (for it would be there, according to medieval superstition, that a weird creature like the Green Knight might be expected to have his home);[6] or he may have wanted to work in a passing allusion to St. Winifred. It is this last possibility which should interest a literary critic most in the problem of the Holy Head. The story of the cutting off and miraculous restoration of St. Winifred's 'holy head' has, in addition to its

[5] *Calendar of Recognizance Rolls of the Palatinate of Chester* (36th Report of the Deputy Keeper of Public Records, Appendix II), p. 253. See also p. 534.

[6] One branch at least of the medieval road from North Wales to Chester seems to have passed through St. Asaph and run through the Rhuallt gap to somewhere near Basingwerk Abbey, between Holywell and the estuary, before turning southeast towards Chester. This was the line of the old Roman road. (See especially W. J. Hemp, 'The Road from St. Asaph to Greenfield', *Flintshire Historical Society Publications*, 9 (1922), pp. 83–87. Also I. D. Margary, *Roman Roads in Britain* (London, 1957), II, pp. 79 f., and W. Rees, *An Historical Atlas of Wales* (Cardiff, 1951), Plate 14.) Giraldus Cambrensis followed this route in the twelfth century, as he describes in his *Itinerarium Kambriae* (Rolls Series, London, 1868), Book II, Chapter X. It brought the traveller out on to the Dee estuary at precisely the point where he might, on the Chambers–Gollancz theory, cross it 'ouer at þe Holy Hede'. So the poet may have thought of his hero as following the line of this road straight across the sands into the Wirral.

quite general likeness to the first part of the beheading game, one or two specific points in common with *Sir Gawain*. According to the most widely-read version of the legend, the *Vita Secunda*, written *c.* 1150 by Robert, Prior of Shrewsbury, Winifred was beheaded just outside a chapel where Mass was in progress, and her head, 'rolling among the feet of those standing in the church and attending to the divine mysteries, filled everyone with the greatest amazement', rather as the Green Knight's 'fayre hede fro þe halce hit to þe erþe,/ Þat fele hit foyned wyth her fete, þere hit forth roled' (427–8). Again Winifred, after her resuscitation, carried a mark on her neck which, like Gawain's 'nirt in þe nek', served as a token of her adventure: 'A very thin white line like a thread encircled her neck, following the line of the cut; and this, for as long as the virgin lived, remained with her always unchanged, as a mark of the cutting of the head and as a token of the miracle'.[7] So the poet's allusion to Winifred, coming where it does, might both recall the first fitt (the rolling head restored) and anticipate, ironically, the fourth (the marked neck). The main point, perhaps, is the ironical one.

There is no difficulty in assuming that the original audience of *Sir Gawain*, in Cheshire perhaps, or Lancashire, would have known about Winifred and her cult centre at Holywell/Basingwerk. One has only to read H. J. Hewitt's excellent book *Mediaeval Cheshire* (Manchester, 1929) to see how closely Cheshire and its neighbouring counties were linked with Flintshire, both politically and economically, during the long period of Anglo-Welsh peace which preceded Owen Glendower's rising in 1400. Chester, in particular, was both the administrative centre and the chief market of the Welsh county; and during the *Gawain*-poet's time Chester citizens were 'buying and selling the lead, farming the lead-mines, farming the coal mines, purchasing land and houses in North Wales'.[8] Now Holywell was not only the centre of the important Flintshire lead-mining industry: it was also a great centre of pilgrimage. Winifred's well was indeed, according to one authority, 'perhaps the most famous well-shrine in medieval Britain'—witness Henry V who, in 1416, 'with great

---

[7] *Vita Secunda*, translated from *Acta Sanctorum*, November, Vol. I (Paris, 1887), 713A (the rolling head) and 714B (the thin white line). On the latter, see Gollancz's note to *SGGK* ll. 2498–500. The *Vita Secunda* is the source of Mirk's homily on Winifred (No. 43 in his *Festial*), and of the nine 'Lectiones' in the Sarum Missal.

[8] Hewitt, p. 86. See the whole chapter ('Wales') from which this quotation comes.

Appendix Two

reverence went on foot in pilgrimage from Shrewsbury to St. Winifred's Well in North Wales'.[9] In the fourteenth century Winifred's shrine was administered by the Cistercian monks of Basingwerk Abbey, which lay close to the main North Wales–Chester road, between Holywell and the estuary. Typically enough, the Abbey held lands both in Wales (Flint and Merioneth) and England (Cheshire and the Derbyshire Peak); and it must have given hospitality to a large number of pilgrims, businessmen, tenants and travellers from both countries. An English guest there might well have learned, if he did not know already, how to cross 'ouer at þe Holy Hede'.[10]

As a postscript, let me mention that the so-called 'Black Book of Basingwerk', a manuscript compiled at the Abbey during the fourteenth and fifteenth centuries, contains, besides Welsh texts of Dares' *De Excidio Troiae* and of Geoffrey of Monmouth's *Historia*, a version of the Welsh continuation of Geoffrey (*Brut y Tywysogion*) in which the original continuation has been blended with a set of annals of English origin.[11] The *Gawain*-poet would probably not have had to go as far afield as Basingwerk for his 'Brutus bokeȝ'; but the contents of the Black Book show the kind of Anglo-Welsh interests which flourished in such a place. Literary historians might well bear centres like Basingwerk in mind when they attempt to track down the *Gawain*-poet's sources for the romantic history of Arthur.

[9] See F. Jones, *The Holy Wells of Wales* (Cardiff, 1954), pp. 49–50.

[10] On Basingwerk and its history, see *Archaeologia Cambrensis,* I (1846), pp. 97–116, and R. A. Thomas' essay in W. B. Lowe's *Heart of Northern Wales*, Vol. II (Llanfairfechan, 1927), pp. 251–68. Like all Cistercian houses, Basingwerk was dedicated to the Virgin, and its arms displayed five five-pointed gold stars: 'argent, on a cross engrailed vert five mullets or' (see J. Woodward, *Treatise on Ecclesiastical Heraldry* (Edinburgh, 1894), p. 355). It will be remembered that Gawain's shield carried an image of the Virgin on one side and a pentangle 'of pure golde hweȝ', symbolizing five pentads, on the other. However, Gawain's pentangle is set 'vpon rede gowleȝ', and there is no gules in the Basingwerk arms. (For a discussion of other possible heraldic significances in Gawain's device, see J. R. Hulbert, '*GGK*', *M.P.*, XIII (1916), pp. 726–8.)

[11] On the Black Book (National Library of Wales, 7006 D), see *Handlist of Manuscripts in the National Library of Wales*, Vol. II (Aberystwyth, 1951), and J. E. Lloyd, 'The Welsh Chronicles', *P. B. A.*, XIV (1928), pp. 369–91.

INDEX

Index